Frank Weston

Do You Have a Return Ticket?

The African Inheritance War

Non-fiction

First test published in New York February 2015
Printed in the United States of America
First Print final addition, May 2015 /
International Multiracial Shared Cultural Organization
(IMSCO) PRESS PAPERBACK EDITION
CreateSpace Independent Publishing Platform, North Charleston, SC
Library of Congress Control Number: 2015906414,
Publisher IMSCO New York City, NY
Library of Congress Copyright © 2007
Do You Have a Return Ticket? / Author—Frank Weston
ISBN-13: 978-1508767657
ISBN: 1508767653
IMSCO Press
4 Park Avenue
New York, N.Y. 10016

Dedicated to the Youth
Own your life and your inheritance!

FORWARD

Mr. Frank Weston, a warm hearted and brilliant man with a great sense of adventure and humor offers us a tremendous work. The history and knowledge that fill these pages cannot be found in schools or universities. The suppressed information contained in this book serves as a threat to White persons grasping to hold on to unearned privilege and power. Mr. Weston shares with us his journey and the journey of millions of people of African descent. It is an odyssey to reclaim what Europeans, North Americans and religions have attempted to conquer the peoples and resources of the African continent. The European and United States government, in addition to corporations, want us to believe that the countries and people of Africa are poor and ravaged by war. Likewise, people of African descent are portrayed as violent, lazy and inferior. Through research, travel and international networking, Mr. Weston exposes the campaign lead by the United States and Europe. Their intent is to oppress the peoples of African descent, and steal the wealth of the African continent.

This book is a movement for Africans to reclaim their inheritance. It addresses the following:
The crime done to the African countries and people in the name of democracy and religion
Wealth available to persons of African descent
Africans reclaiming their legal possessions
Dual-citizenship for persons of the African Diaspora
The wealth in culture, intellect, arts, science and natural resources which belongs to every person of African descent.

As a White, European American who is dedicated to unlearning the racism and lies that are inherent in my person as a result of being raised in the United States, Mr. Weston has served as a tremendous mentor in my on-going journey to freedom. His book is a resource for all to tap into a movement; which can lead millions of people to reconnect with their rich heritage in the African continent.

Meg Knapp, LMSW
PhD Student, Fordham University, Graduate School of Social Service

About the Author

Born in the United States, Frank Weston a graduate of New York University, where he studied geology, economics, anthropology, history, political science, and foreign policy and graduated with honors. He reads and writes ancient Egyptian hieroglyphs. Weston is the founder and CEO of the International Multiracial Shared Cultural Organization, a United Nation ECOSOC affiliated Non-Governmental Organization (NGO) since 1995. He has written and implemented the historic "IMSCO Establishment Agreement" being signed by a growing number of African nations designed to ensure "people of African descent" (PAD) re-entry and family linkage in Africa. He has also written the all important "African Inheritance co-development Treaty" design to assist African and PAD in renewing direct trade linkage to avoid conflict and war. Weston has worked in and visited nearly seventy countries—including China—for the research and adventure of a lifetime for his work and to gather information for films and books. Weston is the writer, producer, and director of his first independent film, *Man in the Mirror,* about the broken American dream. Alongside Michael Dunn, Martin Sheen, and Johnny Brown, Getting his start in the movie business as an actor in Paris Weston holds his own in *Man in the Mirror* with these professional actors. His main mission is establishing cultural, economic, and political foundations for all people especially exiled PAD people from across the African diaspora to obtain dual citizenship and the right to self-determination to flourish and help build a better world.

Contents

Preface

PAD Pooling Efforts to Develop Africa

People of African descent (PAD) are also owners and full partners in all that Africa is, and they have inherited and retaken Africa and the continent's vast land, wealth, and opportunities—enough to rebuild African people's lives and economic and political empires worldwide. So vast is the African kingdom— over one hundred million Africans claiming African ancestry across South America to America's fifty million African Americans to Europe and Asia coowning Africa and foreign wealth and lands—not a single African on earth should have to live without having the basic needs met in education, health care, quality of life, protection, food, or shelter. In fact, Africa's vast wealth can place over one million dollars a year as annual living expenses into the hands of each and every one of the 1.5 billion Africans presently living on the planet. As much as the Western world and other partners in crime against African humanity claim to represent and promote democracy while carrying out such evil deeds before, during, and after slavery, at no time have people in Africa or people of African descent had legal counsel in an accepted court of law before or after the titles to their African property and opportunities were taken.

The International Multiracial Shared Cultural Organization (IMSCO) is an NGO affiliated with the United Nations Economic and Social Council (ECOSOC). This representative of basic human rights and African property rights states concretely that it is important for the world to realize that while PAD are still locked out of Africa and until those existing in exile have been properly represented in a recognized international court of law, no African or PAD share of African private property—in fact no part of Africa—is for the taking or for sale. This book is about Africans reclaiming their legal possessions and will serve as a guide with help from my research and qualified independent African organizations in assisting exiled and impeded African people to reclaim their birthright: Africa's vast land, wealth, and opportunities.

Presently, most Africans are trapped between the Cross and the Koran, a metaphor foreigners imposed on Africans as legal and cultural realities, not our own realities while trapped outside our homelands without having a return ticket to self-determination.

Mandated by the people, IMSCO, with its United Nations–affiliated links through ECOSOC, seeks to link Africans with allies and tools, such as this book, to join forces with all concerned to close the final chapter on PAD external economic and cultural impediments and suffrage. Throughout this book, I hope to encourage the youth and all others concerned to engage themselves in the act of taking ownership in protecting their human rights by taking back what has been (or is being) taken or stolen regardless of the item or its location, the size of the foes we must face, or the amount of the prize. I have found in my global travels and search for answers that there are powerful tools at hand that the most damaged among Africans in Africa and those exiled in the Western world possess for claiming victory. One of those ready-made tools, apart from vast wealth ownership, is dual citizenship. .Dual citizenship affords exile PAD the power to manage needed international economic and political links, foreign policy links that feed nations, people and economies. African people's ownership of vast property, land, and wealth is their key to opening doors to better education, business, and trade opportunities, which before now was never possible. Dual citizenship, one's birthright to foreign trade that creates business and sustainable development and employment, can and does make political and foreign impediments (such as sabotage and biased governments controlled by private multinational companies) go away and remain away from free lives forever. Since the World Bank and IMF are managed by biased teams and funded by greedy investors to lock out PAD often using taxpayer dollars, they fear dual citizenship. Dual citizenship even makes old and bad debt burdens go away, and debts due get paid in full. The impeded people held for over a millennia in darkness own the right as true owners of a continent's land and vast wealth that the black youth and their families are locked out of by systems denying them basic education and opportunities. By publishing the basic knowledge about these human rights, I have been criticized and attacked by governments and private organizations for sharing this basic knowledge with the billions of people I most identify with: people who can now begin to comanage Africa's vast wealth, property, and land.

This book provides important information for many people from early education extending to college. It can offer the student of color links to this basic knowledge of one's culture, inherited land, African land, wealth, and economic power. If the founders of companies like Apple and Google tell us anything, it's that one does not always need to wear a Western university cap and gown to succeed in life.

      This book points out how people who have suffered and lost so much deserve and can have much more with their basic skills and knowledge presently at hand so that they can be more in their lives than they are now. The author once impeded asks the impeded reader and those who seek to better understand the oppressed or be understood by the impeded to rise above oppression in order to trade and codevelop with other cultures, using all available opportunities as families and professionals, and most of all help lift the marginalized person by providing them with the motivating knowledge that they own continents bathed in gold and opportunities three times the size of America or China. I hope this book and my experiences will aid many, not just African people, to understand that they do have a return ticket to the place so many have been torn from and can journey there for a clearer, better understanding of themselves.

PAD, Africans, and allies are regrouping as witnessed in the United Nations December 10, 2014, global event titled "International Decade of People of African Descent." Demanded by NGOs like IMSCO and representing PAD from around the globe, they met to affiliate and help each other end all forms of racism, racial discrimination, xenophobia, and related intolerance. I came to understand at that event that the system that did the harm to so many cannot repair the damage done; only we the people can. The best way to end such impediments is to beat your foes with your economic game. The once impeded people will now begin controlling their vast land by demanding an equal economic partnership in any and all trading, business, and management opportunities. It is written with the blood of our ancestors that African families, professionals, and the youth have controlling ownership of the African people's vast land and wealth to grow sustainable development, banking, business, technology advancements, and institutions, which will produce

unlimited opportunities for all to ensure and manage
strong families and welcome responsibilities and the
right to self-determination.

Introduction

It had taken this native son's rite of passage
over four centuries to return to the great Serengeti
Plains in East Africa. It's near impossible to describe
the feelings of joy I had when I first set foot there,
carrying my ancestor's DNA. Setting foot on the soil
and taking my first breath on the Serengeti in the
shadow of Mount Kilimanjaro was like being plugged
into the energy-providing sources that created the
universe.
My first trip out of America and the
Western world turned out to be a welcome out-of-
death experience. A rebirth! How uplifting it was,
still is, to see, feel, and walk in the footsteps of the
billions of animal and human inhabitants, past and
present, crossing the great Serengeti Plains as they
expanded beyond my vision's capacity to take in the
vastness of the splendor before me. I was finally
witnessing life from my perspective. The sun, the
moon, and all life was free in our solar system in
perfect balance. I smiled so broadly and proudly that
my sunbaked lips and cheeks started to hurt again.
The wonder of it all placed me in a peaceful cocoon,
enveloping me with the natural world around me; I
was free traveling again in the first hours of creation
after death during slavery in the West. I was home
in my Africa! I was exploring being consumed by

Eden's magnificent ever-evolving human and animal natural kingdom, beholding the last unpolluted river on earth. This was the beginning, a new beginning of the new me, as I explored the animals' land, my ancestors' land, my people's land, my land as yet unmapped in my mind and eyes. I saw no Kenya or Tanzania, no Ugandan or South African lines on a map drawn by colonialists and exploiters of my African Eden. I was the explorer exploring the unexplored as a returning African having just jumped an American ship still carrying over forty million African Americans. The wider African diaspora community numbering some five hundred million exiles are still chained, inhumanly denied basic cultural, political, and economic access.

Spring! My favorite time of the year. The season on the Serengeti when nature was in full bloom, and the southern migration had begun. The great animal herds were on the move like some giant seismic plate uplifting itself, birthing itself from some ancient sleep and drifting south. It carried with it all kinds and forms of animals, birds and insects, prey and predator alike, grazing, mating, being born, and dying, all in one big bold sweep toward an area known as Zambia and South Africa, half a continent away. Once there, they will turn and repeat the process, like the seasons, again and again as they have done for millennia before evil winds blew in from the far north to upset the natural balance on the continent. To survive, we Africans in the diaspora, exiled and in Africa, need the land, our land, like the animals to migrate, to survive, and to know our mother, the earth, and all that makes us who we are; in my case, who I was and will be again.

The Serengeti is home to the ancient zebra and wildebeest, the graceful antelopes and gazelles, the spotted hyenas, the hard-to-spot leopards in constant fear of the golden lion, and the prehistoric, majestic elephants standing twelve feet or better at the shoulders carrying precision, six-foot-long ivory tusks. So plentiful were the herds in the 1800s, the invading Europeans slaughtered animals by the hundreds of thousands using the elephants tusks as their hard currency minted on coins and iron brick bars used to trade human beings. The ivory was also used to make the keys on musical instruments and walking canes. Sometimes, it was just for the selfish thrill of seeing the great beast fall and die a horrifying death while placing a foot on the beast proclaiming superiority. It was these majestic elephants who witnessed the arrival of mankind, my ancestors, when they first stood upright here under the baobab tree protected by eight-foot elephant grass.

Following alongside the herds were the dancing light-footed impalas, jumping four to six feet high to entertain the rest of the animals and in celebration of being alive but also to see above the tall grasses to escape the ever-watchful eyes of the golden jackals. The king of the animal kingdom, the golden lion standing forty to forty-five inches at its powerful shoulders is flanked by the great buffalos, zebras, and bashful but deadly alligators lying in wait at the break in the river embankment of each life-threatening crossing for the great herds. As the large herds crossed the great Serengeti Plains, they constantly stirred up tens of millions of insects that in turn attracted the endless flocks of local and migrating birds from as far away as Egypt, Europe, South America, and North America, where I had been held in captivity with five hundred million of my present-day African family members still in exile.

After centuries of Europeans slaughtering these magnificent animals, creatures like us not yet totally free from European guns, were once again reaching safe survival numbers. It is near impossible to get an accurate count of the millions of animals on the move. I felt a kinship, a part of them all going back millions of years, and I was happy, very happy to see the animals roaming free with me like the wind. Down on the great plains as far as the eye could see, to the southeast of mother Mount Kilimanjaro, was what was left of Mount Ngorongoro Crater's outer rim. It rests now cracked and torn from countless violent blasts in the ancient past after a billion plus years of giving and taking life, providing present-day Africa and its inhabitants with a bountiful food supply, minerals, and wealth in its continual cycle in the mantle evident by the steam and smoke seeping upward, a constant reminder from Mount Ngorongoro Crater that deep sleep benefits the surface. This ancient, extinct volcano was still home to millions of unique herds of animals that have evolved and roamed here before mankind walked in its shadow long after it blew. Scientific research suggests our human visit, our journey across earth and time, began only seven million years ago. Yet, there she was taking a deep well-earned rest from nursing the multiplicity of life Mount Ngorongoro Crater and Kilimanjaro help create until the next natural recycling process already on the way. This was Africa, the birthplace of the ancestors, evident by early human remains and footprints recorded in the gray ash that still blows past the great Serengeti Plains north to what is known today as Ethiopia. The early human footprints that were discovered moving away from the hot ash are of two adults and one juvenile: the first branches anthropologists believe on our family tree. Here I am a native son crossing, this wonderland in East Africa on foot and in a powerful four-wheel Jeep in the rugged bush land trekking through high razor-sharp elephant grass. It's nearing sunset. After many, many pleasure-filled hours on the dusty bush trails facing the rising sun and the Indian Ocean, we would reach Dar es Salaam, capital of Tanzania.

Walking in Ancestors Path

I am an African diaspora man, descendant of ancestors forcibly removed, returning home to Africa from America, the inhumane prison where my ancestors were stolen and taken to centuries ago. Having been violently uprooted from my ancient and modern day African Eden, my ancestors' DNA wills me to search for a way back. Once out of the Western prison, I hope much of the limits and pain I lived, experienced, and felt would be left behind me. Back in Africa, I dreamed I would be free again on my own land where I would no longer live in fear, be forced to march to the sound of alien drums or wear the mask of alien cultures while facing oppression in business and learning from a wounded, failing alien system. In the 1800s, Joseph Conrad, a European adventurer who wrote about the evils committed doings his invading fellow Europeans all of whom traveled a "bridge too far" , beyond their welcome and reach, ability, into the Congo, wrote his book *Heart of Darkness* to document the horrors Europeans, Arabs, Americans, and even some misguided African leaders inflicted upon African people and nature. Joseph Conrad used his return ticket to escape his "Heart of Darkness" back to England. I would use my right of passage to return, escape through a crack in the Western cage door and migrate out of a cultural death experience in the Western world's Heart of Darkness back to my native Africa, for me, the Heart of Light, to find and reclaim my culture, land, and rightful place in nature among humans and animals. It's true. Home is where the heart is!

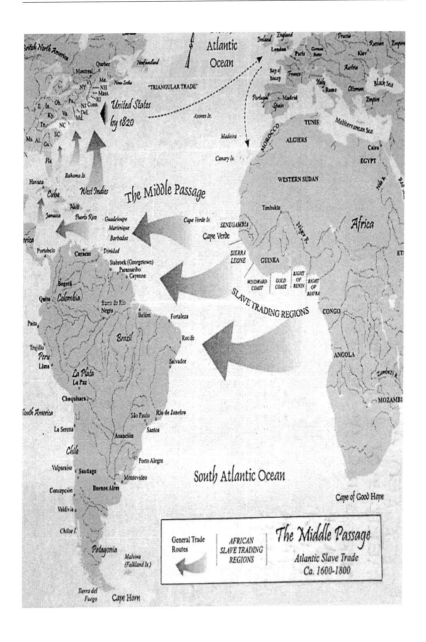

The Middle Passage — Atlantic Slave Trade Ca. 1600-1800

Chapter 1

The Road Home

In this changing world, this is my story, an epic story of one black man's quest to return to his beloved motherland, Africa, and reclaim his birthright, his dignity, his land, his wealth, and his future. If you believe in the six degrees of separation, this is your story as well—at least you will find large parts of your own story embedded in these pages, these years, and centuries. So come along, take the journey with me, not backward into the mangled remains of my African past, but into the future—our future.

Throughout my childhood, my family elders instilled in me a code that was passed down through the millennia to them. It told of a mission that I was to fulfill—a mission that my grandmother said I had been "called" to. I was taught this and much more in the kitchen and around the fireplace of our Alabama home that Africa was the epicenter of human evolution: the land where human beings first stood upright, looked out over the elephant grass, and learned the art of survival and the meaning of life and culture.

My parents wanted me to return to our homeland and locate the things that define who I truly am, so I reached out to Africa and aimed at her heart: the Congo. The journey I then followed mirrors how black men and women are changing the world as they seek to reconnect with their homeland and their heritage. Like most marginalized people of the world, all I wanted was to see a better day. But to get the return process started, I had to endure and survive near-death experiences and almost insurmountable obstacles many millions like me could not have overcome.

It was a quiet afternoon near the end of the summer in New York City in 1988. I sat at my work desk, overlooking the East River, and watched the shadows of the people sixteen floors below grow longer as the days grew shorter. Suddenly the building's intercom in the kitchen rang. It was my doorman announcing an unexpected visitor who identified himself as "Rock from the Congo." Congo? Which Congo? There were two now: the Republic of the Congo and the Democratic Republic of the Congo (DRC). When they were united, they were a vastly rich landmass on the African continent created by timeless volcanic eruptions so massive the Congo River crossed the equator twice. The area is so massive it exceeds the size of the United States of America. Now sadly, they have been torn apart culturally and politically by invading Europeans, Arabs, and Asians, which has been happening since the fifteenth and sixteenth centuries. As I spoke into the intercom in my kitchen, I wondered why someone called "Rock from the Congo" was calling on me unexpectedly.

Puzzled with anxious curiosity, I asked the doorman to admit the stranger. A few minutes later, a man in his twenties, in obvious need of sleep, introduced himself with his Congolese French accent as he held onto a brown, frayed package tucked under his arm.

As soon as I had stepped aside to let Rock come in, it became clear that a distant relative to whom I had been recently introduced from another world and time, Mr. Vital Balla, from the Republic of the Congo, had sent Rock to find me. It had taken centuries of slavery, wars, and horrors too gruesome to contemplate for our meeting to take place. Rock, battle worn but still African strong, had survived the European killing fields to fulfill the mission that brought him to my door that September afternoon.

The frayed package Rock carried— containing typed and hand-written letters and documents, most of them in French from Mr. Balla— would change, enrich, and advance my life forever. I had been informed of Mr. Balla, who lived in Brazzaville, the Republic of the Congo, as a possible contact through a person that knew him back in Congo through the mission representative at the United Nations in New York City a year earlier. I wrote to Mr. Balla via the mission diplomatic express pouch direct to the Congo. My letter was offering and asking Mr. Balla to join me in business cooperation. In addition I was building a pathway back to Africa. Twelve long months had drifted past since my letter was sent, and then Rock stumbled through my door carrying that package. Among the letters and government documents were a number of aging and new maps, some of which were hand drawn. Mr. Balla's letter said I should take the next plane possible and get to the Congo. Mr. Balla had landed something big and needed my help. The die was cast; Mr. Balla and I had bonded for life. It was as if the many voided centuries between us were reduced to a mere few hours. In the end, I knew all that there was meant for me to know at that point, so the only thing left for me to do was decide, pack, and get to the airport. Rock had his work cut out for him as well. His journey was not even close to ending; in fact, it was just beginning in an America I was trying to escape. Rock had been spared from the bloody centuries-long Congolese European war, not just to be a messenger, but to continue on to the future in America's Midwest where he would attend a university that only a few years earlier I had been forbidden to attend.

"I am aiming for a degree in finance," he said.

Before departing, Rock reached into his pockets and pulled out the inner lining, exposing to me that they were empty. Rock was broke, penniless, and hungry. Rock pointed to a line in French at the very bottom of the hand-written letter Mr. Balla had sent. There it was. A written statement that suggested I should advance Rock the funds he would need to reach Missouri, and I did just that with a smile. I made lunch, and we chatted using my broken French and his crushed English. As we ate, I wondered how Rock was going to complete his mission here with all that he faced. I did not know, but on the other hand, Rock's eyes suggested he was thinking about how I was going to survive all that he knew I would face: getting to the Congo and surviving the European death traps and the ongoing European-created and sponsored civil war in the Congo: the so-called "Heart of Darkness." The whole of the global African family was under attack and had been for centuries, and Rock, Mr. Balla, and I were soldiers on the front line defending as best we could our deeply troubled global African community and people. Africa and her global community needed her strongest and most able sons and daughters on our feet at the ready, at the front of the longest bloodiest revolution known to mankind, to guard our people from the great fall and against all known and unknown enemies. Africans were being sent here to carry out missions, while Africans in the diaspora like me were needed and being sent to carry out life-threatening missions in Africa.

The letter Rock carried said Mr. Balla needed me in the Congo to help to protect and finalize important projects with little or no money. We all had fought and partly freed ourselves but would not receive any economic support from the great America or the EU members who showed only disrespect to the descendants of once enslaved people who they had taken everything from. They had even held control over all the printed money in order to hold Africans back and down. This was being done based on the sum total of their fears: the fear of the black man, his women, and children and their rite of passage to be the free self-determining people we had the right to be.

Chapter 2

Into the Unknown

In November 1998, I was feeling angry and tired of being shackled, rendered cultureless for centuries in an ugly America. As I considered the wasted years in America spent chasing false dreams for a white, self-appointed, privileged class pimping anything but a democracy, I realized a black veteran like me just wanted the hell out. As I made preparations to depart the nightmares African and marginalized people regardless of color suffered in an ungraceful nation, I had a stress level hugging a 99.9 and a half out of 100.

Finally, behind me lay racist America and a hell of a lot of angry, lean hungry, uneducated years—and a sea of bad blood between my white brothers and sisters. Like five hundred million other PAD in the diaspora, I was trapped between the cross and the Koran, damned if I did with one and damned if I did not with the other; either being a Christian or hated Muslim, Democrat or Republican. These were the only political and cultural choices, and they were under white domination. I had no cultural rights as long as I remained chained to the burning cross by Bible-carrying Ku Klux Klan members in America. Clan members in America are damned by those they damned. Middle Eastern believers of the Koran saw whites and Africans as nonbelievers or infidels, having no righteous religious beliefs. To this end, Africans are both disrespected and condemned by the extremist believers of both religions using both the holy Koran and the Bible as their reason for inflicting crimes against African humanity from Mississippi, South Sudan, Rio, Haiti, Cape Town, and beyond. My whole life was being pissed on, wasted in America! I had to make the call to Mr. Balla, anyone in Africa I could reach, and in doing so, I learned they were just as victimized and eager to reach back for the very same reasons; so much for human rights and freedom for Africans. It was time to kick ass.

A little more than a week after meeting Rock, I flew out of JFK airport on Air France into what the French still called French Congo. Adding thousands of sleepless sky miles to endless journeys already made, I tried to escape carrying the relentless burden of the "Invisible Man," the black man, in America. The black man's burden is the white man and his oppressive system. I am making every effort to escape America's limitations on me and the lie about America's freedom. Do I hate America I ask myself? The answer is no. I am a soldier. Most soldiers do not hate what they fight, which can weaken a soldier. What I hate is injustice for all living things. I join others in fighting to change a biased system, any system that uses oppression of any kind.

I am thirty-five thousand feet above the earth among the clouds but not feeling any safer buckled into an airline seat, watching overweight passengers consume gout-producing, disgraceful, and intestinally destructive food. The passengers seated on the plane now resembling little faceless dots are fused in my mind's eye, all resembling a giant impressionist painting of a people held in bondage. My face was at the center of this global giant painting. Even though I was at the center of the painting, I knew I was still an invisible man in a Eurocentric system with one mission: escape the European concept of freedom and get my African land and wealth back under the African people's control. I had to get out. Coming out of Alabama schools for black people in the 1960s I was stuck with a second-rate education with more Ds on my high school report card than you can find in the dictionary. Like millions of other Africans in the diaspora at the time, I could not spell "dictionary" at graduation, which ensured no way to earn a living or manage my assets; I sported a life that had no future.

But my folks back home in Alabama had held on to what little knowledge they had kept hidden for centuries about Africa. They lacked education, but their minds were not broken. They could and did pass information on to me to enable my siblings and me to know the direction as humans we came from, a mapped-out plan, a direction back home to Africa. Even though the world's fat cats had taken everything I had, even our ancestral family name, and fed off my ancestors' bones, DNA, and historical discoveries, stolen our memories, African land, and wealth and reduced me and my people's knowledge of self and the world around us to the point of near zero, most of us still stood. With all that, I was still driven to be a man and rise above that near zero and be the man I am. I was going back with the aim to get it all back, my name, my African land and my wealth and make them pay. I was beyond fear and hate since both can slow one down. I was a one-man crusader for one confident reason: African-owned success.

French Intolerance

Eight hours later my Air France flight out of JFK landed in Paris on time for my planned connecting flight. Having arrived at the Paris airport, I found myself entombed in bulletproof glass walkways and cameras scanning passengers' every move. I felt like a moving object in some freak peep show transported by a conveyer belt like cows headed for the slaughter with the rest of the exhausted passengers still suffering from cramped coach syndrome. There was a slight musty stench, evidence of our previously compacted quarters gassed with human farting, combined with jet lag, which all produced stressed-out passengers, like aliens not yet mentally ready for Earth. Suddenly, I see a young African woman being manhandled and deported from French soil by French police.

I slowed my walk out of concern for the woman but could do nothing to help her. I had lived in race-slick Paris years earlier, so I could relate to the African woman. I had traveled to Paris searching for a safe underground passage back to Africa but found the way blocked. I had heard about this Underground Railroad from author James Baldwin, the famed African American who took no prisoners about white America's lies about freedom for all Americans. It was James Baldwin's exit and the writings he sent back that drew me out of America's Christian heartland of darkness more than any other works, even *Black Boy*, written by the legendary hard-hitting author Richard Wright in 1937. Richard Wright had left the scene for Europe long before Baldwin. I did not know beforehand when I first arrived in Paris in 1966 that Europe, specifically post–World War II France, was not the reliable safe haven or the new-age Underground Railroad I had hoped for. Unfortunately upon my arrival, I discovered 1966 Paris, indeed all of Europe, only pretended to place out the welcome mat for African Americans fleeing from "The Land of the Free and Home of the Brave." Paris was not then and not now a place for Africans fleeing from America or from the motherland I hoped to meet and learn from when I arrived.

Watching helplessly through the large cagelike glass that divided us, I could clearly see the police struggling with the young African woman. Her hair was a standup mess on her head. Her shoes did not seem to match, or maybe it was the age of the shoes, and her tattered clothes looks as if she had been through the ringer, perhaps evidence of the years, months, weeks, and days it took to reach this moment. The gloves the police wore made them look more sinister, not more professional, than they were behaving at this moment as they dragged the screaming woman across the spotless floor, likely washed by people of color. I found this theatrical facade to be quite insulting. This was no way to treat the woman! It was a person, a life, and she deserved respect. Didn't they have a fucking wheelchair? This African woman's deportation would cost her everything. Watching this woman's ill treatment by the French police, I felt danger building and anger rising out of control in my blood. I knew I had better move on because even the thick plate glass that divided me from the police holding the African woman would not be enough to hold me back. The evidence of European strategy to control and demoralize people of color was now in the open for world travelers to witness. It all came down to French racism, even though Africa was feeding France. I had to remain focused on my real mission: get to the Congo. I stood erect, swallowing as much of the rage as possible in a large gulp of dry saliva, not wanting to compromise the mission ahead. I took a wide step as if stepping out of the present into the future.

I moved on, regaining my manufactured, international composure. I picked up my exit visa at the arrival station and expected to hop onto my continuing flight for Brazzaville, Congo, without problems..

I made a straight line through a few early morning zombie-looking passengers spread about on the waiting area floor. Some were sprawled near the exit door, partly blocking the passage leading to the bus-loading zone where I needed to take the bus to the Terminal B departing gates. It was one of those rainy, gray, foggy fall mornings in Paris, the kind that makes you want to crawl into bed with a good book or woman. But like the rest of the world, I had to go to work. I had a mission. Like the African woman, I was up against an imperialist postcolonial Western world fighting for survival. Before France took part in enslaving Africans and colonized a number of African countries, France and its citizens were living in a world of crime and poverty. One of their only major food crops was barley, and that was failing them in the 1600s due to overused farming soil and lack of education or resources to do better. The French government started to ship its overpopulated, unwanted people and criminals to other regions of the world to do France's dirty work. What did it get France and its people? Today, France is nearly totally dependent on Africa for its basic needs. Nearly half of France's national budget is dependent on resources from two of Africa's smallest but richest countries: the Republic of the Congo and the Republic of Gabon. Billions of US dollars in crude oil comes from the Republic of Congo, where I was headed with a high possibility of getting my ass kicked if I was not careful.

A Glimpse into the Past

France was assigned its illegal stake in Africa at the Berlin Conference in Germany in 1884, which was agreed to by all its partners in crime: America, Germany, Spain, England, France, Belgium, and Italy (a turncoat country in World War II in near total decline, but no less deadly for African people in Ethiopia). France and all the colonial players weren't just using lies, the holy cross, and the KKK cross. The French and their fellow colonizers used the words "Africans are not human," the Bible, and lethal force to enslave and separate Africans families who were at first willing trading partners with the Europeans. This is the reason I pointed out in the opening introduction that Africans are too rich to have friends then or now. Great Britain, France, Germany and America masterminded to name four of the 1882 Berlin Conference Clan and set out to divide earth's peaceful at ease first family by tribe and skin color, and even sex, while promoting scorn for Africans and their timeless written human history dating back tens of thousands of years. The French and their partners in crime violated every basic person of color and native human right backed up with scorn, mass murder, and rape. The French-colonizing

government and many of France's willing
bloodthirsty citizens went on to spread their evil
campaign throughout African regions such as the
Congo, Cameroon, Chad, Benin, Central Africa, Ivory
Coast, and Sudan. I do not mean the historical
present-day Sudan to the northeast of Chad and
south of Egypt, but an area called Sudan in 1895
that rested between Senegal and the Ivory Coast,
known today as Mali, Niger, Guinea, and Upper
Volta (today's Burkina Faso), Algeria Tunis, Tripoli,
Egypt (for a while), and Madagascar. Mind you, this
happened in 1895, nine years after the infamous
Berlin Conference of 1884, where select European
nations met in Berlin and plotted to invade, colonize,
and enslave humanity in Africa that was more than
willing to trade on an equal footing. My concern is
that France is in just as deep of a sinkhole today, if
not deeper, than it was in the 1600s. Africa, rich as it
is, is the last thing to trust a hungry former slaver
with. You may think I am a bit consumed by history
and wrongs done to humanity, and you would be
correct. I am not writing a love story. Hence, the
reason I wrote this book as I lived it day to day since
1962 is to expose to the youth and the future what
happened to my generation in our passage through
swamps of Western evil.

Exit Visa

Ten minutes later, I arrived at Terminal B
rolling my only carry-on bag behind me. It was still
early, around 7:00 a.m., so there was no one ahead of
me at the Air Afrique counter where a tall, stunning,
young African clerk stood with her head buried in
the computer screen. She seemed to not notice my

presence. I waited for what I thought to be a respectable time before interrupting her concentration.

"Air France sent me," I announced. The words were out before I realized the cultural mistake I had made. I was in the international community, an element in which one would do well to offer respect up front. If you wish to share inject a personal view, an unofficial culture, one can sometimes exploit when you are in a tight spot try it as it may well serve the moment. What I am suggesting in this case is we Africans have not often been able to share cultures on most matters for centuries. It's a way of feeling out the other persons needs or concerns. I should have greeted her first. Although she didn't say it, the look on her face told me she perceived my behavior to be a bit rude. Her eyebrows furrowed into a razor-sharp glare that only black women can manage to pull off with laser precision.

"Good morning," said the Air Afrique ticket agent with a partly manufactured smile that suggested if I wanted something from her, to please use a civil tone and be kind. Knowing I was not on my best behavior, I submitted. There were justifications for her reaction. She had a right to demand respect from the hundreds of faces she encountered hour after hour, day in and day out, and year after year working in an alien culture far from her homeland. Visions of the African woman being manhandled by the French police popped on and off in my head.

"Oh, I am sorry, forgive me. It's the hours I keep. I am forgetting my manners. Good morning," I said leaning over the fading emerald green Air Afrique ticket counter. "My Air France flight to the

Republic of the Congo was canceled. I was told I might be able to fly out with you?"

She seemed more receptive to my new approach and flashed me a warm smile. "It's ok," she said. "The war in Congo produced and funded in large part by Europeans, these French, who now fear losing an aircraft. That is why you are here. Otherwise they would be stealing every passenger out there before you reach an African-managed airline."

"I know," I said playing it cool.

"The war has crossed the Congo River into Brazzaville, Congo...Mr. Weston," she replied, checking my ticket. "The end of your journey, I see?"

Even though I was painfully aware of the war in the Congo, it still upset me, but instead of letting on and risk limiting my opportunity of getting a seat on the flight, I leaned back and relaxed. I already had a bad feeling that I might not get a seat even if the flight did depart. Overbooking and being booted from a flight was a normal occurrence flying into and out of Africa. I know from experience. But please not now. Not on this mission. Not this morning I urged faith. My business in the bleeding, war-torn Congo, war or no war, was too important. In fact, it was urgent that I get there. I had to be on that flight because there was no way of getting a message to Mr. Balla in Brazzaville, who was meeting me at the airport, assuming it was not blown up by now. The attractive African sky angel placed my name on the waiting list, confirming my worse fear that the flight was overbooked. I pulled out my IMSCO badge, hoping she would give priority to an NGO linked to the ECOSOC of the United Nations.

"Miss," I pleaded, "it's extremely important

that I get on this flight."

The African sky angel took my ID badge to inspect it. "Everything should be all right. Come back in two hours," the attractive clerk assured me. "Don't worry."

It was not quite 7:30 in the morning. Out of respect, I backed away from the counter, making a conscious effort not to turn my back to her just yet. People react positively to confidence, and I wanted to show I had confidence in her. We had connected. I knew it, and she knew it. Her smile seemed to indicate she respected what I was doing.

A few hours later I was seated in the departure waiting area, holding my boarding pass. The sky angel for Air Afrique had not only come through for me, she had A-listed me. I had a first-class transit visa. She had upgraded me to business class all the way there. Pleased with my upgrade, I tried to relax and mentally prepare for the long journey.

As these thoughts invaded my brain, I caught a glimpse of three police officers. Then, as suspected, seated wedged between the officers was the African woman being evicted from France. She was relaxed. The woman was not in any way restrained as far as I could see, but she was unusually peaceful—far from the panicked state I had seen her in earlier that morning. I wondered if they had drugged her to quiet her down. However, when they announced for us to start boarding, the young African woman's anger sprang to life again. This time, she let out a cry in her native Republic of Benin tongue. A hauntingly piercing scream, the sound echoed through the crowded waiting room with such a high pitch that even the most insensitive brain could not block out her emotional screams. The stressed African woman yelled all the way down the ramp as she and the officers entered the airplane.

A few African passengers tried to turn away, mostly out of shame I thought, because I felt a sense of shame and humiliation too. It was embarrassing to me that an African woman would be forced to leave any country in Europe after what Europeans had done to and stolen from African people, cultures, and the economy. I had a feeling of dread because I did not wish to follow her onto that enclosed, flying tin box for the six hours it would take to reach the Republic of Benin. I felt humiliation because I wanted to do something, but at the time, I could do nothing but witness and document the inhuman event.

I felt I had failed not only this young African woman, but also all African women in need. I still hear her cries even now, years later. In spite of all France's propped-up, revered hospitality, there was "no room at the inn" for one more harmless African woman in distress. I imagined the worse about this woman's life, reflecting on how tough life can be under European slavery, colonialism, and imperialism still found in Africa. It was fading but still alive in many places in 1998. I could only guess at the woman's real plight and pain. As the rest of the passengers entered the business class area of the airplane, we could hear her cry out from the back of the plane's coach section. Her cries were chilling. I tried not to let on that the woman was affecting me. As all passengers know during flights, all pain becomes one.

Thanks to the African sky angel at the Air Afrique ticket counter who had placed me in business class, I would not have to hear the woman's cries that well, if at all. Business class had removed me if only for a short while from the six degrees of separation. The next six hours crossing the continent of Africa was stillness, peace at thirty-five thousand feet at eight hundred miles per hour. Still anger ran through my veins like molten lava through super-heated tubs deep in the layers of my body. I fell asleep, but my mind, as usual, remained alert.

Chapter 3

Crossing the Mediterranean Sea

My consciousness drifted back in time to 1982 when I first visited the Republic of Liberia in West Africa. A few years before, one of Africa's bloodiest civil wars was fought between brothers over petty cash and diamonds they both owned titles to. They were unable to respect each other's ownership or lacked contact with their African American kin like me in the Western world who is able to add value to such vital resources and be partners, allies in a sustainable global market. In the early 1900s, a group of enslaved and then freed Africans from America had settled in Liberia and remained but never received the proper introduction to each other through education to develop and sustain relations in business and trade such as I was attempting to do in Congo. As things fell apart in Liberia, the whole of West Africa over the years, was the American system, and Asians, lead by Japan protecting Japan take in Liberian rubber interests the best harvest in the end after a war for foreigners was and still is the plunders from war between African brothers. This was America and Europe's way of ensuring the African people's climb to total independence and development never truly took hold.

I was awake. My thoughts drifted back into the future. I was still airborne. I looked at my watch, then out the window, and realized the aging African jetliner was only just now leaving the Mediterranean Sea and entering Africa over the body of water that divided or linked Europe to North Africa. The journey ignited deeper worries about how my cash would hold up. Would I be able to resupply in the Congo if needed? I had been to parts of Africa before, and I knew from experience that a certain amount of cash in hand was a safety net. Wherever I went and what I did, credit cards could not play a role, since they were useless in many cases.

Looking from the window of the plane down at the edge of the great northeast Sahara Desert, I could not help wonder if the Arab invaders truly believed they would not have to pay a price. Pay for invading North Africa and partnering with Europeans in the slave trade and for attempted destruction of African civilization to settle African land with their often very biased culture.

Benin, Land of the Blacks

Six hours later, after flying over some of the most thrilling and vast desert area on the planet, tropical lush green forest appeared as we descended into Contonou, Benin, airport in West Africa. The African airline crew did their job of getting us there safely considering they had so little to work with, given such an aging aircraft. After four centuries, the French were still here in Benin with every other Western imperialist patching up holes in their budgets. Many of them, however, had withdrawn their cash in the wake of the country gaining its independence. Now they were back in full force. First, the postcolonialists withdraw the funds if any and then break or ship out any equipment that might assist the Africans before ordering their personnel to bust every latrine and burn all important records, even the birthday certificates of some African presidents. When departing Guinea, West Africa, the French burned their folk history. The Republic of Guinea took its independence from the bloody hands of the French in 1958 and then leaned to the Eastern bloc for support. This was an affront to France and the all- mighty United States.

Happy to be back on African soil and being processed through passport control in Contonou airport, I could see the deported African woman standing in the lobby. The police had vanished, most likely in the process of taking the return six-hour flight back to Paris. Two other African women were now meeting the deportee, and a white female French missionary shadowed the other two, all dressed in black, not the proper attire for the African cultural welcome I have previously experienced. The African woman had just been tossed back into the African pot surrounded by the hot flames kept burning by the French from centuries earlier. The African woman, like millions of other Africans, had tried Europe hoping to escape what was for me an African Eden where I was headed. But I admit the European evil deeds were still here. They were veiled in aid to hide the death grip apparent by the tight white collars the nuns wore, evidence that France maintained around its colony's neck to this very day.

The aged, busted clock on the Contonou airport terminal waiting room wall waited, frozen in time with the rest of us, for modern time and Africa to catch up. The clock had years of reddish dust caked inside and around its faded, cheap, decaying French-made plastic frame. The clock's aging hands had stopped at 2:45 I noticed, in some moment in the distant past suggesting parts of Africa were still in lock-down. Across the way through the dusty glass, the African crew that piloted us from Paris into Contonou stopped and warmly greeted their replacements, another group of neatly uniformed Africans that were to fly us to the Republic of the Congo. The all-African crews seemed happy about the shift change, as they stood chatting and laughing in the middle of the terminal lobby. During the two-hour layover in Contonou, I did what I often do in most airports in African countries: I visit. I scanned the many faces trying to find a familiar African face that would resemble faces in the Western world. In Benin, there were many such faces.

At 7:00 p.m., Air Afrique departed Contonou for the Congo running late. This was the last leg of my journey. The plane flew down the oil- and mineral-rich coastline of equatorial Africa, crossing coastal Cameroon, a former German, French, and Nordic colony into the heart of Africa: toward the Congo.

The Golden Land Below

An hour into the flight out of Contonou, strong wind currents tossed and bounced the green and white jet around like a tiny Ping-Pong ball above a forest the size of Western Europe. From my window seat, I could see the sun disappear over the green leafy horizon. A moonless night. The darkness set in within seconds it seemed—a bad omen maybe. The billions of years old great African forest wept like the rain that fell like tears as the forest animals were being eradicated a species a day by European logging and mining companies. They used an African modern slave labor force to wipe the forest clean. In the eighties, a World Bank study found that as much as 85 percent of aid that flowed into Africa was used for purposes other than that for which it was initially intended. In contrast to the Marshall Plan's short, well-aimed injections of cash, most of Africa has received aid continually for about fifty years. Aid is a relentless curse, like the busted clock back in Contonou airport with no time limit imposed to work against. Most of the brain-dead African leaders who headed governments should not have had the role as overseers of African land and resources in the first place. America and Europe just did not give a damn about the forest or the life and clean air the forests sustained on our planet. What else could have had such a negative effect on a continent and its people than foreign money changers?

Everyone on the flight that night knew we might not make it into or out of the Congo alive. The US Department of State had warned Americans beforehand of the dangers that awaited them as they saw danger based on their interest. Death was always a real possibility, but dangerous or not, nothing had ever felt this thrilling, this good, to me before. The excitement and adventure—to see it all from the head of the bullet I was riding—in was a best in body experience I had to that date. Was I afraid? Afraid of what? Going home? No! The very thought of turning back—turn back to what? To insult myself?

The bullet-nosed plane inched closer and closer to its target at Maya Maya airport. As it descended, the monsoon rains could be heard smashing hard against the scratched and aging plastic windows of the Air Afrique jet. The wind currents tossed the plane from one side to the other as the pilots tried to guide the aircraft down toward the rain-slicked runway. I was amazed we made it this far because Western airline regulations would have forbidden us to attempt to land in such conditions. But in Africa a rainstorm comes when it wants to. Out here, in the Congo, people were accustomed to doing what they had to do in harsh conditions. The Congo was not for the faint of heart. I had a date waiting with an angel named Ms. Opportunity, and nothing short of a fiery crash or an unmarked grave in culture-rich African soil was going to stop me from keeping that date.

Chapter 4

Landing at Maya Maya Airport

Brazzaville, the capital city of the Republic of the Congo, was named after a Frenchman. The very word "Brazzaville" smelled of French and

Belgian bloody baths, limb amputations, and decapitations during the colonial era of which the stench of unseen horror still lingered. I checked my watch. It was now after 8:00 p.m., December 1998, just fourteen months short of the twenty-first century, and I was not entering the next century as an economic slave! So fly me in. Fly to hell if that is what it takes. I am here, baby. I am here.

The jet made the half dozen or so dips and sharp turns to the left and then right, nose down, then nose up as if a dance contest was taking place to the cue and tune of lighting and deep drum sounds of thunder. Or we could have well been dodging a missile or two fired from below as the plane lined up for the final approach into Maya Maya airport at Brazzaville. As the engines strained, you could hear the stress of the weather pressing against the outer metal of the plane. The pilots demanded more from the aging aircraft and her engines than some would have dared. The aging plane was their sweet lover in the best of times and their dependable allie in harsh weather and times such as these. We all let the plane do our breathing. The airmobile guys women included knew and did their jobs. They had this! The lights on the outside of the jet's wings were turned on, which increased our risk of being shot down by rebels on the ground angry with the government for not sharing the vast wealth we all owned as African stakeholders. With the Europeans in our hair, we could not harvest the opportunities properly for all the people.

You could not see the rebels below with ground-to-air missiles, but they were there hiding so well that they became a part of the bush and vanishing forest they fought so hard to protect in the rain just beyond the runway. The approach to the landing strip, cratered such as it was, seemed to take forever. The landing gear was heard being released just as a loud clap of tropical thunder could be heard. The plane was now dark. The rain was so heavy that we could barely see out the windows. Boom! Someone's carry-on bag shot out of the overhead bins, spilling its contents onto the floor. Somewhere in the rear, a baby started to yell its head off. "Let the baby cry. Fear was behind us Africans," I thought. It's all part of the rebirth I was witnessing. I loved it. I felt alive. What a ride!

The pilot in the cockpit made split-second adjustments time after time as if he could not see a damn thing in the blinding rain. Was the pilot guessing, feeling his way down? Man and machine were locked in a contest with nature's fury over every meter. Then, the seemingly impossible happened. Touchdown! The worn tires I had noticed just before boarding in Benin finally hit the pot-holed runway, jarring the lights back on in our cabin. For a moment, there was only silence in the cabin as the plane taxied down the wind- and rain-swept runway. A moment or so later, someone started clapping his or her hands, causing a chain reaction of applause from the rest of the passengers. I was not one to applaud, but I was impressed with the crew. What sheer fucking genius! These fly boys and girls knew how to fly a fucking plane! The African pilots and crew had come through for their passengers once more, despite being underpaid and underemployed and having to operate an aging fleet in need of repairs, which were kept hidden to cut down on cost out of fear of early retirement for the crew. Few things in Africa lived long enough to be repaired. The Air Afrique airline was suffering the same fate

Zambian Airways had suffered in 1990, forced out of the skies and business for being a threat to the European airlines moving goods from apartheid South Africa: the last European and American holdout. I flew Zambian Airways once from America to Zambia and across East Africa to Kenya. Then it was gone.

After exiting the plane, we stepped into an African monsoon. The passengers and I had to brave the heavy rainfall from the runway to reach the bullet-riddled, divided airline terminal. The terminal had a first class and diplomatic area and a general passenger area as far apart as the African and European visions for Africa and its people. Both terminal areas were about one hundred or so yards apart with no covered walkway protection from the weather. Between the plane and the terminal, we passed a few armed, very young soldiers, probably fourteen years old and up. They were standing guard with no proper rain gear or hats. The tough young soldiers all held Russian-made AK-47s and kept a close eye on the passengers who split into two groups. Their eyes seemed to be more on my group headed for the VIP diplomatic section of the arrival gate.

Africa badly needs these young soldiers to keep it from being overrun by Europeans and freelance assassins of the people and their African dream. Europe and America can yap all they want about child labor and child soldiers. Hell, at eighteen in Africa, you are already viewed in the hood to be approaching middle age. What about American and European use of African children as slave laborers or worse yet as slave sex partners? It is the youth that make up the largest sector of the continual African community. The average American and European live to between seventy and ninety years of age, while the average African lives to between forty and fifty at the time I was entering Africa, so you do the math on how important youth labor and soldiers are to the survival of Africa and its people. Far too many African youth are leaving Africa and not returning. Death due to gunshots and the penitentiary are the two main reasons with higher death rates gaining on the fail return rate. I saw the young African teenage soldiers as having my back. They gave me the feeling the airport was under control. Black youth control.

A great continent needs and deserves great black African youth. Having been a soldier myself, albeit for an ungrateful nation, and moving from one war zone to another, I salute the young soldiers everywhere.

My thoughts remained with that flawless, blindfolded landing. Only an African bush pilot could pull off such a landing. I was all worked up standing there on the wet tarmac. Getting to the Congo had been one hell of a rush. I couldn't help but stare back at the plane as we exited, feeling overwhelmed with respect and admiration for our crew and that aging plane.

Meeting Mr. Balla in the Congo

My Congolese contact, Mr. Balla, a dark, handsome, graying man in his late 60s, was dressed in a dark, fashionable French-cut suit. He was an easily identifiable man and stood out from all the others waiting in the diplomatic entrance as the first-class passengers approached from the tarmac runway and out of the heavy rain. Mr. Balla had checked the arriving passenger list to know in advance how and when I would be arriving. Balla had arranged an official diplomatic ID for me, a privileged VIP pass reserved for men and women on the move. Africa had so much to offer its people, and yet the leaders gave so little in terms of cooperation to the masses who wanted to get moving on building the continent. The pass helped a lot because I could avoid a second nightmare in the same evening after the landing of not having to go through customs in the public terminal, where rain was leaking through the tin rooftop in the baggage area that was riddled with bullet holes. There was no conveyer belt to transport baggage from the plane to the arrival gate, so you had to carry your own luggage in.

It took only a few minutes for Mr. Balla to process my passport through customs, which amounted to a quick handshake and an imprint of the official stamp to seal the deal with the custom officials. My need for a visa and passport had been waived, which I thought only fitting considering. My brother, Mr. Balla, an experienced diplomat had seen to it that I would be honored as a VIP. I was privileged by the gesture, considering my brothers and sisters in the Congo didn't have much to spare.

A short time later, we departed the airport terminal and walked to a waiting car Mr. Balla had arranged to take us to my hotel. The rain had slowed to a near halt. Outside, we crossed the busy street in front of Maya Maya airport and entered a dark-colored car. Inside the car, the driver had an AK-47 on the front seat. I never saw Balla with a weapon of any kind. The drive to my hotel in the light rain that night was like no other I had experienced. Soldiers were everywhere, in jeeps and unmarked cars, standing and moving in all directions. They were standing guard in the pouring rain on most street corners, where each time the lightning flashed, you could get a glimpse of their weapons.

I had gotten lucky and was arriving at a lull in the fighting. However, the locals fighting among themselves could not compare with the large-scale war being promoted by European invaders over the country's oil and mineral wealth Balla and I were after. Vast amounts of crude oil had been in the control of the French and Belgium since about 1946, the year the United Nations was founded. At the independence of the Republic of the Congo, no attempt was made to change French and Belgian claims to ownership of the vast mineral wealth; the wars being fought here were due to the United Nations' mishandling of the meaning of independence, and UN members had deliberately locked uniting families and PAD, the likes of me, out of the African inheritance. From the beginning, wars were planned to maintain control of wealth. The European and Euro-American multinationals that promoted conflict between my African brothers knew the Africans did not know anything about the rich onshore and offshore oil fields, let alone the amounts of wealth leaving the area when foreigners started drilling and production. But the righteous World Bank, IMF, and the United Nations' most powerful members knew because they were the takers.

Though the war was being fought between Africans, we all knew Africans were still trying to repel the foreigners, including the European-invading, culturally dominating church. They all aided in illegally grabbing vast amounts of improvised African people's land, including Brazzaville, followed by wealth and resources, right across this battered, blood-stained land. What they did not know was that African Americans and local indigenous African people were teaming together. I have landed on African soil in order to place the wealth management under African people's control and economically empower the masses at any cost. That is my mission here. The world was probably laughing at us thinking we could not pull this task off on our own. A lot of credit must be given to visionary Jamaica-born Marcus Garvey who called for PAD in the diaspora to make the move as far back as the 1920s.

By the millions, Africans in the diaspora were now joining up with Africans to take Africa back and to control and drive the foreigners out of African people's economic and business culture. Setbacks would be many but we had vowed on our ancestors' graves and needs of the youth to never abandon the mission. Africa was at war and in deepening debt caused by the World Bank, IMF and their blood-sucking Western clients, and get rich-or-sell-out-trying African men calling themselves the people's leaders and representatives. Not one of the African leaders ever gave the likes of me an invite or anyone I know worth his or her salt. I was witnessing destruction. The World Bank and IMF agents for foreign governments and big business is not the best laid plan for a wealthy Africa and its now global people I was soon to learn the hard way on the ground. There was no place for the likes of the black man in the heartless, cultureless, capitalist World Bank and IMF world. It was a basket of thieves in bed with every Western leader and mostly corrupt politicians. Most open-minded African men and women knew the World Bank and IMF to be profit funders. Their partners on Wall Street and many of those investing wanted most black men and women dead, imprisoned, or locked away from the affairs of African business and development. These foreigners were doing nothing positive to assist in global African development.

How is it possible that Africa could come out of slavery in debt to slavers when it was the Europeans, Euro-Americans, and Arab system that stole all that the people in and outside of Africa owned to fund the development? How is it possible that by 1975, Africa was US$2 billion in debt on paper to Europe and America and had nothing to show for it? And Africans were not taken seriously when they demanded payment for the trillions of US dollars in slave labor and human right abuses. The so-called African debt had reached US$8 billion by 1982. DRC President Mobutu Sese Seko had stashed some US$5 billion of that in European banks, bringing the total to US$13 billion in that the Mobutu deposits were all stolen funds from the people. Idi Amin, president of Uganda, had stashed a large nest egg in the Middle East with the Arabs. About the only thing good about Idi Amin was that he stood up and fought the Jewish invaders of Uganda that forced the rest of the African people to band the Israelis from Africa for a decade for their crime committed in the seventies.

These two African presidents are now dead and with them goes the access to their bank accounts in Europe and America. What is needed is a technology-savvy youth to do the search, find the funds, and get them back. For now, the stolen billions remain missing. So the ranting and robbing goes on and on, but the money will not be lost. Why was this war being fought in the Republic of the Congo and DRC at all and for so long at the cost of millions of African lives? Was it all due to African leadership corruption, or was it all due to guns being pointed at African leaders' heads? Africa had some issues all right and lots of them, I give you that, and it extends back to African leaders' roles in the slave trade of their own people before the slavers came back for the African chiefs and their goons that assisted in the trade. Why weren't these African leaders working to better the plight of Africans worldwide? My head was spinning seeking answers to questions held hidden now by Africans, very bad representation, the European cross, the Koran, the International Mother Fuckers, and their capitalist clients.

From Maya Maya airport, it was a twenty-minute drive over moon-sized potholes on avenues and streets to the French Le Meridian Brazzaville Hotel. During the drive, Mr. Balla brought me up-to-date on the latest developments in the war and peace efforts between the government and the bush rebels fighting for a share of the wealth neither planned to share with the masses nor knew how to negotiate with oil companies or manage the state properly. When two dogs fight over a bone in the street, a third dog comes in and grabs the bone. PAD, represented by the likes of Balla and me, and our hidden teams are the third dog. So feared are the Europeans and increasingly feared Chinese, Arabs, Indians, and the others who refuse to cooperate, they must risk sending in supporters of the holy Koran (crop dusters), as we will learn later on. Mr. Balla, a retired ambassador having served in the now US-sanctioned Cuba for the Republic of the Congo government, had hopes of spearheading negotiations with the Congo rebels in the bush using IMSCO and his own NGO to invite rebel representatives to the table. It seems they had agreed just before I arrived.

The United Nations' report on the war had said over two million had died before my arrival, and many, many more were still dying. Still, Mr. Balla thought it better I came in, and if possible, I would accompany him across the Congo River to meet with the rebel leader just in case the government in office lost its edge. The government was not aware of this planned meeting, and Balla and I felt it better to let the meeting remain off the record for now. These were dangerous days.

Inside the Heart of Darkness

The Le Meridian Hotel at Brazzaville was a $250 a day plus hotel. I wouldn't be surprised if that included a tourist and war tax. This was the earlier reason for my concern about my cash reserves. On the rainy night of my arrival, I saw a lobby full of foreigners, seated and standing, all looking for a handout just as they did when Europeans first arrived in the Congo in the 1600s at the point of a gun. The hotel lobby scene mirrored what I once witnessed in Lagos, Nigeria, just after independence in 1974. My visit to Nigeria had had a major impact on my young life, and it was not all good. Back in the hotel lobby in Brazzaville were mostly shady-looking Europeans, Arabs, and Lebanese. A few others has nationalities so mixed I could not make out where they were from. The Chinese invasion in large numbers had not yet reached the two Congos.

Hollywood central casting would have loved the mix for any one of its B-rated, biased films produced in the past and planned present. They were not able to purchase *Raid on Entebbe,* a B movie set in the DRC in 1976 about Europeans trying to steal minerals. Having failed, they are all, no doubt, still looking for African wealth.

The Le Meridien Brazzaville hotel also served as a brothel. It was large for lodging in this part of Central Africa.

African women were reduced to moonlighting as whores in order to remain alive and feed their family during the wars. Some women were smoking and drinking and dressed like Westerners do in peep shows on the seedy side of Paris, New York, Los Angeles, and France. Even the Arabs whose religion forbade alcohol were drinking the stuff and acting like fish on polluted holy water.

The bar sat off to the left side of the large space with tables and chairs made locally of rare redwood trees. The furniture took up most of the space in the lobby. Most of the odd pieces of carved African art were apparently protected, spared from the bullet rounds lodged in cracked window glass and walls. Mr. Balla checked me in at the front desk, and we were led to the aging elevators under the watchful eyes of the foreigners, fearing what could be competition for them. The walk from the front doors of the hotel to the rear of the lobby and then the elevators was short. The bellboy carrying my bag entered the elevator with us, and we all went upstairs to my fourth-floor room. I tipped the bellboy who wore a French-cut, aging, red waiter's jacket a size too large. It was then that I realized the nightly price tag would be way too much.

It was the only hotel not completely destroyed by gunfire and the war bombs that often came like the rains. It was this French hotel or the streets. The French had paid dearly to keep the hotel open and to protect its interest in the Republic of the Congo that fed half the population of the ungrateful French people. The thought of the young homeless African woman at the Paris airport being escorted out of France flashed across my mind. The Republic of the Congo's resources has fed the French people and their long imperialist arm since the 1800s. The French ate well while biting the hands that fed them while it lasted. Now they were back where they started: on beggar's knees with crops dying due to soil hurried by get-rich-quick chemicals ensuring nothing would grow at all that was edible. In the room, I pressed down on the foam rubber mattress bed covered in a multicolored blanket that had seen more action than Indiana Jones. The mattress lay as flat as the watered-down flat beer on tap in the hotel bar or as flat as the bed bugs that infested the beding awaiting a late dinner: my blood.

I stepped to the window in my hotel room and looked out through a crack in the dark red cotton and linen curtain, taking care not to disturb them too much because you never knew what trigger-happy snipers were about. I had a view of the ancient Congo River and could make out the dim lights coming from the besieged famous city of blood, Kinshasa, capital of the DRC. The Congo River that divided the two cities was huge and carried trillions of gallons of fresh water every minute, if not every second, in its timeless flow toward the Atlantic Ocean. One could feel the river's power from far away as it dragged debris for thousands of miles through the dense jungle. It suggested to me that history had yet to record that first human life evolved from right here, in this land as well, and the importance the Congo River played in developing civilization along its timeless green river banks.

Even with the dangers and all the work ahead of me, I could not wait to go near the Congo River. I wanted to smell it, bathe in it, eat fish from it, use it for reliable transport, and most of all to reflect. If only my mother, father, brothers and sister, and grandmother and grandfather long since passed could see this river. I couldn't wait to be near its rich, brown belly full of organic plant matter, logs, and whole uprooted trees, all tumbling to the sea. I longed to see the unique life forms still unknown to foreigners that lived along the great Congo River banks since mankind first stood upright. Sadly, all too often one would see human remains slaughtered by the enemy and reduced to river debris. I stood watching the mighty river passing between the two cities only for a minute, but it seemed like an hour. These two cities were linked but stood apart like Mr. Balla and me held apart by European invaders and forces, like aliens as alien as the political, cultural, and economic force, nesting like competing vultures from hell in the hotel lobby. Mr. Balla and I, like these two cities, in spite of all the horror, stood facing each other centuries on across this broad belly of fresh water waiting until the two cities, two brothers, could remove the divide and unite This great river Congo emptied into the Atlantic Ocean that had once ferried away my ancestors I had just crossed seeking to unite with my brothers and sisters and my great land.

Stay Out of the Light

"President, please step away from the window." Mr. Balla called me back from the window. He always called me "President" on account of the fact that I was president of IMSCO, the NGO we both now supported. Mr. Balla felt I had stood at the window too long—tempting some would-be sniper hiding in the darkness to kill anything that lingered inside the French hotel.

I turned and stepped back into the small room as the fan on the ceiling rotated slowly overhead to find Balla looking directly at me.

"It's good of you to come to help us during these troubled times President," said Balla. He moved to the edge of the bed and sat down. I could see he was tired. The years were starting to show, but still, like most Africans, Balla was strong. He had to be. Africa needed us and demanded that of every well-meaning African who lived here or returned to her shores. The hard years and work could be seen especially on his face. He needed a shave like I needed a bath. Balla's aging eyes reflected a thousand years of the pain and wars the people were experiencing here. As for me I was Mr. Teflon. Mr. Clean. My antiaging coating was lifetime cookware; aging just naturally was not showing or sticking to me yet.

"We are truly thankful for your support, President," Balla said again seated on the side of the bed. I brushed off his remarks as if they were no big deal, but I knew he understood the importance of our hard work ahead and the risk he and I were taking like millions of other poor souls in the African bush and in cities all over the world.

"What are brothers for?" I asked and moved

to unlock my suitcase, taking out two new shirts. I smiled and tossed one to Mr. Balla who welcomed the shirt. It was my small way of saying thanks for introducing me to the adventure of a lifetime.

Later, Balla and I dined in the hotel dining room, quietly discussing our plans for the next day. The dining room had very few people now. We ordered and ate great African food: fish for me, steak for Mr. Balla, and wine for drinks. Later I walked Balla to the lobby door and saw him drive away in the same car that had brought us to the hotel. I had no idea where he lived. He never invited me to his home and from the looks of what the war and looters had done to other homes and buildings, I was not at all surprised. I went back into the hotel, went upstairs, and crawled into bed, imagining the gentle sound of the Congo River. I drifted off into a deep Central African tropical sleep with a chair propped up against the only door in the room.

The next morning, I rose early to the songs of tropical birds hopping about seeking mates in the palm trees just beyond the hotel window. I dressed, went downstairs to the lobby, and waited for Mr. Balla and Jules, another member of Mr. Balla's team and now a member of my team. Mr. Balla had spoken well of Jules over dinner. A car arrived a minute or two later with Mr. Balla and Jules amid the goings and comings of people, taxis, and private cars as deals and appointments were being made, kept, or broken all over the Congo Republic. We were driven to Mr. Balla's office where we began working on drafting an agreement that was supposed to gain us a major oil concession, which we hoped to have signed by the government's minister of mines. A trustworthy man, Jules and I connected with a smile in the blink of an eye. Just like that, centuries of time being apart vanished. There was work to be done, and catch up time was here. Dressed in his traditional colorful Cameroonian dress, Jules was a large well-built man standing six feet or better with a warm smile full of smoke-stained, decaying front teeth badly in need of a dental service. Still, for me, Jules's smile held a welcome worth the trouble of getting to the Congo, even if he was from the Republic of Cameroon, which was reported by the UN to be one of the top most corrupt African nations along with Nigeria. I had not yet visited Cameroon, so I reserved judgement. It's amazing how quickly most Africans and I bonded in understanding and common interests, with mutual goals and aims following quickly. No wonder the World Bank and IMF clients were worried. I am not suggesting that one should be that trusting in matters of life and death and high levels of business.

Mr. Balla's office was twenty minutes away. Housed in a run-down colonial building and shot full of bullet holes left over from the 1800s, it was a stone's throw away from the walled-in Libyan embassy. The glass to Balla's office window had been shot out of all of its colonial-made wooden frames. Luckily the electricity still flowed like the Congo River, providing a lifeline of hope for better days.

A Frontier Welcome

Inside Mr. Balla's office sat a large wooden table and a few oddly mixed wooden chairs. The stucco walls and windows frames were cracked and aging. These frames had been rocketed or shot out long before I arrived, and now weather beaten they rested inside broken shutters that were French or Dutch made. The Libyan embassy and the sprawling city of Brazzaville, consisting of mostly living space, were mostly made of rusting tin tops poorly designed by the human butchers, the Dutch. The African forced labor were lucky enough to still have hands attached to their arms and bodies.

      Later we all were busy at work going over our plan to meet the minister of mines when suddenly the sound of angry gunfire erupted. The sound of bullets next door to Balla's office raced about like Africanized bees, attacking anything within reach. I found myself being pushed to the floor, where I lay shielded under the bodies of Jules and three of Balla's men who had thrown their bodies atop mine—willing human shields for me against the deadly, aimless bullets. Adelaide, Balla's secretary, had already crawled into her usual hiding place under a wooden desk and awaited her unknown fate just like the rest of us. After a minute or so, the shooting stopped. Mr. Balla's men rushed Adelaide and I out the back door of the small office into a waiting car where I was shoved head first into the back seat. Two men sat on either sides of me, sandwiching me in the middle, while two more hopped on, hanging off the sides of the open doors of our four-door car. Handguns drawn, their eyes scanned the streets for the source of the gunfire. Mr. Balla and Adelaide were in the front seat with their heads down. As we drove away, I got a glimpse of a few Congolese soldiers and local policemen dotting about in the streets, firing AK-47s at each other. A few seconds later, the car we were in was on the street and out of range, we hoped, of the shooting.

Blood Brothers

After a busy few days in the bullet-riddled office of a minister of the cabinet, we were finally seated at a table with the power brokers of the government in Brazzaville, hammering out the IMSCO Establishment Agreement. Later we went before the press and the Republic of the Congo and signed the historic accord between the International Multiracial Shared Cultural Organization, AMRE Inc., and the Government of the Republic of the Congo on October 5, 1998. I signed on behalf of IMSCO, the PAD, and the Congo community I wished to see obtain the benefits, and Mr. Jerome Ollandet, the Ambassador General Secretary of Foreign Affairs and Cooperation, signed on behalf of the Congo government. The Congo television on the evening news covered the signing.

"Establishment Agreement between IMSCO and the Government of the Republic of the Congo"

The IMSCO accord was a diplomatic license insurance document known as "Establishment Agreement between IMSCO and the Government of the Republic of the Congo" It preceded the signing of a promised major crude oil concession and service supply contract to be assigned to the African Minerals Resource Exchange (AMRE), a private company affiliated with IMSCO as its economic wing with a focus on sharing the opportunities with the partners. The oil deal being granted carried no imposed termination date and would be used to help fund a bank for African people if all went well.

This was history being made. IMSCO was the first African American NGO that I knew of anywhere in the African diaspora to have such honors exchanged between an African nation on behalf of the PAD's rights to Africa's vast wealth and resources. It was possible because there were no foreigners involved. "Black man gives black man power" should be remembered by all black people as this is true in any culture. The agreement would swing open the doors of success to establish an official IMSCO branch office with full diplomatic privileges that would hopefully lead to the peaceful sharing of the Congo's vast riches between African people. Once this important step was completed, we hoped it would help stop the spread of the constant wars that black men fought here or anywhere.

Stopping the bloodshed was not going to be easy because war was the only way most impeded people knew how to gain or take power. It was not African people's lack of know-how or understanding how to implement development. Africans created development when they birthed civilization ten thousand years ago: advanced farming, road construction, and the refining and marketing of gold and diamonds into cash. We had been doing that for millennia before Europeans knew how to make fire, read, or write down thoughts. How does these two statements or issues relate? For one they relate due to the fact that Europeans have tried and failed at erasing African people contributions being first in cultivating fire, medical history and with the founding of civilization. I am not trying to match points here with other cultures rather to suggest the Europeans hold no higher ground over other cultures contributions. Our main problem was peace and quality of life for the people. It all boiled down to peace, but on whose terms? With the right links to extended family, such as the powerful PAD, and links to higher education for enough people in Africa and beyond, we have the edge needed. Africans can do anything, and Africa's enemies know this; thus, the failure to cooperate with Africans on a level playing field, any field in business, or anything vital to foreigners. If I have reached this far into Africa on the worst high school education imposed on a person ever, just imagine what is now possible for the undereducated black youth. To aid the foreigners in their scams to grab African and all other indigenous land and wealth, stakeholders now pimp globalization as a tool, an excuse to enter and plunder if wars fails. To help build a new Africa and free it of the last pockets of colonialism and imperialism forever, the IMSCO Establishment Agreement is the promised new weapon.

If all went well, the crude oil and minerals deals sort also carried onshore and offshore oil and gas concession commission drilling rights. All this and more had been lobbied for by Mr. Balla's team through his own NGO organizations Féconde and the Association Congolaise d'Amitié entre Les Peuples (ACAP) to link with my team and IMSCO in America and beyond. We had challenged the Congo government and its representatives to share and do the right thing. Share with PAD, and include all the business people in the victory. Include all the qualifying parties in the ownership of African wealth, land, and millions of opportunities in the Congo, and we will have won. Was it brotherhood, the ballot, or the bullet from the bush that had caused the government officials to act positively? I just flat out told the government representatives they were not properly managing the vast Congo wealth, and we demanded a share to manage ourselves. To our amazement, the minister of hydrocarbon, Mr. Jean-Baptiste Tati-Loutard, agreed and threw his full support behind the agreement.

I advised the minister as respectfully and directly as I could that the land, wealth, and resources in Congo belonged to all Africans, regardless if they lived in the Congo, the global African diaspora, or Mars. I argued that as long as they kept placing the wealth and concessions in the hands of the French, Belgian, or American imperialists or in the hands of the new-wave Chinese, there would be war where all the people would revolt as an anti-imperialist force. I argued Africans in America held great economic and political power that the government and people of Congo could now depend on to support and back the Congolese people in times of need like these. In short, African land and wealth and its future would not be left in foreign control regardless.

"Where was it written that Africans in Africa and Africans in the diaspora ever give up any part of their birthright before, during, and after slavery, colonialism, and imperialism?" I argued on national TV in Nigeria, America, Zimbabwe, Zambia, and now in Congo, and I damn well meant it on behalf of the African-impeded people.

I repeated again and again, as I had years ago in Zimbabwe to the British land-grabbing settlers, that we Africans were the victors. We would now rewrite African history and decide our own business culture and future. I realized then that we were treading on Western-established borders, but the Westerners or foreigners had entered and built their greed dreams on my land while they had their feet on our necks in bondage, enslaved even after our ancestors had beaten their asses in the race wars. The foreigners had used the back door to escape from their own hell to enter our Africa to steal African people in the diaspora and those of us here in

Africa's future after denying and outlawing education. Without proper education, they gambled we would never reach Africa again. But here I was about to rewrite every bilateral trade and investment trade agreement ever written in Africa starting with the Republic of the Congo. History was being made to send a shock wave across the rest of Africa and back into the Western world where I was escaping from. It was no wonder the World Bank and the French government were so upset by my arrival, but to hell with those guys who had entered my homeland Africa and pissed on my baobab trees: the African landmark of life I had selected as IMSCO's NGO logo. The foreigners were attempting to erase my team's name as owner.

Mr. Balla had established contact with the minister of hydrocarbon and the office of the president of the Congo Republic and his cabinet long before I arrived in the Congo, and he had done his job well. After a few tense days, word came back that some of the other ministers had agreed to move ahead with high-level talks with us regarding the sharing and sale of and concessions of crude oil and other strategic energy-related resources. We asked for a purchasing and selling agreement to ensure success for our effort in the international market place. I had read and been told that the big oil companies had a system that kept most stakeholders like us locked out of the business unless you had a purchasing and selling agreement to trade with end users. Little did we know that to sell crude oil directly to market refineries was not going to be easy. Then, word reached me that there could be a problem with the minister of hydrocarbon. The elders told me that the return road to African economic stability, designing an economic system, would be a tough but worthwhile fight. And there it was again. The minister was starting to stall on signing the final crude oil concession documents. I do not know if the president and his cabinet caused the stall or if the delay for approval was coming from France, Belgium, or the long and powerful arms of the multinationals that had many spies in the government on their payroll. Mind you, this was still a war-torn country, so anything was possible. The reality was the ministers and government representatives were not certain they would have a job, be alive from one day to the next, or even be able to remain in power. It was a gamble because if the government was overthrown, we had nothing and would have to start all over again.

Seated there in the room full of local Congolese media, we all were eager for positive news to present to the war-torn people. I told myself it was worth the years of pain and disappointment. Africans were not now nor have they ever been a poor people, and there was wealth enough all around to prove that politely to a blind person. I felt that signing such an agreement on Congo national television would give our plan an extra wall of protection from French or Belgian interference. The US government had already stepped up with support for the deal. My presence reassured Mr. Balla, his team, and many government officials that we had some American backup through African Americans if the French and Belgians made a move on us.

Sure as all hell was on fire, with French or Belgian interference already in place, the foreigner agents were planning somewhere in the shadows to ruin the planned mission. I told them America would back us up and even presented a few letters and documents to help make my case. In truth, I really had no assurance that the American government would support us beyond words. I suppose the strongest argument I had was that this agreement with the Congo would help remove any stigma placed on Congo and might help Africans understand that they were not a poor people after all; rather they were programmed into thinking they were poor and helpless as we are brainwashed as such in the Western world and beyond. Well, some of us are.

A Trip into the Jungle

One late evening with a car and driver, Balla, Jules and I headed for the edge of the jungle, or bush as the Africans call this dense tropical part of central Africa. Once we had left the city of Brazzaville under a moonlit sky, Jules placed a white flag on both sides of the car mirrors and drove about two hours before we were stopped by armed men with looks that could and would kill.

Mr. Balla and Jules knew all the rules and the local languages while I hung back taking it all in, learning and growing. In all, we had to go through three checkpoints. At each checkpoint, the car was searched, Mr. Balla spoke, and each time we were waved on. Finally we arrive at a camp well hidden near a bend in the mighty Congo River. At first we saw no one in the moonlit night sky until suddenly a tall African male in his late thirties appeared with two soldiers, a man and a woman who were both younger. Then more ragtag rebels started appearing on all sides, about two dozen or so. We were ordered out and searched. Jules was the only one who had a weapon, and he let the tall rebel leader inspect it. The lead rebel surprisingly gave the handgun back to Jules, who pocketed it. Our driver had an AK-47 on the floor, but the rebels never bothered to ask for it, and we said nothing. The driver remained with the car. The lead rebel knew Mr. Balla and welcomed us into the camp. The meeting lasted about an hour and ended with Mr. Balla inviting him to come or send a representative to the TV press conference and document signing planned two days from that night. The rebel agreed.

Chapter 5

A Coded Message to Black Men

At the press conference, a few rebels wearing African and ill-fitting Western civilian clothes stood in the background with some of Mr. Balla's team. IMSCO and Mr. Balla's peace efforts had gotten the opposing sides in the same room. Among the invited guests was the indestructible team of men and women that had labored hard and long to help Mr. Balla, Jules, and me deliver the project at great expense to this point. We all stood like strong slender pillars of the African society we were helping to rebuild and move our people's lives to a higher level.

The intense lights from the television

cameras exacerbated the already hot room. The air conditioner had been damaged and shut down. Not even the seemingly brand new, French electric fans worked. Just when the heat was starting to get to me, the moment arrived. The government representative, Mr. Jerome Ollandet, Ambassador General Secretary of Foreign Affairs and Cooperation, moved toward the table where I was standing. We smiled at each other, knowing we were making history and closing centuries of economic apartheid imposed by Europeans and foreign NGOs under UN flags to keep Africans apart and on the development ban list. Not a single foreigner was in the room.

Not even the hot, tropical air could negate the mutual feeling of great pride and expectation between Ambassador Ollandet and me. The cameras got in position. Mr. Balla's daughter Paulette, seemingly cooler than the rest of us, kept us in place before the cameras while signing the documents at the table. I was surprised at how well managed the proceedings went. The organizers of the event knew what they were doing, and they respected what was taking place. My French was based on what little I had picked up in my travels and from the short time I had lived in Paris. Behind me, the invited guests formed around the wall to witness the historic affair. Many were wiping the sweat from their faces. I reminded myself that I had been feeling "the heat" in America since I was born, so I could withstand a few more moments under the room's combined man-made and tropical temperatures.

After taking my seat beside Ambassador Ollandet, I gazed at the large red leather folders containing the business and diplomatic official documents we were about to sign. Paulette stepped forward and pointed me to the proper document to sign first. With cameras rolling, the ambassador and I signed the French version and then the English version. Truly, this was a first. At last, at long last, I stood in Africa sharing power and position with another African man, an ambassador on behalf of the Republic of Congo at that. Afterward, a copy was presented to me on camera and the ambassador kept the other for the nation's records. I could not help but smile and think of the years, centuries, it had taken to reach this important moment—a milestone in the reuniting of a people and a culture and it had all gone so smoothly and so quickly. The ambassador spoke first in French.

"Mr. Weston and I have placed our signatures on this historic document in the hope it will help end economic discrimination between the North and South and link our strong family once again. The IMSCO Accord should be only a first step to help reunite the African family in Africa and in the diaspora." When he finished, the ambassador turned to me and shook my hand as I then approached the camera. I quickly got a glance of the people's faces standing about the room. They must have felt the same respect for me as I had for them. And to think the whole event was being captured on tape for history and students to study centuries on.

A reporter stepped up and began interviewing me in French about the history of IMSCO and its aims for the immediate future. "What will be the first area of concentration under the accord, Mr. Weston?" The reporter asked. I picked up some of the French the reporter spoke but not all.

I replied, "This agreement will help link Africans in Africa and in America..."

Professor Leopold stepped up. He noticed I

was not properly understanding or giving the correct answer to the reporter's question and stepped up to the mic to lend a hand. He was a member of our team named after King Leopold II, the evil inhuman Belgian king who butchered Africans in numbers far beyond our ability to contemplate. There is a book written on the subject called *King Leopold's Ghost* by Adam Hochschild, which was published the same year I visited the Congo.

Professor Leopold translated French into English and English into French for my benefit and that of the viewers. Years of being stuck in a one-language country after a year living in France in 1962 had taken its toll on my ability to properly communicate in the language.

"The first area of concentration will be in the field of petrol and natural gas," Professor Leopold said. Those words must have sent shock waves throughout the foreign community when it was later aired. A few more questions were asked before the ambassador waved the reporters away. It had taken Africans more than four centuries to reach this milestone. Following this came the signing of the IMSCO/Congo Establishment Agreement that would benefit Africans in Africa and Africans in the diaspora while establishing a new beginning and an awakening of a badly needed African economic and cultural revolution. I turned and reached out my hand for Mr. Balla to stand beside me. He stepped forward. The ambassador took my arm and pulled me toward a table we had transformed into a minibar with French champagne, and we had a toast to the signing and hopes for a better future. We raised our glasses to the reuniting of our people through the Congo/IMSCO accord. Everything changed for me from that moment on, and the historic moment had been captured on Congo TV news for history. This was to be a milestone, a marker for other travelers from the Western anti-African culture abyss to be guided toward the light, toward a better life, I hoped. Still, there remained so much to do. For one thing the minister of hydrocarbon had not signed the crude oil document, so we had to keep working on obtaining his signature. What was the problem? What the fuck had happened? I wanted to get on with my life! This was a coded message to the black man: get off your ass, take on all foreign domination, and protect family, land, property, and wealth.

Chapter-6

Land of the Dragon

After meeting a number of the Congo officials and obtaining some rushed documents confirming we had been granted crude oil concessions (but no lifting agreement for the crude oil as yet), Mr. Balla suggested we visit the Chinese ambassador assigned to the Republic of the Congo while we waited for the outcome. He was an old friend of Mr. Balla's who he had met while serving as the Republic of the Congo ambassador to Cuba. We met the mild-mannered, always-smiling Chinese ambassador over lunch at the Chinese embassy and were promptly invited to visit Beijing, China, to exchange views on Chinese and African relations with top officials on ways we all might cooperate. There it was again: professional respect I had never been shown by any white male before as owner of anything, ever! We accepted the Chinese ambassador's invitation to visit Beijing. I waited around Brazzaville a few more days and then returned to New York City and started to prepare for the trip to China where I was to fly to Paris and meet up with Mr. Balla to obtain my Chinese visa. For some unknown reason, the Chinese would not issue me a visa in New York City. Later I would learn why. The Chinese did not want the American Department of State to know their business. The Chinese had a master plan for Africa and did not want to expose any part of it at the time. It turned out the Chinese had already booked Mr. Balla on a China Airways flight a day earlier, so I had to travel alone the following day aboard China Airways from Paris to Beijing. The flight was long but friendly, professional, and rewarding with all those beautiful Chinese hostesses floating about the cabin like colorful butterflies at thirty-nine thousand feet at eight hundred miles an hour serving me and the rest of the passengers with drinks, food, and smiles. I don't know what it is about Chinese women from the mainland of China, but I am hooked on their personal culture for eternity.

The next day at the break of dawn, I found myself among a billion and half Chinese. A large amount of them were being processed through the Beijing airport with me, and the odd thing was I was not requested to show a return ticket. I cleared customs, entered China, and was met by a short Chinese man in his forties. He was waiting just beyond the terminal exit all dressed up in a dark, loosely fitting Western business suit that was a size too large complete with red bow tie. He was holding a white sign nearly as long as he was tall with "Mr. Weston" hand written on it. At first all I could see was the sign. He could not miss me because I was the tallest African person at the airport that day. We greeted each other, and the short Chinese man informed me that my connecting domestic flight on Air China was due to depart shortly. Luckily I had only my carry-on bag with me, but how was I to get to the right gate? Finding the gate in 1998 trying to read Mandarin was impossible. Never let anyone tell you that multiple languages are not as important as basic math and any other educational survival tools. I had the basics of a few languages under my belt that I have learned over the years, but nothing when it came to Chinese. China is the most populated nation on the planet and soon to be the most important in business. It's anyone's guess what the Chinese would be controlling in the near future. So there I stood language naked before a billion Chinese people.

Talk about culture shock! I got the surprise of my life standing in a sea of Chinese people rushing about in ten thousand directions with me towering over most of them. The only Chinese I spoke at the time was the word for "Thank you." The short, smiling Chinese man pushed a ticket into my hand and pointed. That is when it dawned on me that I was indeed on my own. Mr. Balla had been flown in ahead of me to some distant location deep inside China, and I was supposed to find him among a billion Chinese on my own without an address or even a map. I looked back over my shoulders for the Chinese man that had pushed me into this puzzle and could not now distinguish him from thousands of other Chinese people. I presented my boarding pass to a lovely passing Chinese girl with long plaits in her hair, and she led me part of the way to where my gate might be and pointed. I moved another ten yards, and there were so many people milling about that I started to get confused. Just then another young Chinese woman took up the civic duty and walked me to my gate. When I finally arrived, I had five minutes to make my connecting flight.

Crossing the Back of the Dragon

I boarded the connecting flight, and an hour later an in-flight lunch was served by smiling Chinese women. I had a great view as we flew over some of the strangest geological landscape I had ever seen. China is the size of the United States of America with a checkerboard of mountain ranges, plateaus, water basins, and seemingly endless green and golden plains and rivers. You know how it is when you are new to a place you like and think you could live there? That's how I felt about my first view of China from the air, and that feeling remain to this day.

I was fascinated by the thought of visiting the Red Dragon, the long-hidden world of the People's Republic of China. In university, I had read Chinese history to a point and had made friends with a Chinese student who always beat me hands down at pool in Greenwich Village pool halls. Even then I saw China as a lesser evil for Africa compared to Europe and white America's multinational and biased cultural interests, so off I flew into the land of Red Dragons.

Hours later, I was standing in the middle of China's Chungking airport greeting Mr. Vital Balla and a party of smiling male and female Chinese hosts who came to meet me. We were pushed into a waiting car, followed by a number of other state cars with red flags flapping in the wind, complete with professional guides. We were taken to visit one active start-up factory after another. All were busy manufacturing goods for export around the world and to serve the needs of the people in China. This dedication to industrialism was indicative of China becoming the world's, dare I say it, next superpower, and I was there representing my soon-to-be-again superpower Africa and the PAD. Whether this was good or bad, the Chinese planned to use Africa in any way it could to reach the development objectives for its people and did not hide the fact.

During a state-sponsored dinner, the Chinese government official suggested an economic relationship between China and the Republic of the Congo. No mention was made of any plans to officially include African Americans, the wider African diaspora, or PAD community in the United States or anywhere, so I was forced to sit and witness while the Chinese official and the acting ambassador to China from the Republic of the Congo discussed select projects to be codeveloped in the Congo. I could see Mr. Balla was none too happy about the arrangement either. The Chinese wanted a bigger piece of the Africa that capitalist, imperialist America and Europe had held for centuries but were now losing due to the same mistake the Chinese were about to make using the evil, inhuman act of exclusion. So why was I there? Guess? I thought Mr. Balla and I were the African American and African link to China, but the future would tell another story. I came away from China with a reinforced vision of the future for African people in Africa, America, and the wider African diaspora, but no cooperation agreement that would include African American diaspora business or PAD, a people who owned half of Africa and all that is in Africa. The blind, confused men who mismanaged Africa over at the African Union based on my contacts with them (in 1998, known as the Organization of African Union) was headed by the president of the Republic of the Congo as interim OAU president. The vision for including PAD was not included as African coowners and the Chinese and the Western world seized the opportunity to use the mistake on the part of African leadership to divide Africa among themselves for the moment; in fact, when I brought the matter up, the Chinese changed the subject. I saw and witnessed the fact that the Western world no longer held an exclusive oppressive business monopoly over Africa and our thousand-year-old cultures and civilization.

I came away thinking the Chinese were only interested in their own agendas, so all Africans should know that China is a little more than the lesser of the two evils between Africa and the West. African people must realize they are too rich to fully trust China or any other country or continent. Before leaving China, Mr. Balla and I were given state visits to the home of the late, timeless Chairman Mao Zedong and the Great Wall of China, among other timeless art treasures that reminded me of the priceless treasures I had witnessed in Egypt.

Quest for Domination

In all, the China trip was a life-altering experience for me. I witnessed things and events the Western world had hidden from the likes of me for centuries, and I met a people in many ways very much like me that had fought hard to win victory over the same enemy and oppressors. The Chinese, like the Africans, are a great people, no doubting that. In the past, we both had made major mistakes. Would the Chinese and African leaders who no one in Africa had properly elected and no African diaspora had granted approval to sell or trade share Africa and its vast wealth? To try and cut out the African diaspora and PAD, China and all others are making a big mistake not respecting their stakeholder rights and not partnering with the entire African family. For now, China grabbing for African minerals and resources seems to overshadow the millions of people the Chinese government are rushing into Africa without one single PAD or African diaspora institution or person in partnership. The Chinese just wish to be the first out of the gate in terms of advance development ahead of Africa and its people for one reason: quest for later domination.

But I kept wondering if the Chinese could be a true friend to African people. They made no attempt to hide the fact that they hungered badly for African minerals and resources, but I did not see that same Chinese hunger or interest to partner with all African people in Africa or PAD in the diaspora, and therein lay the problem. The Chinese were simple colonialists with a touch of refined imperialistic irony. Some call it bias. To tell the truth here, I did have an uncomfortable exchange with a Chinese minister over a dinner he hosted for Balla and me. The man was biased and looked silly as he attempted to divide Mr. Balla and me until Mr. Balla set him straight that he was not having it at all. I will leave it at that for now. I saw the mistake on China's part as an advantage to be played later.

So we flew out of China. Balla set off for his Congo and I to New York, hoping to get a bigger bite of the "Big Apple." During the twenty-four hour flight back, I slept mostly. When I was awake, I thought of life and where it had led me and then of Mr. Balla. I have to tell you that Mr. Balla was all man and as diplomatic as the seasons, giving and taking to gain his aim. Balla taught me something every day I was with him, and even when he was not around, I was thinking of him and trying to take on his style and professionalism. If ever there was a model for leadership, Mr. Balla was it, and he was good at whatever he did.

I was more the Indian Jones or Shaft type: rush in, kick ass, ID, grab, and get the hell out! Living in America, following four centuries of ancestors struggling to stay alive, set the path I was to take in life. My human DNA molded hated injustice. Finding justice was my life quest. Speed was the way I saw out at first. The return trip to America was bittersweet as always. No sooner was I back in New York when my coworker and field agent, Jules, in the Republic of the Congo called demanding that I get back to Brazzaville immediately. I could hear Mr. Balla's voice in the background saying in French, "Tell President Weston he is needed back as soon as possible!"

Chapter-7

The Ugly European

In 1999, I was back in the Congo after visiting China. I was seated by the Le Meridian hotel pool one hot afternoon sipping a glass of monopolized, imported French white wine as Jules showed up with the bad news. The minister was now suggesting the crude oil document needed more review. Jules told me the French, the World Bank, and IMF (naturally aided by some envious Congo government employees who were being paid off) were secretly pulling strings in the state-owned oil company Société nationale des pétroles du Congo (SNPC). Suddenly, everything we had worked to achieve was now threatened; the crude oil allotment, the concession the government promised us, and the needed cash cow were at risk. Without the liquid wealth to finance our planned project's codevelopment, it wouldn't take place as we had hoped. Information kept coming that the hidden hands of the Europeans and World Bank and IMF's bosses policies of control in Africa were behind the scene to block us.

Don't ask me how because I cannot begin to name all the ways they were attempting to halt the progress of black men like us and our teams. Who would be surprised? After all, this was the white man's power, their free ticket to live and remain at the top of the food chain in all their high towers temporarily built on African bones and wealth. They wanted only to maintain their wealthy lifestyles in Paris, New York, Texas, Washington, Los Angeles, and the parts of Asia they now controlled. They wanted to retain Africa and hold the continent and its people in a black hole very badly, but we were still putting up one hell of a fight in spite of the hellish blows we were taking as a team and a people. And here we stood in an independent wealthy undeveloped Africa ready to go to work, yet we were unable to place our hands on a single dollar of our wealth to improve the continent or our wretched lives unless we went through the white and now threatening Asian systems.

More than once, a group of students approached me in different parts of the Congo saying the people were willing to pull together as a team to farm the vast rich lands. They requested that our IMSCO team help them convince the relaxed Congo representatives to help obtain tools and seeds to cultivate a large soil-rich area of the country. The war was over, and the government officials were too busy chasing the Europeans and Chinese for US dollars for their pockets and did not have time to listen to the youth and the people.

The World Food Organization (WFO) has a bias toward Africa. I contacted the WFO in Rome and was refused any cooperation. The WFO is a United Nations–mandated agency. Wasn't the United Nations supposed to help people develop so they could get on with their lives? But instead, I found representatives of UN agencies driving around in the Congo in big air-conditioned cars with houses safely hidden behind bulletproof walls. They had police or military armed protection 24/7 and more servants it seemed than the president of the country. What were these highly paid UN agency representatives really doing here? The NGOs stole and misused most aid and grant money or hung on to 40 percent of the funds for operational use that largely went into their pockets for downtime. What did they know about African people's development and cultural needs after centuries of their European ancestors (in most cases) attempting to destroy the people and culture? Then before the descendants of the formerly enslaved can return, the foreigners, NGOs, and the like rush in and attempt to grab all that is left of this good land? Over the people's dead bodies will I let that happen or remain for long. I had been running into foreign aid workers across Africa since the early 1980s, living in very fine five-star hotels the common people were lucky if they could walk too close past.

In 1999, most employees at these fine hotels and businesses were foreign workers rushing in due to failure of a corrupt Western system still exploiting Africa to feed their own largely uneducated, poverty-stricken, white society. A few African workers could be found cleaning the floor, bathrooms, and walkways, doing kitchen cleanup, driving, babysitting, washing, tending the gardens, or shining shoes left outside the room doors at night; all were low-level positions and locations controlled by foreigners. For years, from South Africa to Congo, I have never heard foreigners in Africa say anything positive about the people in Africa, and nor do I hear Africans say positives things about foreigners. The foreigners and foreign NGOs all greeted me as if I were the invader.

"So you think you can make a difference. You think you can change things?" I was asked and sometimes told by Europeans in social gatherings at the United Nations starting the day my NGO was inducted into the UN ECOSOC in 1995. The ones who voiced these biased remarks were so afraid of the coming links between PAD, the African diaspora, and African people on the continent that they would attempt to invent a false dream reality. I may have been suffering as a victim of crimes of the past, but these Europeans, Indians, and Asians that were trying to steal my space and property were and still are suffering from broken minds about who and what they are. They have lost their humanity while trying to eliminate the humanity of Africans. The facts are found in the lives of these wretched people, self-made victims of their own biased denials. Sad to say, but better to expose it than try and live with a lie as it willingly continues to block our path to healing.

Europeans and many white Americans always wanted to be in charge in Africa, and they knew nothing about the true nature of the people and even less about the PAD in the diaspora seeking to link and return to their cultures and ancestral homeland. It is no wonder we Africans were having problems reattaching ourselves with the land, resettling in our ancestral cultural heritage, managing our lives, wealth, and last but not least, comanaging our vast wealth and business culture.

Chapter 8

Inside Man

One day during my work visit in the Congo, Dr. Jean D. Ovaga, a friend and the private doctor to the president of the Republic of the Congo, seeing what stress I was faced with trying to complete the crude oil deal, invited me to visit his place in the country for a day. I accepted and he and one other friend, the driver and the bodyguard drove an hour outside Brazzaville and ended up at his house deep in the hills surrounded by forest. There was a pond at the back of the house fed by a stream coming from somewhere deep in the forest.

We had lunch and later went for a long swim. Then we just sat for an hour in the pond talking and being refreshed by the running water. Dr. Ovaga's English was not that good, but we communicated well enough and he told me about his life and the horror of having his marriage broken up. His story suggested strongly that his wife had been molested and then stolen by a Frenchman posing as a priest. Dr. Ovaga was so upset, he stopped the story in the middle and would not continue, as it was too painful for him.

"Africans in the diaspora can help develop Africa and the Congo over these Europeans," he said. "After all, the French and white Americans are harming us." How many times had I heard those words in Africa?

That day we visited the doctor's country house on the edge of the great Congo forest was the best day I have ever had in Africa. To sit and bond with my brothers in a mountain stream after four centuries was both healing and heaven. This was the freedom I was in search of during my many escape attempts from Western cultural hell for me. Nothing heals the injured soul better than homeland and a pure African mountain stream.

Touch of Evil

Back in Brazzaville, I was once more faced with the reality and terror of the European-imposed debt on Africa and all its people. The children were hurt the most by the hit men and cultural assassins who worked for the International Mother Fuckers, who called the shots trying to block those of us from the African diaspora from returning to Africa while creating unlivable conditions for Africans to live at ease on the continent. Right behind them was the tidal wave of Chinese, for the better in some cases, as partners I hoped, we hoped. We Africans were tired of fighting, sick of centuries of fighting, but because we are so rich, we must continue to fight to protect what we have, own, and want back. As pointed out in John Perkins's *Confessions of an Economic Hit Man*, I was to discover in real life and read about later how the hit men and women, governments, and foreign businesses inflicted blood debts on Africa. They rigged every bilateral trade and investment treaty agreements that the crooks in Africa and the damn foreign crooks cooked up. International corrupt laws move the success goalposts on any African who got close to success or tried to escape the deep abyss of horror that reached up and pulled us down with the unjust debts. The book *Dead Aid*, written by Zambian author Dambisa Moyo, focused on why aid is not working and how there is a better way for Africa. My take was to send the imperialists a bill for the slavery and colonialist and imperialist damage. Of course these imperialists and their agents will stop at nothing to try and prevent Africa from rising and Africans would stop at nothing to rise. My own presence was a threat, and I knew it. I loved it! While nothing can stop the rising, solutions will be bloody, and it will be costly to us all. Nothing and no one should stand in the way of a people and an army as we are going home.

The Western imperialists tried to stop the Chinese, but look at the Chinese now. They tried to stop African Americans, but look at us now. Even when it seems that we are down, the world tries to be us. At first there will be one or two like me who enter Africa. Then there will be many millions more, and they will keep coming from the African diaspora until Africa is reclaimed as the black mecca it has always been and always will be for the black man and woman. I had witnessed the evil of these invaders firsthand in America, and I knew the cost Africa would suffer again if they were permitted to once again settle in. There were fewer, but they were still here in the Congo, much the same as Joseph Conrad's book had suggested in the 1880s. We must close Africa's doors to the 100% even 50% management of bloodsuckers like Exxon Mobil, the Shell Oil Company, and Elf (the French oil giant) who aims are in fact outdated for the modern day.

Sadly the Chinese now often have proper documents to slip in under the radar and run amok, ruining every drop of ground drinking water in villages across Africa, as they seek gold to patch up holes in their budgets. Water is the life blood and must be saved. The land also cannot continue to be drained from Africa as her rich mineral arteries will be lost from which flow pure gold and natural resources. Mind you, both the DRC and the Republic of the Congo officials did not know then or now how much oil, gas, and other strategic metals were being stolen. I had even approached the minister of mines and asked him to grant me a contract to visit and investigate on the government's behalf to see how much oil was being pumped from the off-shore oil fields and place a counter on each and every oil and gas well. The minister of mines backed down at my request. I wondered why, so I paid a visit to the American embassy. I spoke with the acting US ambassador, a Mr. Shawn, to get a better picture of how much oil was being taken but was told there was no such oil-lifting numbers being shared with the US Department of State. To obtain this information, it was clear we were going to need a bigger political voice: PAD is a bigger voice and fish. Mr. Balla, Jules, and I were ready for the big fight we all knew was coming. During this trip, we had managed to get the government of the Republic of the Congo cabinet to meet and issue orders to the minister of hydrocarbon to draft and sign when complete a crude oil concession agreement for the company AMRE Trade Oil Inc. The concession was to issue half a million barrels of sweet crude oil to our efforts, and the government would have no further control over how the business would be operated. I was pressured to return to New York City on urgent business, so I left before all the documents were drafted and signed, thinking it was a slam-dunk closed deal. I was wrong!

Chapter 9

Washington, We Have a Problem

In the fall of 1998, I flew back to America feeling upbeat to research my idea of an extension to the IMSCO master plan of taking down the walls we were facing. I was not back in New York City a week when a frantic call reached me again from the Congo. It was Jules, my soul buddy and trusted assistant, and Mr. Balla calling again.

"President, there is a problem," Jules said. "The minister of hydrocarbon has the document drafted but refuses so far to meet with us or sign the crude oil agreement."

"Why?" I asked.

"Someone inside SNPC, are trying to block the deal from going through," Jules told me. I could feel the flow of anger in his voice flowing through the phone line. "The French have got a hand in it, President; I am sure. I have reliable, inside information to that effect...What do we do, President?" Jules asked over the phone.

"Fuck the French monopoly! We will deal

with them." I was fishing for answers, solutions. "We will have our oil and wealth. Just give me a little time, and I will get back to you." Just then, I remembered something critical that could perhaps help us. Before departing the United States for the Congo, I had signed a noncorruption agreement with the US Advocacy Center in Washington, DC, and I was wondering if I could draw on the agreement's powers.

"I will take care of it," I said and hung up the phone.

I called the US Department of State in Washington, DC, and asked for their African business sector seeking help in the matter. After a few days of discussions, a US Department of State official advised me to contact the American embassy in Brazzaville and ask the acting ambassador to look into the matter. I had a real problem. Would I receive help from America or the bilateral trade agreement, a treaty between America and the Republic of the Congo? I was able to reach acting Ambassador Mr. Shawn in Brazzaville and he agreed to go in and speak with the minister of hydrocarbon personally. A few days later, Jules called me back. This time, I could hear Mr. Balla's happy voice in the background instructing Jules. They both sounded very pleased. The minister of hydrocarbon had signed our letter of intent to supply crude oil.

We have sent you the fax, President. Did you receive it?" I had received the fax.

It seemed that bringing out the big guns from the US embassy worked. The visit by Mr. Shawn must have moved the minister of hydrocarbon to act. But why did it have to come to this? The minister had promised me to my face he would sign the document! What was happening to African men in Africa? Where were their fucking balls to do business with their fellow African brothers?

Now that the letter of intent was signed, I was told I would need a signed purchasing and selling agreement. To get that, I would have to return to Brazzaville, so I flew back to the Republic of the Congo in February 2000.

Chapter-10

Purchasing Power

Getting the cooperation was easy enough, and Mr. Balla was the man of the hour. I was back in Pointe Noire when Mr. Balla came through the door of the private house. He was all smiles and dropped the document on the table saying, "Now, President, we can have our oil." The director for the refinery CORAF, Mr. Nestor Mawandza, had signed the purchasing and selling agreement without delay. This document would give AMRE the power to lift crude oil and ship it anywhere in the world. It was signed February 9, 2000. Europeans and the World Bank viewed African Americans signing such contracts as a worthy nightmare for the European oppressive system.

From here, I thought we were home free. I flew back to New York City. In July 2000, I received a message from Balla saying I must travel to London where I should meet with Mr. Denis Gokana, head of SNPC, the Congo state-owned oil company. I was to be given a contract to sign that dealt with the discount the government of the Republic of the Congo was offering AMRE and the team. But not to worry, Mr. Balla said nothing could stop us now. But that was what worried me. As it turned out, the flow of oil from the Congo was going to be a major problem, and it was going to take a lot more than the documents we had agreed to before the oil would move. Every block imaginable was in place to try and prevent our deal from taking place.

The World Bank Group and IMF push African countries over the hill in debt with their debt collecting for major oil companies and Western states that are all there picking Africa clean. After all, that was why the war was being fought: to keep African wealth out of the hands of African people, including PAD in the diaspora. But my team and I were in no way going to roll over and let these bandits keep us out of the African business culture, our only path to a future of self-determination. What was the problem? The government had granted the concession and better yet, the people of the Republic of the Congo had made the deal public. But something was very wrong. There was a pull on Africa and the crude oil deal by some hidden object, circling the continent and affecting every important deal black men and women were developing, like some kind of space asteroid threatening to kill everything in its path.

The Fallen Star

In London, Mr. Gokana handed me a typed unsigned crude oil contract. I gazed upon the document for a while thinking so this was what the approach to real economic power felt like.

Mr. Gokana said, "You will receive all cooperation from this office." I thought to myself that this should rush the approval to lift crude oil from the Congo. Upbeat, I hung around London for five days before I flew back to New York City thinking I would soon be sent a letter inviting me to travel back to the Congo to receive a lifting agreement from SNPC. Instead, I received a letter a few days later on August 15, 2001, stating that the Republic of the Congo did not have oil to provide me at the moment, but as soon as they did, they would contact me.

I assumed that meant they would be willing to sell (note, I said sell) to my company AMRE, the company established to be IMSCO's economic wing, and assist in the flow of business contracts and concessions into the wider black community with the allotment of crude oil the government had agreed to. But that was not to be. My brothers from the Congo seemed to have their hands tied or could not or did not wish to honor the binding commitment made by the Republic of the Congo to supply the crude but were not giving me any details. The crude oil when obtained would help IMSCO and AMRE and the team and I start any number of businesses and schools in the Congo and continually educate an endless number of students, which our community badly needed. I began to flood the office of SNPC with a continuous stream of letters, faxes, and telephone calls, but nothing would bring them out of the holes they were dug into. There was another hand. There had to be a hidden hand of power that called the shots for all the oil sales in the Republic of the Congo. I did not know it at the time, but the president of the Republic of the Congo and his family were not in direct control. They had done as much as they could for us at the time I reasoned. Regardless, I was by now near bankrupt and decided to dig in and wait for a better day to continue the fight to obtain our oil.

Could I get the American ambassador in the Congo to back me up or push the Congo government to honor its full commitment to my team? Could the UN be counted on under a black man's watch (Mr. Kofi Annan), the UN Secretary General, to support an African NGO that was already seen by many as crossing the line compared to the way other NGOs in the ECOSOC did things around the world? I did not care for the way other NGOs did business or treated people in developing countries. I disliked the way they omitted Africans in the diaspora from taking part, wanting to replace the African diaspora role in his and her own lives, and I was not afraid to let it be known how I felt. Why not? It was not going to help by saying nothing to people who did not respect black people anyway. It was a disrespect not for the color of our skin but for what we owned and the power we had but could not yet use. Yes, humans do hate for the strangest reasons. These people, not the United Nations, feared the black success actually taking place.

There I was swimming in a sea of questions with few answers. I did not wish to think of any NGO as an enemy. The whole matter was confusing. I felt out of control and without guidance. How could it have had guidance? No one wanted to accept the fact that people like me wanted to go home to Africa and regain control over our land and wealth and have freedom forever from the Western world's madness that wanted to hold black people in their grips of culture in which we could not partake. This was a nightmare on steroids.

Consumed by angry feelings, I moved to the large window of my combination office and apartment. Looking down from the sixteenth floor onto 34th Street and Park Avenue, I wanted to shout out at the world. Up and down the avenue, I could see the constant flow of four-way, bumper-to-bumper traffic, yellow cabs choking the city like the anger flooding my body and soul. They all needed energy I was being prevented from supplying even though I owned a major concession of the nation and life building energy. Because of a limited budget, I could not move away from New York to set up in Africa yet, so I was forced to endure. It was cheaper to come and go than remain in either location. At any given time of the day, I could hear the overpowering foghorns from the red fire engines burning energy I was forbidden to supply anywhere in the nation racing under my windows, followed by any number of other emergency vehicles painfully grinding past my building, lasting well into the night. It was even worse whenever there was a game or concert at Madison Square Garden over on Seventh Avenue five blocks away.

The good thing was my window looked southeast toward the direction of Africa. Looking out the window, I would think only of Africa, that wonderful continent that gave me something worthwhile. It was something more meaningful to my life. Over the years, because Africa was not all that economically stable, I stayed put at my New York City address. Besides, the prestigious Park

Avenue address saved me money, and it was at the center of Manhattan with connections to every subway, bus, and airport. The United Nations was my international base so I could quickly zip in and out of "the land of liberty." But I am a sun person. Like millions of other exiled PAD and Africans in the diaspora, I wanted to be home in Africa with those who now had but did not realize they could have dual citizenship and the right to vote to change their lot in both Africa and America. How could they know? Hell, I did not know at first. My aim now was to help take back African business culture. Take it back with the continent!

Chapter-11

Survival Instincts the Early Years

Once in the shower, I started feeling something soggy. I looked down at my feet and saw I had done it again. I had forgotten to pull off my socks. An old childhood habit even my mother could not rid me of when I was growing up. I laughed and pulled the socks off and dropped them outside the tub. I am a teenage boy again in the 1950s, where I was growing into young manhood seemingly without a care in the world.

I was walking with my best friends: Joe Branch (the singer in the group), Chester and Joseph (both brothers), and my two younger brothers.

Roosevelt is the youngest, Reb, we called him, and over to his left is Robert, the brother two years younger than me. We were returning from an unsuccessful fishing trip from one of the fishing holes in the area. The fish were not biting that day, so we ditched our fishing poles and clothes and had the time of our lives splashing about in a creek on that hot July summer day. Carefree teenagers, we didn't think twice about the snakes in the water. We were naturalists, and we were black kids so nothing in nature could harm us. Fortunately, the pond was not that deep because some of us couldn't swim worth a lick anyway, but we were trying to learn.

Once out of the water, we horsed around a bit and then got dressed in our scant summer outfits. Picking up our fishing poles and bows and arrows, we headed home across a field, laughing and carrying on, as youth often do. Thanks to our loving parents, we were virtually shielded from the mean, racist, Jim Crow Tuscaloosa, Alabama (named after one of the twenty-million or more murdered Native Americans; the few still living whose land this still is. What an honor!). Halfway across a farmer's field, we stopped and decided to play target practice with our bows and arrows. Joseph, the youngest of the group, started playing around, accidentally shooting an arrow into Joe Branch's right temple. Almost immediately, his temple began to bleed and quiver. Branch sunk to his knees in pain and shock and begged us to pull the arrow out. Before we could come to his assistance, Branch yanked at the slender bamboo stalk, dislodging it from the nail tip that remained embedded in his skull. It was at this point that everyone except me ran home. I stepped up to Branch and pulled at the bloody nail with no success. The nail was in deep, and blood was gushing around it. I tried a second time to dislodge it. I nearly panicked, but Branch regained his composure, grabbed my hand, looked me in the eye, and waited for me to complete the process.

"You hold still, Branch," I said.

"You better do it right this time, damn it!" Branch demanded.

I pulled a sweat rag from my jeans back pocket, wrapped it around the bloody nail, and yanked hard, dislodging the nail. I stood over my friend Branch, who sat for a moment holding my sweat rag over the nail hole in his head. Then he stood and started walking toward home, swearing every step of the half mile or so away. I relaxed somewhat because as long as he was walking and swearing, I knew he was not dying on me. He was understandably furious. Branch kept saying he couldn't see with all the blood in his eye. I was afraid I was going to be blamed because I had made the bows and arrows, so I kept asking Branch if he was ok.

No Health Care

We got to Branch's house, where his father and a group of men sat playing cards and drinking rotgut moonshine (locally made whiskey, it is sometimes called). Black men sometimes passed the time this way while between jobs. Work from these mostly Irish- and German-owned businesses, the sawmills and harvesting companies, was as unpredictable as the weather. So the black men sat and waited and waited and waited and drank, having few or no options. Only the women worked regularly as domestics. Cotton was still king in the South, but the need for black field hands had gone down considerably. In the 50s, it was the start of the industrialization of the South, an economic death trap for any black man that had not yet fled north.

I stood by my tearful friend as he told his father what had happened. His father could do nothing for hours but clean the wound and place cold well water on Branch's swollen eye and face. Branch father did not have a car or telephone, and the nearest white doctor was ten miles or better away by car, which Branch's father did not have. My family was just as poor, and even if we had a telephone, calling for help was not an option in those days because the white-only emergency vehicles would have refused to come to pick up a black person anyway. Our predicament reminded me later of the controversial death of blues singer Bessie Smith in Mississippi. Though it was before my time, my father and the black men of the community often educated us kids about the ways of the world around us by repeating the stories they heard from the "African news grapevine." The grapevine was the Internet system of our time. This was one of those stories. While traveling to Mississippi, Ms. Smith was involved in a bad car accident. The car was totaled in the crash. According to the grapevine story, by the time people got her to the closest emergency location, a white hospital, it refused to admit Ms. Bessie Smith to its emergency services. By the time she did reach a black-operated emergency location that would treat her, she had already died. Although the validity of the events surrounding Bessie death is still debated today, I, and many in the black community, believe she was left to die. For us, this was unforgivable. A dangerous day in the land of the free that God loved so much. Remember now, this is as much a report for future generations as it is for the now living.

Heard It on the Grapevine

My friend Branch's mother who worked as a domestic was still at work. Had she been home she might have been able to help. African American women in those days usually knew what to do because they had more access to the white community and systems than most black men. The black woman has always been considered less threatening to whites than the black man.

I went home and told my parents what had happened. I got fussed out at first and then later called a "good, brave boy" for staying with my friend Branch in his time of need. I was ordered not to make such dangerous toys in the future.

The rest of the summer was hell! My friend Branch lost his eye, but he could still sing better than most singers I heard on radio and TV. Most importantly, he and I remained friends. After the accident, something starting changing in Branch. He got meaner. Every time something harmed him physically, he would snap and try to hurt that person or beat that object to a pulp unless I stopped him, and I was the only person that could stop him. Seeing the effect the accident had on my friend, I don't think I ever played with a bow and arrow again. Those sad and sometimes happy days of my youth vanished as the times demanded we kids grow up quickly. We needed to get on with our lives and not be held back by a dying, racist system operated by a group of foolish white folks that did not accept that they had lost the war with African people over slavery the day slavery had begun.

Chapter 12

Attempted Sex in a Hen House

As time passed and we kids grew into our midteens, we changed and developed new responsibilities and interests, among them high school, girls, and work. For me, the only jobs that I could find were picking cotton in the hot fields or mowing white folk's lawns. There were also jobs working on the new federally funded interstate highways planting grass by hand on roadsides and sloping embankments to prevent erosion and beautify the "lynching state." However, you had to be lucky to get one of those jobs because the federal and state prisons had most of the local black male prisoners on chain gangs doing that work for free or hired out for big bucks to Irish or German private businesses by the state representatives who took a bribe or kickback. That left picking cotton for $2 a day in the boiling hot sun, with no water, no food, and no place for people to relieve themselves for nine to ten hours straight.

Through it all, young black men had to be

ever mindful of the evil intent of white men, mostly Irish males, in that they were and still are the largest group of white America (followed by Germans) who wanted to lynch and castrate as many young black men as they could cowardly reach and railroad as many others as they could into state prisons. Our fathers often reminded the young black men in the community to be careful because most white men in the area did not have an IQ that would equal that of a country goat. Racism, evil under white sheets the brand of Ku Klux Klan (KKK) a European dress code, an export worn by the hidden faces of Germans and red necks of the Irish. Both groups Irish and Germans, many were banned from Europe were with many women north and south the card-carrying members of the Ku Klux Klan continued this evil upon arrival in the Americus. Somewhere in this mixture of the white man's imagined heaven, a diseased brand of the American dream, the black man's living hell, I discovered girls. I fell in and out of love at least once a month with the girls in our community. First attempts don't always work!

One hot summer day of my youth, I turned fourteen. There was this one older girl with big boobs and a very large African butt, who lured me into a small chicken house in the back of her home. It was then that I learned the do's and don'ts of sex on a 110-degree day. We both fumbled around the cramped, smelly chicken coop among the roaming, confused chickens. I was nearing the point where I thought I could insert myself inside of her, a first time for me. The girl, whose name I can't quite recall due to lack of interest in names at the time, was just as willing and ready. You'll never believe what happened next. Before I tell you, I must confess that

Chicken Little was right: the sky does fall, and it fell that day on me.

The girl's mother kicked open the chicken coop door behind me. Startled, I looked around holding my steel hard pecker that stood out in space like a rocket in flight. There stood the older girl's hairy, wide-legged mother, blocking my only exit with a homemade broom handle, harder than my pecker, that she was stabbing into the dirt and chicken droppings.

"Boy, I know you!" She said standing over me with her big tits sticking out a mile in the summer heat and busting through her aging, flowery print dress. "I know your Mama, boy. What are you doing with my daughter in here?"

"Who me? What am I doing to her?" Shit, I am about to get fucked! I thought to myself as blood rushed rerouting from my erection no longer hard. I prayed to my legs and got ready for some fast action to get me the hell out of that chicken hut. The whole thing seemed surreal and heartbreaking. It was disappointing to be that close to a home run and strike out! What would the fellows think of me?

Blood retreated from my penis and returned to my one-track brain, where it was truly needed to come up with an immediate escape plan. There was only one of two ways out: right between the mother's legs and out the door or make a hole in the chicken hut wall. I took off like the Road Runner TV cartoon character right between the mother's big hairy legs: not a fitting place to be after just coming from between her daughter's legs. But, being the guy in the fix I was, I had to find a way out. Forcing the mother's long dress up with one hand and crawling between her legs with the other, I created a space just large enough for me to squeeze through. Praise

God! "Please God, save this young sinner," I prayed with little hope of having the pray answered. During the escape, I thought I heard the girl laugh, or was it the mother? Funny or not, the shit was not funny to me!

Having made it to the opposite side of her hairy legs and beyond the door, I ran bare feet for dear life, kicking up the Alabama red clay dirt road that led to my house a few miles away. I knew my behavior would rub the self-righteous members of the community the wrong way as much as the way I was running. Many believed sex should be kept in the closet. Well, guess what? It was out of the closet now. I think I heard my name being called as I sped away, and it did not sound like the mother was calling me a church-going child of God. The mother never caught up with me, but the modern-age technology did. By the time I reached home, the bad news had spread by telephone that my parents had made sure of getting after the bow and arrow incident. By the time my mother reached home that evening from working as a domestic maid in some white woman's house, I was wishing I had gone the other way in the chicken house. My mother planned to whip me with Pop's belt. The only problem was Pop had only one belt, and he was wearing it at the sawmill where he was working. When he finally did come home, he was tired from working a 16-hour day in the dilapidated sawmill. All he wanted was some peace, a hot supper, and some sex if mother was in the mood. My mother, however, was still thinking about my romp in the chicken coop. I couldn't understand what the big deal was. It wasn't like I was with the Virgin Mary. The girl was of age, 18, I believed. She was old enough to attract any able-bodied interested man, and from what I heard around the community, there were lots of takers. After Pop was told the exciting tale, he must have started thinking about his own sexual needs.

"You wanted to whip the boy for becoming a man?" He asked. "What will you do when he does have sex? Kill him? Leave the boy alone woman and let's go to bed. You are more likely to turn him into a faggot...leave the boy, woman."

Well, Pop got his supper, and later that night I heard that familiar bumping sound of their bed hitting the wooden wall of the room I shared with my brothers. I got the feeling lying there awake that my father might be sending me a coded message. My sister's room was farther away near the front door of the three-bed room house we built brick by brick with our own money and hands. I won't even begin to reveal what my best friend Branch and the other guys in the community had to say about the whole messy very public matter. I became so depressed by it, I became a snake catcher for the neighborhood whenever the nasty pest slithered into their rural yards. Back then, I thought it easier to risk being bitten by a snake than to face the jokes some of the guys were tossing at me.

Surviving the Hard Years

The strong union between my parents had to be the reason my siblings and I survived to complete high school and reach early adulthood. Most black people knew how to survive and taught their children how to survive under the most difficult situations imaginable in the 50s Jim Crow South.

Our parents and forefathers were denied any education at all and had passed on their survival tactics and instincts to us to pass to future generations for generations to come. Stories were told around the dinner table, and there was always time for those around the table and the fireplace. These discussions more than made up for the bad education I was receiving at the local school for brainwashing black youth. I wanted action in my education so badly that I started to develop short movie scripts in my head. Then I stage produced and filmed them using a still camera and cast my two younger brothers as the Cowboy and Indian.

On Sundays, my mother would call us all around and ask one of the boys to take out the ice cream maker, and we would hand crank for an hour or more at the bucket until a gallon of the best ice cream ever was formed. We would all eat until our hearts were content and bellies full.

On the half-acre of land we owned, we planted a garden and raised a few pigs and chickens. When that was not enough to put food on the table, we would just head for the closest forest to find food growing in the wild. Along the roadside in summer, we would search for berries. In the forest, we gathered nuts, edible plants, and even plants for traditional medicines based on knowledge passed on to us through the centuries by Africans ancestors. Some of this knowledge and skills were shared from the few surviving Native Americans still in the area. Then, there were the squirrels, rabbits, and wild boar we hunted, although we were careful not to be caught hunting on the land stolen from the Indians by Irish and Germans mostly who claimed they now owned the land. I once found a finely carved, bone, white Indian arrowhead while I was digging out our basement, which proves to me the Indians owned the land we lived on and not the Irish and Germans. Case closed as far as I was concerned.

Becoming Interested in Earth Science

I remember one winter when we fell behind one payment on a new potbelly, a coal and wood-burning stove father and mother was paying off in installments from an Irish-owned business in Tuscaloosa. The owner of the store showed up one cold winter morning at our house in his pickup truck and demanded the stove back. My father pulled the live firewood out of the stove, and I helped him haul the hot stove out of the house and into the truck. Then, the Irishmen drove away with the stove. It was kind of hard on the family that winter since we no longer had a heating stove. At times we would ask sharecroppers to let us scavenge their fields for leftovers after the sweet potato and corn harvest ended. Later on I found work with a printing shop in the nearby city of Tuscaloosa. It was an Irish-owned company called Randal Publishing Company, where I learned to slightly improve my writing and reading skills the high school had not taught me. What I learned at the publishing company would later help me to venture deeper into the outside world.

In time, the full force of the second civil war, the civil rights desegregation movement, reached Tuscaloosa, Alabama, upsetting the University of Alabama and the already-thin foundation of local white power. The white community panicked. They were losing their one remaining weapon, their pagan God—a false sense of superiority held in place by racism, murder, segregation, and intimidation. The white community and the US government had used these illegal criminal methods to deny African Americans human rights and the opportunity to reach back and reclaim our cultural heritage, so naturally we, as a people, were going to have a long road back ahead of us. No one in the outside world, not even the United Nations, came to our aid or was allowed to enter America and offer African Americans a helping hand. I was starting to develop anger and uneasiness. I was a young black man growing up in Alabama whose energy and dreams could not be contained by the system and the evil it tolerated and promoted. All hell broke loose as every black man, woman, and child in the failing nation stood upright across the land that bled, led by a young Dr. Martin Luther King. They placed their lives on the line to support sister Rosa Parks who sat down. I would meet her later in life. The revolution moved into direct confrontation with white folks and made all America seem a racist nation.

It was in this era that I grew into a man with a longing for wider knowledge of the world than Alabama could ever offer me. I had finished high school and had helped my family pay off the home we had built with our own hands. It was the first plot of land we owned outside Africa, so there was no longer any reason for me to hang around. For what reason would I remain in Alabama, on a half-acre of land that took less than five minutes to walk across? My grandmother told me I must try to be myself, find myself by any means, and reach Africa. I was visiting her in Falkland, Alabama, recovering from a foot accident that happened in a church of all places. Africa was nearly half the size of the world according to a local elder African man who was the keeper of the records of exiled Africans in his area of enslaved people. My older brother Willie, who used to work for the Coca-Cola Bottling Company, had already split for New York City. He was over twenty years old, and it was time he moved out on his own. Soon after Willie departed Alabama, my parents and grandmother wanted me to leave. I had outgrown the South and all its low IQs. My impeded undereducated parents saw the danger of me confronting and losing the battle with the local white low IQs that threatened to destroy us all.

Chapter-13

Getting the Hell Out of Dixie

It was the summer of 1959 when I boarded a Greyhound bus and got the hell out of backward Alabama. It was my "Underground Railroad" out of the pathetic American South. Little did I know what awaited me along the way I had chosen. I was among the first African passengers to ride in any seat on an Alabama bus in the 20th century thanks to Ms. Rosa

Parks, born in 1913, the year Harriet Tubman died in Auburn, New York. Tubman, like Parks, stood up when black men were so oppressed under slavery and Jim Crow laws that few black men could hardly take a piss in a ditch anywhere without being watched.

I was departing the South with my young manhood still intact and, regrettably, still a virgin, but only just thanks to my father and the women in my family who taught me the culture of being a man in battered black America. I was headed out of state on a well-traveled path that had become the great African underground exodus north for Africans trying to escape the extreme Jim Crow laws. It seemed the only way out from under the Irish-controlled KKK-riddled south was to head north. I needed a lot of knowledge and training before heading into the unknown across the Atlantic Ocean to Africa, a place I then knew little about but for stories told around the fireplace or potbelly stove in the evenings.

I had finished high school a year late and had yet to read my first complete book. Thanks to Alabama's horrible racist school system, I could barely add, multiply, read, or write. At one point, I was good at math, but then something happened that placed my motivated love for math on hold for decades. The math teacher went after a young woman in class with a board larger than both my hands to beat her for some silly game kids play, and I was not having it. I could not allow that. I did manage to stop the math teacher, but it cost. He lost my respect as a student and with that went my interest in math. Before the event, I was an A student in math. I imagined the white-controlled state, not the black educators, were proud of that accomplishment. I will always be thankful to the majority of the black educators for giving the black kids all they had to give. There I was, near functionally illiterate, not yet having read my first book, graduating high school. Yet, I was determined to start out on a journey to carry out a mission not knowing where it would lead.

All Aboard! Back of the Bus!

My father picked up my one small suitcase with his large, overworke,d muscular hands and carried it onto the bus with his head held high. I think this was the first time he had been on a bus headed north out of state. Like so many other brave black men, he had passed on the great African American migration north and west taken by so many. From outside the bus windows, I could see him inside working his way through the black and white people to a seat as close to the center, but clearly at the back of the last white person. After placing my bag in the overhead rack, he turned and exited the bus.

The white bus driver emerged from the white-only bus station bathroom, adjusting his cap that had over the years and thousands of miles molded itself into his persona. Now, the bus driver was all business, whereas minutes before he was seen joking with the older white station manager.

"All aboard," the driver called out glancing at his pocket watch.

"You will be on your own, son, from here on, you hear me," my father said.

"I hear you, Pop." Holding out my ticket, the driver punched it. There was something final about that hole in the ticket as if I had reached the point of no return. I placed one foot on the bus doorstep and climbed aboard, not looking back until I was walking down the center aisle near the seat selected by my father. Glancing over out the window, I saw a few hands, black and white, waving good-bye. I sat down and was no longer able to see my family, and they had lost sight of me. The driver closed the door and searched the gearbox for first, and the big bus slowly carried me away from the segregated hell and my loving family. This would be the last time I would see my father alive. That was it; the first trip out of that hellhole was the end of my childhood, my youth, and my claim to innocence of any kind. The bus rolled out of the station onto the main avenue. We passed white-only segregated shops and restaurants that gave no hint of African American or black business culture or that we even existed, even though our slave labor had built the south. As the bus headed north, it passed the state's parks. These beautifully manicured parks had benches that were for white asses only. As the bus moved, it passed Confederate flags and segregated University of Alabama buildings anchored in soil and soaked with African, Native American, and white blood that clung to a failed state. Africans had won the slavery war. It was the early 1960s now, and the black south was gearing up for the final push to win the second civil war in the nation, the so-called civil rights movement; so-called, because in truth we were fighting a second civil war for land and the right to manage our own economic future. I was proud of my family and the whole community it took to raise me. They had taken on the world superpower with bare hands and no education or iron or steel weapons. And no one in the outside world, not even the UN members, came into America to assist us.

The large Greyhound bus strained under its own weight as it pulled away from the city of Tuscaloosa onto the main highway, away from what had been a fucking dry white nightmare for me and so many alive and dead. I just wanted to get the hell out! I had a life to find away from this empty shithole. I had a mission in life that had to be carried out even if I had no idea where to begin, and I was just about broke. I had not much more than $2.50 before Pop slipped me what most likely was his last five bucks just as I was entering the bus. I had a near worthless high school education, $7.50 and was still on the banned list. America banned education for the likes of me to help hide the systematic crimes against humanity and guilt of the many human right crimes committed over the centuries on African people. The black, not African cultural training, my parents and community provided me was all there was to carry me into the world. I had to deal with it and make the best of it.

Chapter14

New York City

Finally, we reached New York safely, a city so big and famous they name it twice they told me. The person who said so was right. New York City to me was another planet. I located my mother's sister Aunt Darling, she was called, a church-going woman who split the South to live in Far Rockaway, New York, with her gay only son Johnson. She received me with open arms, burying my face with joy into her chest, her expression of total joy at seeing me.

There I was in the city of speed where anyone could come and nearly everything goes. New York in the 60s was a greed-stricken concrete jungle of cultures, good and bad, and rich and poor, as James Baldwin noted in many of the books he authored. Lucky for me, New York City had opportunities even though corrupt, white, European political management played a major role in blacks being held back in New York. There was enough to get over and excel I soon learned or saw cracks in the walls of the "Big Apple." I had the mind of a person with dual citizenship to *Another Country*, a book James Baldwin would write about in time. In the mix of it all, I somehow remained on my feet. I learned quickly to swim in the currents of human greed and anxiety.

To support myself, I found work at a

chrome-plating factory in Queens, where I inhaled the plant's poisonous fumes eight fucking hours a day. Concerned for my health, I sure as hell was not going to stay in that poisoned gas pit, but many men of color did. They had to. They had families to feed or just could not do better. Later, my two brothers followed me from Alabama, and we lived with my aunt until we could save enough money to get our own apartment. While working at the plant, I earned more money in a month than I was earning in a year in Alabama. Since it was at a great cost to my health, I quit. The system of oppression was more under cover in the North, but the intended outcome was the same: keep the blacks and Spanish down and out so a few white males could hold on to ill-gained, fading power a bit longer.

Like most African American enslaved immigrants moving north to an advanced American city out of the backwoods of an oppressive rural system, I learned to survive. No thanks to Presidents John F. Kennedy (JFK) and Lyndon B. Johnson (LBJ) who sided with corporate America and passed an immigrant bill to flood the country with non-African immigrants from around the world in an effort to protect America from what most whites saw as a very aggressive African population now demanding full shares of the American pie. This was some cold shit to face for anyone. This was just a plain monopoly.

The new immigrant policy in America would grant jobs, free educational scholarships, and honorary white citizenship status to mostly non-African foreigners, many who used their dual citizenship and free education as an unequal advantage to return and help build their homeland. It was unbelievable to me that the US government could give all this to those who had not had a hand in building this nation's foundation! But I did not know then the reality of foreign policy. Protecting even a racist America had global needs. More and more I was meeting people from all cultures around the globe but had little connection with them because as united as America would like the world to think the country truly is, it is not united.

Working hard, my two younger brothers and I saved money and soon had our own apartment on the beach in Far Rockaway, New York. It was near my aunt's apartment so she could keep an eye on us. I met a girl named Goldie. We dated and luckily there was no chicken house sex and hairy-legged mother blocking our adult development. When my new girlfriend and I were not together, I would drift into New York City, observing what it had to offer a newcomer like myself.

Sidney Poitier, a Role Model

Time passed while I got to know the city much better. One day while on a run from one of the many messenger jobs I held, I ran into actor Sidney Poitier, Hollywood's top black superstar at the time. He was at a parking lot on 53rd and Broadway with his first wife and two daughters. I just walked over and introduced myself and asked him for a contact in show business as an actor. He asked me to wait until he could put his family in the car. He came back a few minutes later, and we chatted for a short time about me wanting to break into the movie business. Sidney advised me to try my luck in Los Angeles and look up an old friend of his named Ivan Dixon, an actor and director. I thanked Sidney, and we parted company not knowing I would meet him again later in life on two of the many films he went on to star in after I got into the business. One was called *The Lost Man*, which filmed in Philadelphia in 1966. I worked with Sidney again on the film *For Love of Ivy* in 1968. What I did not know at the time was that the US government Selective Service agents were stalking me.

Chapter-15

Go Kill the Yellow Man

During the time I spent in Los Angeles, I had no idea the Selective Service, the army police, had put out a wanted poster on me. It seems by American rules, I was ungraceful. I had skipped out on taking a bullet in Nam, and I should have been grateful for not being drafted sooner to be sent to Vietnam to kill what Europeans called the "yellow man." I was moving so fast to get my life started, it seemed the system could not keep up with me. Then these US Army guys came knocking on my hotel room door. I was asleep that morning when they came. I thought it was the hotel manager looking for the room rent, which I did not have. I told the army guys I would come with them, but they had to pick up my tab at the hotel because I was flat broke. They did and I was driven away to the army induction camp. Naturally, my life and all my plans were placed on hold.

While doing basic training in Fort Ord, California (the goddamn South again), I quickly learned the army did not give a damn about us guys. Even though the training was paid for by taxpayers, we did not get any. I mean we were not trained to win at anything. We were expendable. No wonder our guys were getting their butts shot off in Vietnam. There was so little respect for the black guys that I caught a sergeant taking the firing pin from my M·1 rifle during a drill and placing it in the rifle of a white guy. I called the sergeant on it, but it was washed over. With that done, what could we black men expect on the battlefield?

About the only thing good that happened to me in basic training was I became a weapons specialist. I was also given the job of producing live entertainment shows for the guys when the officials found out I worked as an actor before being drafted. Then, things kind of fell apart. I didn't want to be in the army fighting the white man's war. Besides, I had no problem with my Asian brothers who were pretty much in the same fix we African Americans were in. Dr. Martin Luther King Jr. felt the same way. He was all over the TV and in the newspapers telling black men not to fight this white man's war and kill our Asian brothers. It was all designed to make white companies richer and more powerful so they could go on slaughtering indigenous people and their diaspora family members for their stolen resources America and Europe (if they were smart) should have been paying and fair-trading for. The black men in my army unit were doing everything we could to support Dr. King and remain off the battlefield, but we never let the people of America down by putting the nation at risk while finishing our tour of duty with an honorable discharge from the service. Like most, I knew there would be hell to pay in American society if I came out of the army with a dishonorable discharge.

I GOT YOUR BOY!

Shortly before completing basic training, a few African American soldiers and I got into a very big fistfight with a group of white GIs. Mind you, the white guys, all from the ass end of racist America somewhere, did not want to eat in the same integrated army mess hall with the African American soldiers in the first place. I felt these guys were scumbags, and no doubt they felt the same about us. The fact is, white and black males in America, then and now, just do not know or respect each other and, to this end, do not trust each other. Anyway, our guy was shy and too afraid to defend himself from the white soldier. Ironically, I had got a bad vibe when I stepped into the mess hall, so I had decided to skip breakfast. As I turned to leave, I noticed the black soldier kneeling and leaning toward the eggs. I called out.

"Hey man! What are you doing? Don't do that!" I yelled. "Let him pick up his own fucking tray."

"I will pick up my own tray," the white soldier responded. "But this nigger is going to pick up my eggs over easy and eat 'em."

"If he must eat the eggs, you will eat the tray," I retorted, advancing toward the white guys. I must have been out of my fucking mind because all six of them were as big and strong as country mules. Fortunately, the ancestors were with me that day. As luck would have it, Dale and Sleet, two black army buddies I hung out, stepped into the mess hall and saw that I was about to get my skinny black butt kicked. They were the size of Mack Trucks and pissed at being in the white man's army. Seeing them gave me the courage to walk over and push our guy away from harm's way.

"Get the hell out of the mess hall, brother!" I ordered the man on his knees.

Just then, one of the white soldiers spat at my face. I do not remember very much after that because I was pretty damn busy with Dale and Sleet burying our feet and fists in those good old boys' asses and faces. Food trays and chairs were flying everywhere. It was a hell of a good fistfight. The only fight that might have been better than this one was in a movie I had seen a few years earlier called *Shane*, starring Allen Ladd. Both sides in this fistfight fought hard, as if we were fighting for the World Heavyweight Championship. We ended up making a mess of the taxpayers' mess hall. The fight, which involved seven or more guys, spilled out onto the veranda of the mess hall. It was here that the deciding blows were landed. Dale was a martial arts specialist and struck the massive guy he was fighting in the chest with a kick that sent him flying backward through the railing and three feet below to the ground. Being the skinny six-foot, boney kid that

I was, I was hard pressed to finish off the guy I fought until Dale shouted at me to end the fight.

"Move in close, Frank, and work upward and clip him good," Dale shouted. I did as ordered. Again and again I struck with a right upper cut to the jaw, finally sending the guy down for the count where he stayed. I turned and saw Sleet, strong as an ox, pick one guy up and slam him into the wooden deck. Then he grabbed a second soldier who was trying now to flee and picked him up. Just then, the captain and two other white soldiers ran into the mix of what must have been thirty or forty soldiers calling for a halt to the fighting. Sleet had the last man in the air over his head and was about to break his back over his knee if Dale hadn't stopped him. Instead, Sleet slammed the soldier down so hard on the oak deck that I flinched. Bloodied and pissed, all of us soldiers were bruised up. The captain called for someone to get a medic. Our side had won the fight, but no one dared say it then.

The white American system was concerned and rightly so in my mind. Countries like China and the USSR were already focused on Africa and had been for decades. The question was would this support benefit African Americans and how would they react? The 1960s civil rights movement was heating up across the country. I mean, brothers and sisters were burning cities; all hell had broken loose in the "land of the free." And all the time China was smuggling propaganda posters into black American communities urging them to burn Washington to the ground. I even collected a few of these well-crafted posters printed in the 1960s in China, and I have a few original posters to this day. We African guys were mad as hell about being drafted into the American military in the first place because we had our own war going on in America. Before the mess hall fight, the army brass in Washington, DC, had ordered the black soldiers not to go out and get involved in any civil rights demonstrations while we were away from the base, but we defied the army rule and demonstrated anyway. This pissed them off, but there was nothing they could do about it. What were they going to do? Shoot us? They were already doing that in the streets of America and losing the war in Vietnam for their sins.

Assignment Day for Our Sins

The top army brass must have been angry at us for the fight and disobeying their orders about demonstrating in downtown Louisville, Kentucky. For our sins, they shipped Dale and Sleet to Germany and shipped my skinny ass to Thailand, where I spent a few months of hard labor building bridges. In the end, I survived the war in Asia and missed doing a tour in Vietnam by a city block. My younger brother Reb did not fare as well. He was sent into that napalm hell and was socially and culturally alone with other black and brown men, treated worse than most captured Vietcong.

Chapter-16

Underground Railroad to Europe

I left the US Army with a disability but so far had been denied disability pay. I did not know then that my disability deserved compensation since no one in the army shared that information with me.

It was early spring in 1966 as I stood alongside the massive SS *France* ocean liner saying good-bye to an old friend. Willis, a sixty-something-year-old African American who worked at the Manhattan Shirt Company, had given me a job both as a shipping clerk and messenger after returning from the army. He was forcing me to quit and depart for Europe where I could learn something about life and the world around me. I would be embarking for Paris, France, on my second trip outside of the oppressive United States of America. I had earned just enough money to make the fare. I saw this trip as an extension of the Underground Railroad, built by Harriet Tubman back in 1865 and used by Africans escaping north to Canada and beyond from the horrors in America's South and North. I had less than a hundred dollars in my pocket after the purchase of the one-way ticket out of New York just as I had when I entered. It seemed I was always holding a one-way ticket. I lied to Willis telling him I had a lot more cash and a return ticket. I didn't want him to worry. He had become like a father figure to me, and I was like a son to him. We said our good-byes, and I boarded the ship.

The SS *France* drifted out on to the Hudson

River and into the belly of the great Atlantic Ocean, as easy as Sunday morning. At a distance, I could now see Willis walking toward the hill he strained to climb due to old age and one too many cigarettes. Suddenly, he stopped and turned to look back at the SS *France*, straining to find me somewhere on deck as if he had changed his mind about letting me go. Perhaps he forgot to tell me something, but could not find me now. But, I could see him, and that is what mattered most to me. Then he turned and was gone—swallowed up by the city.

I reached the cabin assigned to me and entered. There was my friend Maria from Sweden standing there unpacking her bags. Maria was about my age, twenty something, maybe a year younger. Maria and I had met the day I came to purchase my ticket a month before the departure date. We hit it off so well waiting in the long ticket line that we decided to save money and share a cabin to Paris, where she was planning to spend a few weeks before taking the train on to her native Sweden.

"I see you made it, Maria. I was looking all over for you," I said, giving her a bear hug and receiving one in return.

"My hotel would not let me stay past ten o'clock, so I came aboard early," she explained.

Maria and I sailed together and bonded closer than I thought we would. We would join the other students on the dance floor at night, acting as if we did not have a concern in the world. But, there was some hostility between the whites and Jewish students aimed at me who did not wish to see a fine-looking friendly girl from Sweden and me getting along so well. Maria and I decided to avoid the "Children of Darkness." The few misguided students and I went on with our lives, enjoying and learning from each other.

At times, Maria and I would go up on deck, stand in the windy rain, and talk about our lives and the future of race relations. To avoid the Children of Darkness, we sometimes missed meals and ventured onto the dance floor long after everyone else had left. Both living in New York City and the various army tours had taught me that friendship was a powerful weapon over low IQ when faced with racism. I had made lots of friends from all walks of life since arriving in New York City, and society be damned if they did not like it or envied it. The ship guests would always notice when we entered the dance floor. Maybe it was because Maria and I were more entertaining dancers and we were a mixed couple. We were so popular with the guests on the dance floor that when the captain heard about us, he invited us to visit the captain's table and later dance with the first-class passengers. Afterward we got invited to dine with the captain and a few of his VIP passengers. You can imagine how this affected my brain that was already dancing on a high wire miles above but feeling like my footing was slipping on glass. We reasoned this was why the others showed so much resentment toward us. Maria and I would spend a lot of time in our small cabin studying dance moves and having great sex for hours on end as the SS *France* approached Paris, the city of love. We even walked hand in hand on deck and counted the heads that turned while making jokes about it. Once the ocean liner reached shore, Maria and I, still happily excluded from the white American clan, traveled by train to the city for lovers. We ended up at the same youth hostel with the group of white youth from the SS *France*. We stayed a few days at the youth hostel, avoiding contact with my fellow Americans but soon moved to another hotel where we were much happier and looked less like tourists.

After a week in Paris, Maria and I ran out of money and lies she was telling her parents in order to remain. In the end Maria had to go home to her native Sweden. I promised to visit her in Sweden once I got settled in Paris, but it was a promise never kept. Ever since the last time I saw her at the train station in Paris, she keeps returning in one form or another: a smell of a certain blend of coffee, a dress shop on a Paris street, or a smell of fresh-baked bread Maria and I would steal early morning before bread shops would open. I will always remember Maria as my shipmate and first love in Paris, but life goes on. As I discovered Paris, I realized the French were much more open socially than white Americans, but all things were not turning out to be exactly what they seemed in France. I learned early on that the French were sly with their evil intents and racism. They had to be, as I later learned. Their national pride and pocketbooks depended on young African lives, stolen African wealth, and resources. A thief is always uneasy around his victims. It makes the thief sweat, exposing himself to the thought of justice. In time, however, it was through a white American, named Sally Wilson, living in Paris that I was able to find part-time work dubbing films and earned enough money to keep my hotel room on the Left Bank of Paris for a while. I avoided most Americans, who were almost always white tourists. Few African Americans were traveling this far at the time, but those who did make it this far certainly left their lasting marks on French culture. As my knowledge about the world expanded, I learned more and more about France's and other European nations' assaults on my African paradise. In my spare time, which I had a lot of, I met many people. Some were Europeans, others well-known exiled Africans and African Americans. Willis said they would be there trying to exhale the same nightmare I was trying to escape. People like author James Baldwin and nightclub singers like Ada "Brick Top" Smith, a classy, heavyset African American woman who operated a fashionable nightclub called Chez Brick Top in the Left Bank. Then there was theater director Gordon Heath, a tall, well-mannered African American. It was Gordon Heath who gave me my first onstage walk-on role. I played a role called "the Negro" in Arthur Miller's *After the Fall*. I never knew most of these famous, exiled Africans existed until I reached Paris.

Born in Harlem, New York City, with a class and style that would put most men (ok, gay men) to shame, author James Baldwin was by far the coolest. Baldwin was one of the most famous and important African American writers of the time, and many feel he still is. I first met Baldwin in a Paris cafe with his French male lover. Baldwin told me he had left America years earlier to save his own life and sanity and develop into a more successful writer. He had reached his career goals and was enjoying the success of it, but I could see that something was still missing in his life. I told Baldwin I was trying to find the path over the same mountain: to live free and develop as a productive human being.

While we sat at this West Bank Cafe, seemingly free men, the new independent nation of Ghana was just emerging, hardly a thousand days out of the slavery death grip and British and European human right and economic oppression. Ghana was the first African country out of what was to become fifty-four divided and exploited African states.

Paris gay life flowed around us that sunny day like bees around a honeycomb, dripping with love or trying to find love in Paris to wash away the pain, the kind of reality that bites.

"France is not the answer for you or me, Young Blood. Rather we have brought the solutions with us; we have to step up and sort out our new reality," Baldwin said. "We must now grow our new culture, as hard as that will be."

Baldwin and Brick Top became my mentors, and they often gave me the kind of advice I truly needed. It was in Paris I learned later that a gay person like Mr. Baldwin and his many friends could live their lives free of sexual harassment and oppression. Though I wasn't gay, neither Baldwin nor any of his friends ever tried to influence me to join their unique sexual culture. Rather, they sheltered me, and this was before Baldwin took me to meet Mama Brick Top. Brick Top provided shelter and food for me over the course of a few weeks. When they felt I had it together, they gave me a few employment leads, one of which was Gordon Health. In those days, Africans in exile living in Europe were a connected community.

We were all from oppressed communities in the United States, and it became natural for us to be concerned about each other. The more established, older ones in the community made sure young bloods, like me, got safely through the first few weeks or longer if needed; in fact, they sometime spied on us to provide hidden protection. They had all gone through similar experiences. I was warned never to let my guard down, even in white Europe. These are the people, I was reminded over and over again by Baldwin and Brick Top, who stole our land and enslaved Africans for centuries. And now they only tolerated African Americans in Europe to the extent that we had an American passport or served their interests to keep the postslave states afloat. When I asked them about African details, it was like asking them about moon rocks. Baldwin wrote about what he knew in America: racism, the church, politics, and sex. He seemed to know very little about his homeland at that time. At least he never lectured me about it. Brick Top knew little and what she did know she sang about in the blues. Their final stop was Europe. I pushed. I wanted more. I had heard and learned enough to want to see Africa; I wanted my wealth, culture, and land back. Brick Top and Baldwin introduced me to some African brothers my age and older that they had helped or who had helped them. In turn, the Africans helped me to gain a better understanding about who I was. For the very first time, I could see how I looked from the perspective of indigenous Africans. They each told me about the cultures and hardships the people faced in their countries and what I could expect when I returned. They told me which countries they thought I should visit first. Naturally, we exchanged contact information and saw each other often in the many cafés and nightclubs of Paris. Not one of us knew enough at that time to survive on his or her own. They taught me everything from how to survive the mean streets of Paris to what cafés to eat at to make my money last longer. I slowly found myself drifting toward a light that my African friend pointed out at the far end of the tunnel. It was a light even Baldwin and Brick Top could not show me because they had made Paris and other cities in Europe their final destinations. But not me; I wanted more. I wanted to ride the bull: go all the way to the end of the tunnel and come out of the white hole into Africa.

Chapter 17

Gaining a Grip on Self-Confidence

My self-confidence was beginning to build despite the European culture of closed doors, open sex, and economic end games designed especially for black people. Despite all this, I learned some French and found a great one-bedroom apartment at last. It was on the fashionable Left Bank of Paris. I began planning a limited future for the first time. The American horrors I endured and painfully remembered began to fade with every day that passed. But then some French people would remind me all over again that I would not get off so easily. The French had a few horrors to offer as well. Sadly, I still had a long way to go before being welcomed into the French or any other European culture, if I would ever be welcome at all. As it turned out during the year I was there, I never felt welcome. I still couldn't find gainful employment, and all bets were off on opening a business in Paris. I lived, like most I guess, day to day.

When not finding work, I settled for visiting the French museums. Once there I saw firsthand just how much the French had stolen from my fellow Africans and me. Post-Nazi and postcolonial Paris was overflowing with stolen African wealth and artifacts. Most notably, the zodiac ceiling was blasted from the Temple of Hathor in Egypt and then stolen and stashed in the Louvre Museum. The zodiac ceiling has since been returned to the temple, but only after the French were told their institutions would not be welcome to research in Egypt if they refused to return it. The zodiac ceiling is an almanac displaying wisdom beyond the understanding it seems of the French who used explosives to release it from the ceiling of the holy temple in the 1800s. The temple is a cultural icon. The zodiac was, still is a tool in the correct hands and minds to study the cosmos, stars, and heaven long before Europeans entered the study of caves, let alone the cosmos.

I walked the streets and avenues of Paris, dreaming and waiting like many of the young people from around the globe who had ended up in Europe like I had. We had a lot to balance and a lot to figure out about our lives now adrift after World War II and the Vietnam War. For one thing, the youth and the outsiders did not know the war in Nam was fought to enable Europeans and Americans to advance economic enslavement into people's lives more than anything else.

French xenophobia

One evening after losing my one-bedroom apartment due to budget problems, I was returning to my cut-rate hotel room on the Left Bank when all hell broke loose. Things were starting to go from bad to worse. The hotel manager, a fat, chain-smoking French woman, went into a fit when I walked into the hotel a few days behind with my room rent. She had dragged my half-opened suitcase from my room and into the street. The manager stood with hands on her super oversized hips and began calling me every name in the book of bastards. I didn't speak French that well, so most of the insults the vulgar woman spat out got past me. Naturally, people began to gather around. If I could have I would have just entered the hotel room gathered my belongings and left. I knew she was getting off on this public tirade, so I had to play it cool. A young French woman and a tall guy from Port-au-Prince, Haiti, named John Calverton, a few years beyond my age, had been watching from the shadows across the street under the awning of a nightclub. John walked over to me from where he had been standing and spoke to me in English.

"Do you understand French?" he asked me calmly.

"No, well, not so much." I replied with a half smile.

We exchanged names and looked each other in the eyes, sizing each other up before deciding to join forces. The French woman had crossed the line for John; she had played the race card, and John was pissed about it.

About that time, the young French girl that had been standing with John near the nightclub moved up closer beside him and waited. She watched with interest as this ugly face of her French people was exposed. A small crowd had gathered by now. The hotel manager, realizing she was on center stage, regained her breath, shifted her apron that covered her repulsive bulk, and lashed out at me again. With only two blacks in a sea of whites, she had nothing to fear. Forget the fact that so many African men died helping France liberate their flag and people from Nazi-controlled Europe in World War II just twenty years earlier. The hotel manager must have felt like a Nazi superstar by the gutter language she let roll out of her mouth. Suddenly her dull life had meaning, if only for a moment. John moved closer, stepping between the manager and me. John spoke calmly to me in English.

"How much do you owe her?" John asked.

"A week's rent, seven days." I told him an amount in English the manager understood.

"I demand payment in advance," she said.

John turned to the hotel manager, called her a few insulting names in Creole French slang I learned later, and pulled out a roll of French francs. John counted the notes and pushed the money into her fat, smoke-stained fingers that were still holding her cigarette. As the manager eagerly counted the money, John turned to me.

"Go into the hotel, and get the rest of your things. You can stay at my place for a while."

As I turned to enter the hotel, the hotel manager went into a long coughing spell, choking on nonfiltered smoke from the stub of the French cigarette. She lashed out at me again. Clearly all her attacks were provoked by more than just a late hotel bill. The manager had crossed the line for the French girl who turned out to be a close friend of John's. The French girl shifted her small body and unleashed a personal attack in French at the manager. She told the fat lady she was about to get her fat ass kicked, or something to that effect, I learned later.

"You should quit while you are still standing, bitch," the girl said to the hotel manager, as I entered the second-class hotel lobby. "You insult France with your very presence."

This sent the fat woman racing back into the hotel. When I came out of the hotel a short time later with my personal belongings, the hotel manager was nowhere to be seen and the people standing around had all left. The street was quiet again. John and his girlfriend were waiting for me beside my half-opened suitcase. The girl assisted me. John invited me inside the nightclub where he was performing and asked me to wait with his girlfriend until he had completed his last set. Here, I discovered what everyone in the club already knew. John was a damn good singer and entertainer! I relaxed with John's girl as the evening passed and enjoyed the cocktails he sent to the table that did not stop until John completed his last set. I put the fat French woman out of my mind and enjoyed the remainder of the show.

Paris Streets and Lovely Nights

Later that warm evening, we dropped my bag at John's place and the three of us went for a walk on the streets of Paris. It was a warm summer night, and lovers were out in full force, kissing it seemed under every streetlamp. During the walk, John's girl pointed out the hundreds of bullet holes in the building walls as we walked past. Signs of resentment attacks on the French city from Arabs and Nazis were everywhere. She told us the older bullet holes were from German World War II guns. Many were mostly plastered or cemented over. She said the Algerians had a right to kick the French government's butt. They invited me for a glass of wine. After talking until sunrise, we went to John's place and slept until noon. I listened and learned and slowly better understood the fears of others trapped in the same world of misery and shit I was trapped in. John didn't say much at first, but later he opened up and told of the horrors the French had inflicted upon his people in his native country, Haiti. I didn't even know Haiti existed, let alone that it was an island in the Caribbean where enslaved African people were taken after their long journey from Africa. In Haiti and its neighboring islands, John said the women were systematically raped and worked like mules with their children. The African men fared a lot worse he said. Historical documents and eyewitness records indicate Haitians being systematically beaten, castrated, and lynched if the African men, women, and children refused to obey.

All across the Caribbean, the same horrors were being repeated day and night. The horror took place twenty-four seven for four centuries or more. All this was designed to force the black man and woman to submit to produce uneducated children: human mules to work for the French. Fast forward to the 1960s, and France was still being occupied by Americans. Who was controlling the whip while the Africans in Haiti were forced to grow and make sugar bound for the fine coffeehouses in Paris, Germany, New York, Sweden, Rome, and all Western cities and markets? Slavery and the colonial era extended right into the oppressive post–World War 1966. Only a few bloody hours later in 1968, the so-called civil rights bill was signed by US President L. B. Johnston, an act that did nothing really worthwhile for African people the world over. We still had to face being banned as international immigrants flooded our areas and took away jobs and business culture we haven't seen in fifteen hundred years. I was in Paris because I had to flee America to save my soul.

As we departed a cafe and walked under the dimly lit streets, John told us how the Haitian people had risen up against the French in a bloody revolution and defeated them in the eighteenth century and become the first black island nation in the Americas to win its independence. John went on to suggest that no cooperation was forthcoming from Western democratic countries to help Haitian people develop and feed themselves. The Western democratic oppressor even went so far as to impose global embargoes on the new country and refused to recognize Haiti as an independent nation of free men, women, and children with human rights. American and European politicians had refused because they did not wish to be seated in the same room with black men and women on an equal basis.

John's voice grew angry in the late night air, and his French girl moved closer to him as he described the fate of African people in Haiti following the bloody revolution that left them ragged, hungry, and industrially handicapped to this day. This was the start of my education at the "University of the Streets." It wasn't just the Haitians. We all were angry and felt powerless, but we remained defiant. The 1960s was a time of rising violent social change in Africa, Asia, Europe, and North and South America. Those were also the days of the Cold War between the Eastern bloc countries and the so-called free Western world where John, his French girl, and I were still enslaved. Little did we know at the time that the Cold War was really about African resources.

My First Job in Paris: A Movie Role

As time passed, I spent my days looking for work in the French film industry as an actor. One day, while out seeing work, I walked into a French film production company and got lucky. I landed a job on a major film called *Martin Soldat* directed by Michel Deville. I was cast in a bit role playing an America GI in a World War II comedy about the Americans liberating France. How ironic to be accepted more as a man in the movies than in reality. As luck would have it, that day the director of the film was coming out of his office just as I was entering. The director, though I did not know it at the time, carefully looked at me and asked.

"Are you an actor?"

"Yes," I replied. Hell, I needed work so badly I would have said I was Martin L. King Jr. at the time.

Chapter-18

Stolen African Treasures

Acting on a tip and holding a letter from a casting agent, I drifted over to London on a ferry that operated between France and England. While in London, I decided to visit the British Museum. It was there I discovered Africa's rich cultural and wealthy past. Locked behind bulletproof glass were Africa's stolen treasures: gold, art, books, priceless records, and royal mummies—bodies of my dead African ancestors who produced the wealth the Queen of England now claimed as "Crown property." Just the thought of it made me angry. I nearly screamed out loud in the museum full of people that day. It took all I had not to. It was also here in the British Museum that I first came across the Rosetta stone, and what a bittersweet discovery it was for my tormented life.

It was winter 1966, and I was in London like a few million other black people all of whom were stolen from Africa and dumped there to work for free for centuries. The failed links to economic and missed education opportunities were a special treat Europeans and Americans dished out to defenseless Africans: the less education, the less competition for whites. I was surrounded by billions of US dollars and trillions in African gold and assorted wealth, with emeralds and diamonds the size of chicken eggs, and I was near penniless. I saw sapphires as large as human eyeballs and lapis lazuli that would make even King Tut envious. In fact, most of the loot there might have been stolen from the African boy king. Rubies glittered behind the bulletproof glass as my hungry eyes tried to adjust to all the gold, gold, and more gold. Mind you, Great Britain is beggar poor in most vital minerals needed for the state to survive as a state. Gold, brass, cooper, and tin had to be imported at a growing cost as the UK tried as best as it could to hang on to apartheid South Africa and Rhodesia, later to become a thorny, independent, defiant, mineral-rich Zimbabwe. The list and value of the wealth stolen and held here seemed near endless, and I could not reach out and touch a gram of gold or claim one diamond as mine to establish enough credit to get me through the night.

In the 1800s, Queen Victoria of England and a long line of British queens and kings wore the so-called "Crown jewels," all stolen from African queens and kings. The gemstones had all been gouged out of African holy temples and tombs. The wealth was taken from every part of African cultural heritage over the millennia it had taken Africans to fall. All this and more were now in the illegal possession of a thief that gave England's mythical Robin Hood a bad name.

Carved from basalt stone and taken from African soil, the Rosetta stone holds the most important information ever written by the most advanced humans in Africa. Written in Egyptian hieroglyphs, the writing on the stone was used as a break-through code enabling modern humans to read and write the ancient African text and provided the only key to a world my ancestors had created and built, which lasts even to this day. The hieroglyphs were also the key that helped to gain access to knowledge to what Egyptian ancient language meant and sounded like.

Though stolen centuries earlier than the enslavement and theft of my people, I felt as if I had found priceless treasures just in time to save my life and turn it in a whole new direction. The Rosetta stone for me soon ranked above all others, even the Holy Bible and the Koran. It was indeed the most important object in the British Museum and stood out the most among the stolen African treasures. Years later when I established my NGO IMSCO at the United Nations, I sent a letter to the British Museum demanding that it immediately return the Rosetta stone. Today, the Rosetta stone remains captured in the British Museum. What did happen was that for the first time in my life after reading the inscription on the stone, I felt a link to a cultural and power second to none. My long-lost culture. The rush I got from that cultural jolt started me on a path of motivated rediscovery that has lasted to this very day.

The next day, I had plans to return to Paris, but first I had to get through the rainy day and night. I didn't have money for a hotel, but I was longing to grab a few hours of sleep, remembering the French woman who had kicked me out of the hotel in Paris. Later that day, I kept the appointment with a movie talent agent that had invited me to London after hearing of my work from an agent in Paris. No sooner had I entered the office, the English agent gave me the brush off. His disrespectful eyes dotted about like daggers as he scanned my presence.

"Your agent in Paris must have misunderstood me. I have no such job in a movie for you," said the slender, pale, more pink than white talent agent.

I held out the letter the agent sent me. There I was trying to get accepted into an imaginary Western world when I was banned from the real Western word. Now, it just didn't get any more fucked up than that. Even though just a few blocks away from the British agent's office sat proof at the British Museum that I was the original star and had written the stories that history and present day rested on.

"What do you mean I misunderstood you?" I queried. "Here it is in writing. A wire signed by you inviting me to come," I said, demanding a correct answer.

"My secretary must have made an error," the agent replied. Oddly enough, I still have that original wire the British agent sent me in Paris inviting me to England.

Guest in a British Jail for a Night

I walked out of the agent's office onto the wet London streets questioning my life. What was it that truly lay ahead of me? I was scared stiff for the first time in my life. Apart from the few African and African Americans I had met in Paris, I had no community to fall back on, no education to speak of, and no money in a money-mad-driven world. On the damp fall streets, I melted into the mass of faceless people. I spent the day moving around London. I tried to keep dry by spending as much time as I could under shop awnings and moving only when the shop owners' eyes suggested to me they thought I was planning to rob the place. The only money I had remaining was the fare needed for the ferry trip back to Paris. Later that evening around 9:00 p.m., a police officer stepped up out of the fog and dim light as I was drifting up and down some nameless London street.

"Excuse me, sir, may I ask where you are going?" the officer demanded.

"Nowhere," I replied. "I am just walking around until 8:00 a.m. tomorrow morning when the ferry leaves for Paris."

"Why don't you check into a hotel? It's drier," the officer replied.

"I am broke," I said standing in the rain. "If I spend what little money I have, I will not be able to leave tomorrow, will I? Can you put me up for the night?" I asked the officer.

The policeman agreed, so I spent the night at the police station in an unlocked cell as their guest. About 6:00 a.m. the next morning, I was awakened by a station house sergeant standing over my bunk with a hot cup of tea and sweetbread. After I washed and ate, the sergeant ordered a police officer to drive me to the ferry. Back in Paris, I wandered about, hanging on from day to day, and I soon realized that France for me was not worth hanging around in. I had a life ahead of me, and though I did not wish to, I had no choice but to return to the abyss: America. For a young black man, more traveled and somewhat more learned, America was as terrorizing as being waterboarded. There were some people of color, and the lighter shades and stringy-haired people fared somewhat better when they tried to pass for white—whatever that got them! So I tucked it in and got ready to face the American songs of intolerance aimed at humanity, affecting all concern humanity. America was still holding on to slavery as a doctrine. It was no longer for free labor, though Africans and most whites, like it or not, were working for slave wages. It was America's transition years. All hell was breaking loose, and I had traveled outside the country for a better view and got that view for better or worse.

To my knowledge, nightclub owner Brick Top never returned to the United States. James came in and out of America mostly because he just did not give a good goddamn about whitey and his selfish fading American dream. What the so-called privileged citizens calling themselves white did behind these iron gates that hid a false freedom for African people even the UN or member states were not allowed to penetrate was anyone's guess.

America claimed to be saving the world, and yet the world could not enter the land of the free and help save the oppressed black man, red man, or yellow man. America's dark secret was systematic physical and mental extermination of woman and children. It was a horror for the blacks whose identity was stolen and stripped of their rights to humanity. Know your history, or be buried in it.

Chapter 19

Back to America

Crossing the Channel back to Paris, I realized a year had passed. It was then that I first got the urge to start keeping notes for this book. Right then and there, I pulled out a pen and starting writing down what had happened to me in life and where I hoped my life path would take me. I hadn't remained long in Paris after London. It was only a few months at the most, long enough to put together the price of a plane ticket via Ice Island, the cheapest air route out of Europe then. I flew back to America.

After a day in New York City, with confidence overflowing, I walked into Warner Brothers Pictures Distributions office at 666 Fifth Avenue. I requested to see one of the vice presidents of the company and hit on him for a job. The vice president sent me down to the film distribution department, and I was hired on the spot, much to my surprise. I was not sure if it was the newly found confidence I picked up in Paris or the new US laws that had been passed during my absence, compliments of the second civil war in America. The civil rights movement now demanded white companies hire African Americans in the film industry. Warner Brothers was not that far from the Manhattan Shirt Company on Avenue of the Americas, where I once worked. One day at lunch time, I walked over to see if I could locate Willis to thank him for the advice he had given me a year earlier and to say he was right in pushing me to leave. Willis had died a few months earlier in his sleep, or so the news through the Harlem grapevine reported. A younger African American man who had replaced Willis offered me my old messenger job back. I smiled, declined, and left.

The job at Warner Brothers was ok except that I could not stand the fucking cheap cigar smoke coming from the older man who was assigned to teach me the business in the windowless room where we worked. After a few weeks on the job choking on the smoke, I soon realized the company would keep me in the back room for years and never give me a sales post. I knew they favored white salesmen over me, which was cool because the gig really did not suit me anyway. I resigned from Warner Brothers Pictures and soon after entered the world of production, working for a TV commercial house on West 57th Street. There I met a Greek guy named Jim, who was the studio manager and a few years older than me. We hit it off. Jim hired me on the spot as his assistant running the production studio where we managed the crew and oversaw all the operations behind the scene of the company's TV commercial productions. In the studio, Jim called the shots and quickly trusted me to do the same, and I did. Jim had gone to college, and I had not, not that it mattered because the film production business came naturally for me.

One day, I got a call from the Directors Guild of America (DGA), the labor union for film directors in the movie industry. They told me I had been selected to become a member holding the title of Second Assistant Director, (A.D.).

"What?" I asked them. "Why me?" I was told that the union was very happy with the work I did and thought I would make a good member. Truth be told, the DGA had been ordered by the federal government to integrate African Americans into the union or face government fines and boycotts of Hollywood movies from the black community. It turned out the NAACP had put a lot of pressure on Hollywood and its racist clans to ensure African Americans a future in the film industry. This was huge power, so just like that I was in the DGA union. I knew I had earned it the hard way like all African Americans who had labored long for centuries from Paris, to Alabama to Harlem, and L.A to get those doors open. It meant I could now be paid the same wages as the whites at any wage level and be called to work on major film productions. I saw this as a way to fund myself to leave America again. I was able to get hired once in a while, but the Irish, Jews, and Italians who mostly controlled certain levels of the movie industry were not about to show much cooperation toward African or Chinese people, as I later learned. They were going to guard their racist trade as long as they could, and that meant keeping blacks and other people of color at bay.

My First Career Attempt

Because I held the keys to the studio on 57th Street and could order industry equipment when I wished, I gained in status and made a few allies. I started making deals with camera houses to loan me camera equipment on weekends to shoot my own short films in exchange for renting from them. I also raided the film vault of the company where I worked for raw film stock to shoot. I then directed and produced a number of short films and learned a lot about how to make a complete film from start to finish. Jim knew what I was up to and did everything he could to assist.

"You got balls, Frank, and you use your head," Jim often told me.

However, the DGA did become an opportunity, and I used it to better understand how movie propaganda worked. I began writing complete screenplays hoping to use the medium as a tool or as a weapon. Although I was writing a screenplay, this voice in my head would not go away.

"Go to Africa." The voice kept repeating over and over to me.

About a year later, with the help of the DGA, I left the TV commercial production house to try my luck full-time in the larger motion picture industry. However, making the move from TV to movies would prove to be not as easy as I had hoped. In my spare time, I wrote twelve pages of a treatment for a screenplay and began thinking about a cast and crew to produce a big-screen independent movie.

Meet Actors Martin Sheen, Michael Dunn and Johnny Brown

The summer of '68 in New York City was hot and gritty. Work had been slow. It was two years after the signing of the Civil Rights Bill: an agreement between white and black power in America to end the second civil war and the fighting over the rights of African Americans to be employed and live where they wished and do what they pleased anytime they chose. Finally, we had power; finally our efforts were paying off.

I had just completed work as an assistant director on the Hollywood big-budget movie *Hello Dolly*, directed by Gene Kelly. Soon after shooting was completed one midsummer day, I found myself in New York City working as a second assistant director on the motion picture production *The Subject Was Roses*, starring the legendary actors Patricia Neal, Jack Albertson, and Martin Sheen.

After a few days on the set, I walked up to Martin Sheen and asked him to read the twelve pages of a screenplay I was working on titled *Apple Man*, which I later renamed *Man in the Mirror*. The story is about a man who happen to be a dwarf named Apple Joe who is a society dropout in search of a more meaningful life than he was living as an assistant university professor in New York City. He quits his secure job, builds himself an apple cart seeking to earn his living as a street vendor, and goes into the streets of New York City to escape all the lies he does not wish to face in the so-called upper class. Minutes after arriving at his new gig on a Manhattan street corner in Greenwich Village, thinking he is free of responsibilities, he realizes he has stepped from the frying pan into the fire of his inner demons and social responsibilities. The script also addresses the issue of the endless gauntlet of New York's disposable and marginalized people struggling to obtain a slice of the elusive American dream.

The next day, Martin came back to me. It turned out he liked the screenplay and agreed to costar in the film after *The Subject Was Rose* had completed production in New York. After the film had wrapped, I turned producer and worked hard to raise funds toward making the independent movie, my first feature-length film. After a few weeks, I raised some money, got Martin to sign a contract, went into preproduction, and then rushed into production. I had gathered a strong supporting cast starring well-known TV star Johnny Brown, known for his many leading roles in TV series such as *Laugh-In* (1968–1973) and in the role of Bookman on *Good Times* (1974–1979). I also managed to get Michael Dunn, a famous film, TV, and stage dwarf actor, who rose to fame in most homes in America via the TV series *The Wild Wild West*, and Mr. Dunn, my star, who was nominated for an Academy Award for best supporting actor in the film *Ship of Fools*.

I had cracked the glass ceiling as far as I was concerned. What was even more impressive, I did it with the best emerging A-list actors America had at the time. Martin Sheen was a rising star if ever there was one. I had used much of my own money to find a mixed cast and crew to start a near impossible job I had no budget for production to speak of. America was changing for the better. Lots of people were sick of the old ways that pitted human against human just because of the color of their skin, or so we were led to believe. Despite some people's futile efforts to stop it, a better life was emerging for all. I had pushed the cast and crew hard to get as much filming completed as possible because I knew I was in a tight spot to complete the project. Martin Sheen was great. He flew back and forth from LA a number of times to do nine roles in the film and completed them too. Then the production company ran out of money.

Having completed most of the filming with Martin, Dunn, and Brown, I placed the project on the shelf and decided to wait for a time in the future to try and complete the film. I tried calling on a lot of Hollywood studios to assist, but none would. They sent a lot of letters but no takers. There were a lot of hard feelings still in the industry about African Americans entering the business. Fear of black America was hot, so hot that I found it near impossible to find a production job in the New York City film industry when I closed the production. A lot of guys resented me for trying and were happy to see the project fail to be completed, but little did they know, I never quit at anything.

At this point, I was fed up with the entire racial and political nonsense in the United States and began planning to leave. Why waste my time catching hell in America when I could face the same hell in Africa helping to raise a continent? If successful, I would help rebuild my stolen empire and produce whatever I wanted.

Chapter 20

Back to Africa

By now, it was nearing the middle of 1974. A Nigerian man visiting New York introduced me via mail to his uncle in Ibadan, Nigeria, who was thinking of building a cinema on a site in his home state north of Lagos. He invited me to fly in and advise him on how to obtain American films. I prepared to leave America once more. I took the money I had saved and climbed aboard Pan American Airways for what was certain to be the greatest adventure of my life. I wanted and needed a change and a new area to land opportunities and what better place than Africa? I felt like I was off to help save the world or at least take back the part stolen from me. I felt I was going to help preserve African cultures. I was going to Africa to join the war on the political ground and any other. How? I did not know. I would learn or die trying. I was willing to learn and do anything to help stop foreign invaders—Europeans, Lebanese, East Indians, Jews, and a host of others including Arab and African traitors—who blocked my development. From the bits and pieces of news I had gathered and learned about Africa, I realized that Africa at least at the start was not going to be the land of milk and honey. At the time, I had not anticipated the mess created by the UN members (a.k.a the colonial masters still in absolute control). They had even written African constitutions to keep the likes of me out of my own homeland. Little did I know then that these European masters of horror and American racists were leading companies and cheating Africans in the diaspora out of their birthright. How could we know?

Uneasiness started to swell up from deep within me as the big Pan Am jet lifted off from the runway and the extended silvery wings entered and split the night sky above. It glided over the Atlantic Ocean like an angel with its wings spread headed south to its first stop: Ghana. I was taking my first trip back to a part of Africa called the Gold Coast, still famous for its vast gold deposits used by Africans for millennia to build and trade in the first civilizations. A few minutes into the flight, the first black steward touched my shoulders since I had drifted off to sleep.

To my surprise, she asked, "Would you like a blanket, Mr. Weston?"

"Yes, please," I replied to the smiling host. I gazed down at the Pan Am, blue, wool blanket that had just been placed in my lap and then out the window. I could see only blackness—emptiness in the cold black belly of the sea that cradled millions of my ancestors' souls and bones that would never see their African homeland again. I imagined their restless bones pleading for someone to discover them, avenge their honor, and restore their self-respect if only on the pages of history written by Africans. I woke up and noticed the plane was nearly brushing the tops of the tropical trees. This was it! I was home at last. After centuries upon centuries, I was seeing the shore of West Africa.

Chapter 21

Missing Warrior

The plane was scheduled to stop in Accra, Ghana, before flying onto Lagos, Nigeria, our final destination. In the process, we flew over one of Africa's number one tourist attractions: the "Door of No Return," a seventeenth century ghostly fort built by the British that was used to hold and ship millions of families out of Africa into the horrors of Western slavery. Formerly known as the Gold Coast from the 8th to the 13th century, Ghana's precolonial empire lay north of the Upper Niger. Millions of Africans were captured and enslaved from all areas of the continent including Ghana. Every African kingdom was burned or rearranged, and the people were scattered to the wind and into many lands as the diaspora. God only knows where I was truly from, and only DNA testing could identify my family today.

In 1957, modern Ghana was the first tropical African country to gain its independence from the British's bloody colonial rule and genocide eras. Ghana's first president, Dr. Kwame Nkrumah, a visionary and Pan-Africanist, called for the unification of the African continent soon after Ghana's independence in 1962. Had other African leaders cooperated with this vision, I would have already been home and reestablished. Sadly that was not yet to be.

I will never forget that moment when the African American stewardess, the only one working the flight, pushed open the back door of the jet just opposite from where I was seated, and the rich tropical air rushed in carrying a kind of damp, salty taste of a coastal forest. Out on the runway, I could see a group of black men working. I could not help noticing for the first time not seeing a white man overseeing their work, an insult most Africans in the diaspora have had to endure for centuries. A few of the African men came on board to clean the plane. I felt an immediate bonding. I watched as the dark-skinned men with their natural, curly hair scanned the cabin for waste left by the departing passengers, gracefully moving about doing their jobs.

As soon as we were airborne again, I fell back into a dizzy anxious sleep. How could I sleep peacefully, even nap, for fear of missing a single glimpse of a homecoming to my great continent that I had not seen outside my ancestors' DNA for centuries. It had been a long journey: from 1960s Alabama to New York, to crossing the North Atlantic Ocean on the SS *France,* to Europe in 1966, back to the United States, to finally reach home on the west coast of Africa. After a short nap, I looked out the plane window with bloodshot and tired eyes and pants that hugged my thighs a bit too tight from the long flight. There was a sea of nothing but green, green forests as far as my eyes could see. The natural wonders of the world here stretched for thousands of timeless miles. I felt a transformation in that moment on the plane. I felt at peace with myself. Suddenly, my body started to heal itself of all the stress and pain of all the centuries my soul and DNA had been imprisoned. Now my body and mind were reacting as if an injection of natural life had entered into my bloodstream, nourishing every starved cell in my body. Then the big jet suddenly started to descend into Lagos, Nigeria.

Cultural Shock in Africa

I was more alive now, relaxed from centuries of stressed-out genes mutating from being and existing in America and Europe. I was freer and feeling better than I remember having ever been in my whole life.

Outside the plane, my lungs pumped more easily as I descended the stairs of the plane and felt my feet land on the concrete runway leading to the main airport terminal. My feet standing on concrete felt like clouds; Africa was truly a reality. Standing on the concrete clouds meant that Africa was a specific personal reality for me, not a vague, abstract, emotional, dark continent one had heard about or imagined from the many biased Tarzan movies. One cannot imagine Africa. Nigeria, the second stop on my journey into myself, was heaven and hell all rolled into one nightmare that carried me back to a past I had not wished to see, but could not avoid. That past was how I came to be put in a position of having to escape America and the Western world in the first place.

Suddenly, hundreds, it seemed like thousands, of black people were pushing, yelling, and grabbing at oversized luggage, stacks of suitcases, and boxes. I could see African women dragging their babies to reach their loved ones. This was a bizarre sight and foreign in more ways than one to the eye, but deep down I felt I fit. I was at heaven door's while still alive. I had never seen so many black people in one place belonging and interacting as they swarmed about, passing between them hugs and kisses. I had arrived in heaven, and it had no white man with long white beard. I had arrived with a bang, like a planetary probe fired from some faraway planet, and landed at what is said to be the most notorious airport in the known universe: Lagos's international airport. I may as well have been on another planet because as the story went if you could make it through the gates of Lagos airport alive and pockets unmolested in the 1970s, you deserved the "Survival of a Lifetime Prize" for making it through the eye of the needle.

Four times the size of the United Kingdom, who had enslaved and colonized Nigeria since 1861, Nigeria is said to be Africa's most important country. Black gold of another exploitive kind (crude oil) rather than human black gold had been discovered here. The official language is English, and Hausa, Yoruba, and Ibo are also spoken. The religions at the time were Sunni Muslim (45 percent), Protestant (26 percent), Roman Catholic (12 percent), and African indigenous (11 percent). What a mess these many belief systems under one God would make later.

The natural resource wealth was nearly unlimited. Though I did not know it in 1974, Nigeria holds a number of important minerals and natural resources, among them gum arabic. Gum arabic is a natural gummy substance obtained by tapping the branches of the acacia tree. It only exists in certain parts of North Africa with the larger supply produced by the trees in the Republic of Sudan. Gum arabic grew in demand because of its widespread use in soft drinks and beer and in the medical, pharmaceutical, and confectionary industries. Nigeria is also known for its groundnuts, maize, cocoa, cotton, millet, cassava, livestock, rice, timber, gold, diamond, iron ore, oil, gas, tin, and coal to name a few of the thousands of vital minerals.

Then there are the massive amounts of sweet crude oil for export with a reported 80 percent exported to the United States today with not one drop in concession to an African diaspora business that I know of. However, few of these riches reach Africans or Africans in the diaspora. Nigeria at the time of my arrival had a population of about 160 million people.

Back on African Soil

I had reached my final destination, but the stampede-like greeting at the airport had thrown me off-kilter on what seemed to be one of the hottest days of my life on earth. A large black hand holding a dirty sign with my name on it came straight at me. I thought the sign a mirage until I heard a voice.

"Here, my brother, Weston. Let me help you out of here. My taxi is just outside."

I was in luck that my letter and picture sent ahead had reached Chief Okendla. Chief of what, I did not know, but in time I discovered he was chief of his village or clan where he lived somewhere in Ibadan, Nigeria, where I was eventually expected to arrive.

"Chief Okendla has arranged your hotel in Lagos. That is where we will go, and you will wait for the chief's arrival in a few days to fetch you," he reassured me. I envied the glowing skin color of the stocky, very dark- skinned Ibo Nigerian. He carried my bag with one hand and held on to my hand with the other, determined not to lose either as we plowed through the maddening crowd. A few minutes later free of the airport madness, we were stuck in an awful traffic jam of cars and pedestrians.

Adjusting

I could hardly breathe from the diesel fumes and heat swelling up through the holes in the back seat of the battered taxi floor. The holes were big enough for me to see the potted uneven paved street below. To make matters worse, the holes in the floor of the taxi seemed to suck up every bit of dust and trash as the vehicle noisily crept along. Nigeria, like the rest of Africa, was battered but not beaten. The fumes carrying death wishes combined with the dirt-pitted, tropical, midday heat above coming right through the taxi roof seemed to force me in and out of consciousness. I could not help thinking this was not the Africa I had dreamed of, but here I was in it now right up to my neck. Strangely enough, I was fascinated, loving every minute. It was an adventure of a lifetime I thought to myself, knowing this was just the beginning. The first drop of sweat with billions of drops to come cleansed my polluted body of all that Western pollution it did not want to let go. How great it would have been if a few of the guys back in the states had agreed to come along instead of remaining trapped in the American style of apartheid capitalism.

It was the summer of 1974, the summer my true liberation began as we inched toward the hotel. The bloody Biafran War had been between North and South Nigeria over the wealth and power Nigerians already had but were too greedy to realize they should share the wealth as all Africans globally had suffered in European and Arab slavery for four centuries. Not just the Nigerians, but all black people and most people of color shared the pain, blood, and vulgarity of European and American inhumanity to mankind. It was my personal responsibility as an African man to return and take a stand to do my part in rebuilding a global foundation for all Africans to stand on. I could see the lasting effects of colonialism all around me among the ruins of the recent bloody brother against brother against sister Biafran War, a war that nearly bled Eden to death. Nigerian author Chinua Achebe wrote about the Africa I was now witnessing. His books *No Longer at Ease* and *Things Fall Apart*, a Fawcett Crest Book published by Ballantine Books 1969 were bloody spot on! Was I crazy for being here? Yes, but it was a good kind of crazy.

There was a putrid stench from the open sewers, gutters, and holes in the sidewalks and streets as the aging poorly British-made taxi crept forward in bumper-to-bumper traffic. The exiting British foreigners had done a bang-up job of leaving Nigeria worse off than they found it. I could see row upon row of rusty brown tin-roofed shacks that made up homes and storefronts for millions. The imperialist Coca Cola brand name was plastered everywhere with its deadly contents for African DNA boldly going where most American-made products would not go. There were massive signs of poverty all around me. What a shame! Nigeria was a country rich in crude oil and all manner of natural resources, but it was unable to use any of it for its own poverty-stricken people. Most natural resources were being shipped abroad to Europe and America through white trading hands only. I knew one thing was for certain as we drove through the streets. The now-dead Chinua Achebe was right. Nigeria was "no longer at ease." The people in most need walked close to the taxi windows begging for money. I pushed a dollar bill into the dirty hands of a little Nigerian girl about ten years of age. She grabbed at the bill like a scared squirrel would for nuts in a city park of strangers and vanished. Anger began to swell as I thought of the Europeans that invaded Africa and put us in this hellish state of existence. Relax. Take it easy. I kept telling myself over and over again. Progress was being made. Or was it? I took great pride knowing that I was becoming a part of the grand plan to get Africa and myself out of the European nightmare once and forever!

Poetic Justice

Uneasiness crept out of my damaged, restless soul and clung to my ribs, vibrating from the pounding of my heart as the aging taxi pulled up in front of the brand new Lagos Hotel. This was to be my hotel during my stay. It was like arriving on another planet. There was a young African man about my age (at this point in time, late twenties), who was the hotel bellboy. He rushed to the taxi wearing a smile a mile wide and grabbed my bags from the boot. I tried to pay the driver, but he waved my hand away and drove off into the wonder of the strange, brave, new foreign world I was standing in; yet it was not so alien after all. I did not even know the taxi driver's name and could only remember his smile, the back of his sweaty, gritty, black neck, tattered shirt, and the profile of a young face. I was now on my own. I followed my faith and the bellboy into the five-star hotel and tried not to look so out of place. I failed at fitting in, but that uneasy feeling I used to get in America and Europe whenever I checked into a hotel was no longer with me. I felt at ease as if four centuries of European and Western oppression and shit had been washed from my body, mind, and soul, and this was only the first hour of being in Africa heaven.

"Welcome to Nigeria, brother," the bellboy said on the move, bags under his arm.

"It's good to be home," I said, hoping it all came out right.

"You are Nigerian?" the bellboy asked.

"I am not certain," I answered. "My identity has been stolen."

The bellboy laughed and shook his head to the sad, truthful humor. Here, you can get a new identity. By now, we had reached the center of the lobby crowded with all white males of all European nations. They appeared to be businessmen no doubt hungry for African wealth and contracts. Other people, mostly Europeans, were still arriving from the airport. Some of the people in the lobby on the same plane with me had already arrived. Inside the grand Lagos hotel, visitors were panicked. It kind of reminded me of the scene at the Lagos airport I had just narrowly escaped. The word was out: there were few or no rooms left, and dreaded Lagos nightfall was fast approaching.

"The desk clerks are holding rooms to force more money out of whites," said the bellboy.

I could hear the businessmen complaining quietly as we crossed the hotel lobby floor to the reception area. A push and struggle was taking place at the reception desk. The bellboy quietly told me that this was one of Nigeria's scams to rip off Europeans for money and to get even. It sure was good and rewarding to be black for a change I thought. As we approached the front desk, my bellboy winked at me—an indication for me not to worry even though there was a big sign placed on the desk counter saying "No rooms!" One has to give it to some Nigerians; they are smart enough to see a cash opportunity when it comes alone. He asked me for my given name.

"Wait for one moment, please," the bellboy said to me and stepped away, leaving my bag beside me. My bellboy went to talk to the front desk clerk. A minute later, a finger and a smile from the bellboy beckoned me toward the front desk.

"Would you like a pool view or one of the city of Lagos, Mr. Weston?" the African clerk asked me from behind the counter.

"The pool view," I said. No way did I wish to awaken each morning to the dry, rusty view of Lagos. I saw enough coming in from the airport. A few Europeans standing next to me could not believe their ears and eyes. The bellboy took my key. All eyes in the room followed my key as if it was the grand prize, and it was. As he picked up my bag and pushed his way through the mass of foreigners, I overheard a white man ask again for a room.

"Do you people have any reservations or don't you?"

The clerk behind the counter smiled and said, "Maybe we do and maybe we don't, sir. What is your name?"

Evidently, the European finally got the message. I glanced back as I was trailing behind the bellboy and saw the white man place some bills into the clerk's hand. By the time we reached the elevator bank, I was relaxed. I felt safe, like I belonged to a place for the first time in my life. It's a terrible thing to live in fear! Being black and powerful again was one hell of a great experience to feel. That is when I realized that only black men gave black men power. As we stepped into the elevator, the fat French woman that managed the seedy hotel I was evicted from in Paris in the 60s flashed across my tired brain. I remembered the evening on that narrow street in Paris and how humiliated I had been made to feel being kicked out of that cheap hotel in a strange land. I saw the same look on the faces of the white foreigners in the lobby. To me, their rejection was poetic justice.

I didn't sleep much the first day or so what with the excitement of being home in Africa and all. I ventured out poolside and met a German girl named Renee. She invited me to a VIP business party at the German embassy where I saw firsthand the plotting to rip off African people and the wealth of the continent, my wealth. In this case, it was the major infrastructure contracts, roads, and phone national system being passed for cash under the table between the German businessmen and Africans who had gathered at the embassy to do these major shady deals. What little I learned came from Renee, the daughter of the German ambassador to Nigeria. At the event, Renee witnessed me trying to enter a business discussion at one point and then being denied cooperation by an African ambassador from Somalia. It seemed I was not human in his Muslim view. I was an infidel. This was my first lesson about the postcolonial mentalities of Africans from different regions around the continent. Renee stepped over and pulled me toward the large doors leading to the large green lawn outside, studded with tropical flowering trees and a sweet smell of lilac not native to Africa and no doubt brought in by the English. Renee and I had decided to escape the party. Outside on the veranda, the intoxicating mixture of cocktails, expensive perfume and aftershave, intermingled with cigar smoke all vanished and were consumed by the delightful tropical night air.

"The hell with them. I am back by the grace of the ancestors and my own hard earned effort goddamn it! I will get what is rightfully mine," I said and thought, taking a deep breath of Nigerian night air full of the smell of sweet flowers. "They pose no threat to me. The day will come when I will be in control of my land and wealth someplace here on the continent, maybe all over the continent." I was up against it. I knew that, but somehow I was determined to last until the last round on my feet. I was fucking angry and motivated, very motivated!

Chapter 22

Rite of Passage

There were some positives things about my first visit to Nigeria, and there were the recurring nightmares of times past that would not leave my hunted soul and mind. First, the good news: the visit helped me understand I had to fight for my rite of passage as an African man. What it did not tell me was that I was in for a rude awakening. My visit to Nigeria proved to me that no one was in control of anything in Africa at that time. Everyone was for him or herself in this stampede of wealth and madness. Justice and human rights had no chance at all. The place I considered my homeland knew little about me, did not seem to care, and worse yet did not even seem to notice I was there, although some made me feel welcomed. Still, I felt something was missing. I met lots of Nigerian men and women, but they were all struggling to make ends meet and fighting bad government, local tribalism, and lawlessness. There were not enough day-to-day resources to go around. No one seemed to have the power to take charge of his or her life. To top the confusion off, the people of

Northern Nigeria that had just fought and lost the war with Southern Nigeria, or you might say with the British and Americans, were hit so hard, the crimes against humanity were best left unseen even by the United Nations. This was Africa's first step out of former colonialism in central Africa into the new wave of madness governed by greed.

I soon learned Chief Okendla was a respected attorney. He arrived early one sunny morning to collect me, and we drove to his private residence in Ibadan. Renee had wanted to come with me, but that was not to be. The trip through the Nigerian bush took a day's drive through a rain forest of giant trees, many of which were being chopped down as fast as grass grew for export to Germany and all points in Europe. We zoomed past the destruction of thousands of falling hardwood trees with large trucks carrying two trees at the most due to their size. Each tree was worth millions of US dollars but cost Europeans, mostly Germans, only a few US dollars per tree. The chief's Mercedes finally reached his large, impressive residence late that afternoon. His family of six wives and many children were waiting to welcome us. The chief had told me he had expected an older man. Right away I took that to mean youth was not a Nigerian priority. The chief was looking to get something he felt I did not have. At the chief's residence, I was lectured on the new Nigeria and the role he thought it could play in Africa's future. He had written a short book about his life, and he gave me a signed copy.

A few days later, I received a surprise honor. Chief Okendla had planned an elaborate traditional Nigerian welcoming ceremony complete with dancers and food to celebrate my return home, as he was dead certain I had been "stolen from

Nigeria." After several hours of African cultural dance, I was taken into that hidden world of rituals to help cleanse my mind, body, and soul of the evils of the Western world, which in Nigerian were still all around the people.

No mention was made of the bloody history and horror of selling members of the PAD family, me included, that were birthed here in the fifteenth, sixteenth, eighteenth, and nineteenth centuries and to this very day at the return of this descendant of enslaved ancestors who were likely sold off to the Europeans near this very location. Mind you, I knew some of the short history that had taken place between Africans but admittedly like most Africans in Africa and the likes of me in the PAD exiled not yet enough. That education would come painfully later and would extend across Africa where my ancestors' faith was set by those Africans who played a role here in the slave trade, referred to as the transatlantic slave trade or just transatlantic trade. Lacking the skills or tools to create huge amount of capital, Africans were not producing enough trade with European transatlantic merchants in the fifteenth to nineteenth centuries, so they turned to a "trust system" supported by both Europeans and Africans under the guidance of the Chiefs.

The Europeans would advance European-made manufactured goods to the African system in this area called Kalabari Inc. It was a system of middlemen to carry things into the bush and the hinterlands and return captured slaves, palm oil, and kernels as payment. At the time, the African Kalabari middlemen were well informed about current prices and were good negotiators. Ship documents from the Albion frigate, manned by Captain James Barbot, recorded a meeting with the king of Kalabari Inc. in 1699.

"He gave us to understand that he expected one bar of iron for each slave more than Edwards (the captain of another English ship) had paid him. He also objected to our metal basins, mugs, beads, and other goods and said they were of little value at the time." Negotiation and bargaining proceeded. The next day "we had a conference with the King and principal natives of the country about trading, and this lasted from three o'clock until night. But it had no result. They continued to insist on having thirteen bars of iron for male and ten for a female."

Source: Book – (The Mind Of African Strategists, A Study of Kalabari Management Practice.) The Making Of Kalabari Incorporated,) By Nimi Wariboko, Book publisher: Madison / Teaneck Fairleigh Dickinson University Press 1997, page No. 35.

The experienced African traders would generate capital from the margins they were able to build and generate from sales. The interested reader today might research the history of Kalabari Inc. for more details on the nasty business created in this area by the Nigerians, Cameroonians, and other parties right across the Central African belt; in fact, trading went on right across the entire continent by Arabs, aided by some Africans and masterminded by Europeans. Mind you, Europeans were in control and urged on the trade for profit that spread like the plague birthed in Europe centuries earlier as the profits from the trade led to the mass exodus of Europeans into Europe and Americans into Africa, South America, and Asia in the sixteenth century. I admit I can be a bit rusty on this subject as I am not a historian so do some research on your own.

Centuries later, here I sit among the

African descendants who sold my ancestors, chewing kola nuts for luck and drinking palm wine, drifting in and out of a wine trance that made me think I was seeing the spirits of the ancestors who did indeed protect me and had led me back to my ancestral homeland on this mission. The big chiefs all sat around in a row checking me out and saying with some degree of certainty that I was Nigerian based on my youthful looks at the time. These chiefs still held power and wealth, and they still lived much as they did in the earlier years of the arrival of the Europeans but for the electricity and the European-made automobiles. The chiefs, no longer kings as the British had taken that position, denied the Africans that had sold their own people, now slaves themselves, the right to use the King and to this end, they were not able to do a hell of a lot but sit and wait. Even doing this, the chiefs, presidents, and local leaders evident in the meetings being held by the German embassy and others in Lagos still sold or sold out the people for European bits of iron and diamond now used on drill bits to drill for minerals and oil as the people were no longer needed for labor. Strangely the same process was now taking place among the Europeans themselves as they are no longer needed as technology is replacing their presents. Changing times were creating conditions that promoted low wages among the African masses and the European working class to be exploited in the twentieth century.

Although the bloody Biafran War (1967–1970) had ended, evidence remained that the bloodletting was not yet over. In years to come, the group known as Boko Haram would rise up to stick again at the heart of darkness in the oil-rich Christian Nigerian south. My returning put the zap on many of their minds of the chiefs who knew even less than me about their own history. If you do not know your history, it will come back at you, and among the chiefs it showed. One of the exiled had returned. I had survived and returned to tell the story of the victimized and the dead to the living Africans.

In the years that followed, memories of that summer of 1974 in Nigeria and the rites of passage have never left me. Luckily, I had a camera with me and snapped a few pictures that I have to this day. I remember thinking how good it would be if all Africans in the diaspora came home to Africa, or at least visit to partake in their own rite of passage. Chief Okendla and I discussed the possibility of me staying on and opening a cultural center that would include a cinema on his property. I could see right away that the plan had flaws. The chief had a good idea, but I had had enough of the film and theater business for a while. Furthermore, the chief was too old, and I was too inexperienced to live in Nigeria on the edge of the bush. In the end, the chief was not able to induce me to stay. Years later, I would reach out to Chief Okendla's offspring, still living in present-day Nigeria. They seem to have developed as a family.

I left Nigeria with no wealth but a hell of a lot of experience, survival savvy, and knowledge I could use to start my own bank one day. I was being empowered. I could feel it building, growing inch-by-inch, word by word. I felt I had been saved—something the church and all the prayers had failed to do. My father said I could save my own soul if I searched for truth within myself and live by that truth. Africa had reached out to me, and I had saved my own life. Reconnecting to Africa set me on a path that would in time wash away much of the dirt the Western world, enslavement, and European injustices had injected so brutally into my culture and being. Fighting, surviving loneliness, homelessness, hunger, and joblessness, and staying out of prison as a young black man in America took strength and focus! Protecting my new-found freedom and the education I was getting cost a lot of money and time away from my family I was torn so brutally from at such a tender age. I can only imagine what slavery was like as families were being ripped apart in Africa and beyond years ago. There I was standing on a continent of nearly a billion Africans and unable to select one single one as a direct family member. So far removed, we Africans and those in the diaspora needed a fucking DNA test just to locate our bloodline. When we do link with that blood, for some of us a royal blood line can be traced back for millennia, not a measly century or two. I was kind of like a lost wildebeest separated from its mother in a sea of ten-foot tall elephant grass. Being on the edge of a newly forming African society gave me a unique prospective that few Africans were seeing or understanding inside Africa or the world outside. Something great was starting to happen to me, swelling up inside me like a storm of Biblical proportion. How much more documented proof could be needed to prove Africa belonged to me as well? I owned something I thought, left it at that, and returned to New York.

Chapter 23

Return of the Invisible Man

I landed back in America a new but invisible man and in many ways saw a new invisible America no longer as reverent to PAD African future. I was proud to have ventured back into Africa, my homeland. Even though I was treated as the Prodigal Son, I was still an invisible man in an America that held on to me like chains biting into my flesh, my soul pulling me back into the fires of New York City, now homeless and without money. But I was saved. I had broken out of the system and saw wonderful things that motivated me like nothing ever had. I said "fuck it" to fear.

Being broke, I went to Queens to spend time with my two brothers. They were two great guys who had no idea what I was doing with my life, and they were not doing too badly. They were both married and building businesses in the gas service station business. They had cash to spend, and one had a wife that told me she did not want anything to do with those Africans when I suggested they visit the continent. In fact, I got laughed at a few times when I wore colorful Nigerian traditional dress to visit. The reaction was not welcomed by me, and I did my best to inform, but like most, even most non‑Africans, their minds are broken. I split for Alabama, a place I dreaded, a place that once put the zap on my ass, and spent a week with my sister and mother. Then I returned to New York City and dived back into the rat race. My father (not my biological father) had passed on earlier, and I had sadly missed the burial. Sadly still, I never knew when my biological father died. But Henry, my live-in dad, what a man. I met my biological one just once as I remembered my mother introducing him to me with a distant "This is your daddy, Mack." And she left it at that.

That was it for fatherhood, but I had no problem with that knowing the hell black families were going through just to stay alive. What to do now? Get lost in New York City with its population of mixed cultures from all over the planet and try and get my hands on enough funds to leave for Africa again where I felt I truly belonged and wanted to be at any cost. I was soon back on my feet and living in a studio apartment on Grove Street in West Greenwich Village. A few years drifted past, and I started to read, write, and paint. I even sold some of my artwork to earn a living. I had a few relationships and hung out at the local cafés that dotted the colorful Greenwich. While hanging out in the village around New York University, some students encouraged me to read more, so I read everything I could find about Africa and how the world related to Africa. I even enrolled into New York University but soon dropped out. I had little motivation, money, or lack of direction to focus on what to do in a Western society when I finished school, and I felt I just did not fit in. In many ways, I was like most young black men of that time. I was a lost man in the wealthiest nation in the world, and I was unwanted. I could have moved to Queens and got a thirty-year mortgage if I survived, and I am not knocking those who did, like my brothers. That is all many of the black men and women knew what to do, and most of them failed.

I remember going on a job interview I had arranged with an international, New York–based construction company and making a pitch with one of the VPs on how I could travel in Africa and obtain construction contracts for the multinational company. The tall, balding, white Irish male, Mr. Big with the degrees who received me, quickly told me, "What do we need you for?" He basically told me the world belonged to white males, and there was no place in it for the likes of me, not even in Africa. Well, that was the headbutt that busted the dam. I left the office on Madison Avenue swearing I would never ask another white male for a job or to partner as long as I lived. I would spend the rest of my life making it as difficult as I could for this kind of mentality to do anything in Africa or with African people's wealth and resources.

"To hell with him. Fuck them all," I thought to myself, walking back to the Village because I did not have subway fare. I don't know what culture he was from, Irish or German most likely. I was still only seeing white people as whites, not as Irish, German, or having a different cultural linkage. I was brainwashed like the whole world in that way. We all are still brainwashed today. We, especially African people, are blinded by color, not the person or culture, so much that it limits us.

I left the construction office disrespecting all white males. I felt like a fool. Why was I going into the office of a white male asking for a job in the first place when Africa was there with all its riches and resources I owned that his company needed? I decided to take my share. I would remember that day and that insult like a hot iron on my ass.

I still needed sustainable income. The white-controlled system still exploited me and my people even those who thought they had it made like members of my own family. Not to knock anyone mind you, but exploiting me with their brand on my ass just did not work for me. I could not get stuck in one place, so there was only one thing to do.

In 1978, I met this fine woman named Tamara from Traverse City, Michigan, in the city trying her luck at being a model and as futile in her search as I was in America. Tamara and I linked up and moved in with each other, becoming a team living and working out of my new Park Avenue home and office. I established a contracting company on my own and headed to the United Nations in search of contracts at the African missions and residences.

The African ambassadors' residents mostly dotted the Upper East Side along Madison Avenue and Fifth Avenue. I worked hard and ended up obtaining cooperation with ambassadors who personally controlled most of the important contracts that came and went to their African missions in New York City. At first, I was only obtaining small contracts from the missions to supply office supplies and items as such. Tamara did the books, and I obtained the concessions and ran between the United Nations and the supply houses I got my wholesale supplies from. It was when I went for the bigger contracts that things started to get a bit testy. But I stood my ground and demand respect and first right of none refusal in the name of Africans' right to the service and any contract. I began to receive larger contracts to repair the homes and missions of the ambassadors and staff, and it was working until some of them started to demand kickbacks from my already cut-rate prices I was giving them. One ambassador I personally knew from Sierra Leone was so corrupt he even went so far as to sell the country mission offices without informing or gaining approval from the country, and he pocketed the cash. Mind you, this ambassador had for a year or more refused to grant me a foot in the door of his mission service needs. Then his new landlord started to raise the low rent the new owner had agreed to let him continue to operate the mission under. One day I got a call from the ambassador's secretary asking if I could come over to meet with him. I agreed thinking the ambassador was going to offer me a contract.

"Brother! Come in. Come in. Would you like a coffee to drink?" he asked as he approached me from behind his desk in his private office.

The ambassador wanted me to help him out of a major corruption jam. A road jam I was not foolish enough to go down as there is never a bottom. The jam he was in was that the illegal selling of the mission had bitten him on his ass. The new landlord had sold the mission building and was now demanding immediate much higher rent than the ambassador could justify based on what he was receiving from his war-torn country where his people were being butchered and murdered by the thousands. The ambassador wanted me to sign a half million-dollar receipt for services rendered, so he could use my name and that of my company to blackmail more money out of his struggling country and a bleeding Africa. I played along and asked him to give me time to look over the paper to make certain of what I was about to do. He smiled and offered me contracts he could no longer provide, and I left the mission. What the ambassador did not know was that his secretary, who I knew well, had told me everything before arriving at the mission about the ambassador's secret. Earlier I had helped the secretary's close friend rid herself of another ambassador who was raping her. I won't go into details, but the problem was resolved. The ambassador I had met with was called home for selling the mission and was either shot or sent to prison. Despite these examples, there were some good African ambassadors who did or tried to do the right thing.

Chapter 24

Cultural Wars

We all felt the effects of the last kick of the dying European buffalo globally, the apartheid stench flowing out of South Africa, and the oppression of Africans in the diaspora. The murder, beatings, and destruction of black businesses were meant to be a final blow to our homes. The denial of educational opportunities, I suspected willful destruction, was the extended apartheid foes' target. Africans, PAD, and diaspora families were being held in imprisonment daily in the thousands with the system calling this progress, the order of the day. Fed up, I decided to try and drive a burning spear directly into the demented brain of those who were behind this human and cultural slaughter from where I stood in New York City the only way I knew how. I decided to use culture to pull together a force of black and brown people. I decided to create and produce a major jazz festival in Harlem to support the culturally oppressed people in Harlem and across the African diaspora.

After discussing and informing a few people, including a number of top jazz musicians, I contacted my old friend, a Jewish attorney named Walter, who had worked on my movie *Man in the Mirror* in 1970. Walter had soul, and he loved art, especially if it was going to reach a multicultural world. Walter agreed to team up with me again. I do not know why other than just to prove his friendship and the love of the adventure I brought to his office he once told me. Walter was the only lawyer I trusted to be straightforward and loyal to his word in business deals or just as a friend to me, so it was Walter and I again teamed on a project I would call the First Harlem Jazz Festival Inc. I contacted every jazz musician and their agents in America and in Europe that I could find. Many of these musicians had never set foot in Harlem, let alone performed there. Yet, they relied on the legendary name of Harlem and the culture of its people to make a living. After I had a few musicians booked, I contracted a Jewish ad marketing guy who knew the business of promoting festivals, and he went after sponsors and Chase Manhattan Bank. A few others came on board, but not nearly the number we needed. Still, I moved ahead with plans to bring a jazz festival to Harlem.

After a few hard months of work, the First Harlem Jazz Festival was set to open on August 17, 1978, with the Ahmad Jamal Trio. Jazz great Dizzy Gillespie was signed to close the festival on August 31. In all, more than fifty jazz artists had been booked to play at the festival in legendary Harlem. As far as I knew, New York had never seen anything like it before or after that event. The festival was set to play at a number of clubs in Harlem: Small's Paradise, The Cotton Club, Vincent's Place, and the Harlem Hospital Auditorium. Unfortunately the festival did run into problems. To begin with, the American Federation of Musicians Local 802 would not willingly cooperate with me because I wanted the festival to play in culturally and economically oppressed Harlem. I really did not understand it at first, so I just did battle with them and got on with the production. After all, I had faced off with racist union guys before when I produced *Man in the Mirror*. The money I had obtained ran low, so I could not properly promote the festival. However, I could not let on that the festival was having money problems, so I decided to ride out whatever waves came my way and keep the festival light on green. My film had taught me how to survive in the business art of promotion with little money. It takes guts and being able to show and sell people confidence; after all, it is confidence that people buy most of all with trust. Done correctly, it works. Just don't blink when the going gets tough. I lived in Murray Hill on Park Avenue, and that was a big plus. I had good loyal friends and a kick-ass Jewish lawyer. Due to the United Nations African missions, I had a recognizable name in the community and reasonably good looks helped. Being in the media over the struggle to obtain UN general contracts for needy people was an international passport widely accepted across the city.

To help free myself from my cash squeeze, I felt the festival needed a community cultural media star. I learned that my old friend James Baldwin, a native of Harlem, was back in America writing a book in Brewster, Massachusetts. I sent Baldwin a letter. He remembered me from Paris. I asked him to be the keynote speaker for the festival, and he agreed. Baldwin and Dizzy's name gave the festival the professional, celebrity status it needed to gain the interest of the media. The dark side to putting together this event was dealing with Local 802. They resented the fact that I was taking the festival to Harlem, where they had no control over the clubs.

One club I could not book was the Savoy Ball Room on 125th Street in Harlem. I had stopped in one day to book the festival, but when the aging, Jewish owner looked away as an insult to my plan, I knew I did not have his support. This was July 1978. Jews and blacks had been fighting a war over Harlem since the Dutch pulled out in the 1900s. The style of the Dutch townhouses was evident all around the area, even in Murray Hill where I now lived, including the historic Brick Carriage House on 149 East 38 Street in Manhattan. Then,

Just as the festival was about to get underway, one of the checks I had written to a musician was refused at my bank. All hell broke loose. I knew the funds were there because I had just borrowed $5,000 from Robert Brooker, an old roommate who had picked up the monthly rent on the Soho-rented apartment more than I liked to remember. When the news of the check got back to Local 802, they thought they had me. I had informed the bank to pull funds from a protected account to pay bills only as the checks came in. I had more than enough in the second account to cover the check. I can only assume that word of this got out to the media through the festival enemy Local 802. This action threatened to halt the festival.

At the time, this was hot news because there was a culture war between the African American community and the white community for control of Harlem and African American culture stood in the way. Officials of Local 802 contacted the radio and television stations, hoping to damage me. They wanted to stop the First Harlem Jazz Festival and blasted me all over New York City airwaves. The media aired the union's biased, doctored complaints without first contacting me to check to see if the Local 802 story held up. After a few days of being blasted to hell and back by the New York media, I launched my counter attack through WLIB, a then black-owned and operated radio station in New York. The aim of the media and my enemies was to drive other musicians away from the festival as I was trying hard to host an event that would be an economic boost to Harlem. I was not alone under these attacks. The black people of South Africa were also facing even worse treatment under apartheid, only South Africa blacks were arrested and even killed for trying to hold a cultural event. The brainwashing against supporting anything black was so bad that even many local black and white people from Harlem and the Greater New York City failed to show up and support the festival. Was it just the name "Harlem" the controlled media trashed in an all-out attempt to lower Harlem property values so certain nonblack groups could purchase them from New York City.

Redlining banks could make a killing while locking blacks out of any future claims and profits from the culturally rich community they built and fought for in most every war America entered. Not even a single politician, black, white, or Spanish, set foot in Harlem during the entire two-week run of the historic festival. Despite the lack of support from New York media, the story of the jazz festival coming to Harlem attracted international tour companies and airlines. International media got word and came in droves from Italy, Japan, France, Sweden, Germany, England, and as far away as China and South America, all spending money in New York City hotels and black clubs uptown in Harlem.

Excited about James Baldwin and Dizzy Gillespie, the jazz great, joining the team, Tamara and I began planning for a big press conference gala that would coincide with Baldwin's respected birthday.

James Baldwin Returns to Harlem

Finally, the moment arrived. Baldwin stepped up to the mic at Small's Paradise with a grace and style where countless entertainers had performed over a half-century leading up to this moment. His long, silk, white scarf dangled around his neck and reflected like a flash of lighting off his dark complexion with a matching French suit. Baldwin owned the stage; this was his crowning historic moment to Harlem after a half-century or so. He had returned to Harlem in the style he told me in Paris that he had always wanted to. Baldwin began by repeating some of what he had been saying all along in his books. He started off slow as if making love to ever word he was saying.

"The Harlem that I grew up in, poor and despised as we were, was yet a life-giving community," said Baldwin. "We have met grave, even mortal challenges before. That is our history. Our children have always been our principal responsibility and our invaluable asset. We, who are the old folks now, are and must be the bridge, which makes the past coherent and the present surmountable..."

Baldwin delivered this address August 8, 1978, at the First Harlem Jazz Festival.

"So the purpose of the Harlem Jazz Festival is not a return to the past or an attempt to rebuild that community, which was Harlem at the time that I was born. That community has done its work. Otherwise, we would not be here, and our responsibility to that community is not to imitate, but to build anew—armed, as we are with the authority of the past, to enable our children to excavate in the present the great wealth of our inheritance—that inheritance produced by the unprecedented travail and triumphs of our ancestors on these shores as a universal inheritance and place us in the vanguard of a new morality and a new world..."

From the affirmative looks on the faces in the audience, Baldwin's words had hit home. There seemed to be an air of pride in the room, one of admiration for Harlem and its prodigal son James Baldwin.

Al King, a local Harlem jazz musician on sax whose timeless face graced the festival poster, eyeballed John Hicks. Following my offstage directions, they smoothed out the grooves in their music to honor the legendary James Baldwin. Baldwin moved over to the birthday cake that I (being so excited) had cut by mistake for him. No matter how hard we tried, we could not get Baldwin to tell his age.

Bill Tender, the African American who had worked for years to make Small's Paradise a success by serving fine food and drinks and promoting great music, always stood off to the side but managed well the links between his workers and my special hired team. Bill groomed them to look after the local and international guests, and they did just that in a style that got them James Baldwin–approved smiles. Bill was a good businessman, one of a kind, tall handsome, and a hit with the ladies. The kind a producer from anywhere would want to work with. He stuck with me through all the attacks and picked up enough money during the festival to cut his losses. On the last night of the festival after paying off the festival employees and staff at Smalls', Bill and I sat at the historic bar and toasted our victory. Never quit! Never take a step backward. Keep moving forward!

"Well, Frank, we did it; we pulled it off," Bill said, holding his glass of brandy toward me with a big smile on his face. After a few sips of brandy, Bill broke the silence in the club only he and I remained in. "You fucking did it, Frank. You are some fucking producer my brother." Bill just wouldn't stop. He went on and on. "Frank you were like that crazy captain in that movie *Moby Dick* who went after that white whale. You won't fuck'n quit. You had the whole damn city in your hands watching your ass to see if you would fail, but you held up. You stood up to them."

"Yeah, we did all right," I said, taking a long sip from my brandy glass while loosening my necktie. Louis Armstrong's gritty velvet blue voice was flowing from the colorful 1960s jukebox. As the last worker left with the bartender, Bill got up and locked the glass doors that looked out onto Eighth Avenue where the historic club had been for as long as anyone I knew could remember. This location of Smalls' had seen Harlem through some mean very lean years: the 1920s depression, the Billy Holiday years, and World War II when the black soldiers returned home to Harlem and other all black-communities to escape Jim Crow in the South, New York, Alabama, and beyond into Mississippi, goddamn! The last of the international tourists had left with only great fun memories of a unique experience in the "Big Apple." City bosses and businesses downtown had spread the word that Harlem was not safe to visit during the festival to scare people away. The fix to grab was being planned even then. Harlem was as safe as the rest of a corrupt and badly managed, fenced-off Manhattan held by the city hall bosses. I had gone to great lengths to keep everyone safe. I had met with Harlem underworld black bosses, and they had assured me anyone who attended the festival would be safe; they had kept their end of the deal. The pain Baldwin spoke of reflected the pain of all the great writers and families living in Harlem, Mississippi, Texas, Kansas, Alabama, and Chicago. After closing the door, Bill looked as if to say a prayer and walked back to the bar where I was seated. It was getting late, and the people and traffic moving up and down Eighth Avenue slowed with the sound and speed of the music coming from the colorful music box. The people of the greater Harlem Village were retiring with their pain and joy for the evening. Bill stepped behind the bar and placed two fingers of brandy into my glass.

"I am going to miss New York City, Harlem, Smalls' Paradise," Bill said as if he would be leaving the club and restaurant business. And he was. Over the years, Smalls' had had its share of owners who had come and gone, leaving a lot of stories behind. Now it seemed Bill might be the last of that breed to serve the Harlem residents and tourists who came uptown to the historic club.

"I want to thank you, Bill, for sticking with me through this important festival and cultural event," I said.

"I should thank you, Frank, for helping me get out in style, with respect, with Dizzy as my story ending soundtrack," Bill said sipping his brandy. It doesn't get any better than this, the pride of being complimented by a brother in business or war I thought to myself.

"What will you do next?" Bill asked.

"I'll be around for a while and settle a few things, but before long I am headed back to Africa," I replied.

"You love Africa. You are always there," Bill said.

"You should come over to Africa for a visit."

"I have always wondered what Africa was like," Bill said.

"Then get off your butt and come out and see what you own, see the future, what we left behind is our future. You won't regret it once you make the trip." I assured him.

Bill sat motionless in the dim light of the club, sipping his drink as Louis Armstrong's timeless voice and music flowed like the twenty-year old brandy we were sipping, complementing the aging music box that would forever be silenced. I felt great, like a winner, but at the same time I could not help but feel a sense of sadness looking at my friend Bill who had just helped me through a difficult time and never once bent under pressure from the media, Local 802, or other New York bosses and bullies. Then, Bill broke the silence.

"Don't tell anyone I said this," Bill said. "You know black folks. They will have it in the streets that I am seeing ghosts in here, and that will be the end of my sex life, but sometimes at night after everyone has left and I am alone, I get the feeling a lot of the old-timers come in and join me at the bar for a drink. I can't see them, but I get the feeling I am not alone at the bar. Hell! I think I have even heard the older timers flush the john." We both started laughing.

"This club and Harlem have a lot of black history, stories to tell, man. Now our story can be remembered by the old-timers who haunt these walls," I said, still chuckling. "Just kidding, Bill, but if you don't give me your little black book, I will release the recording I just made of your ghost story."

"The money holders and lenders or the city will rip the joint down soon anyway, so go ahead," Bill said with a grin.

The next day Bill and I split the profits from the festival. The media had done us a big favor by reporting we had lost money. Only the IRS knew the truth. As a result, no debtors came after us for money. The festival received good reviews in European media, no media support from New York City, and that was the end of that. I never saw Bill again after that, not even a phone call. He said he would drift south. A place I would never go for fear of vanishing into the American void where many black men now go to die. Instead they could return to Africa, have the grandest adventure of all times,

open an international business, and join the new
African cultural and economic war. I hope he did not
pay a dime to the redlining banks and bloodsuckers
in Manhattan that had fucked him and so many
people of color over the centuries that James
Baldwin had written and spoke about; the centuries
and history of black people and Spanish all stuck
with high rents, bad service, and rotten food. These
are supplies often sold to the struggling business
people in Harlem, the Bronx, Brooklyn, and beyond.
I hoped Bill reached the South and fared well. I truly
hoped he would find his way back home to Africa one
day too. I hoped. As for James Baldwin, he finished
his book and split for Paris. I never saw my friend
again. The festival behind me, I had one last move to
make before I would leave for Africa again.

Chapter 25

Establishing IMSCO

In 1978, I established the International Multiracial Shared Cultural Organization (IMSCO), an NGO to promote business and help link the underdogs and the oppressed people of the world. It would help give a leg up to the disenfranchised. I decided to conduct some research on how to put together a summit for IMSCO and invite African and other foreign ambassadors and representatives at embassies, missions, and consulates in the United States. Why target the African and South American embassies to the United States and missions and consulates to the UN? I felt an IMSCO summit face to face was the fastest and best way to introduce the African diaspora, Spanish, and people from South and Latin American cultures to the men and women from our homelands. The summit would also give direct access to knowledge to air our disagreements and seek jobs and business opportunities for the diaspora people in America who did not know who to reach out to in these international links. It was through these embassies, missions, and consulates in the United States where a large available part of the money coming from Africa and South America was being spent. Even in the eighties, the amount being spent was in the billions collectively. Today that number is in the multi-billions of US dollars. These foreign embassies, missions, and consulates in the

United States were direct links to the wealth, jobs, and business contracts in the global African diaspora and in the homelands of the diaspora people. One did not have to buy an expensive airline ticket and pay a lingering hotel bill and face denial as I had in Nigeria to obtain or pay to obtain a meeting with an ambassador or representative and gain some success and place a bid or demand PAD rightful economic share.

After I finished my research, invitations went out to all the African ambassadors in New York and Washington, DC, announcing the IMSCO summit. I also invited European and South American ambassadors. Mind you, I had no idea who would show up, but out of some sixty invitations sent out, forty ambassadors and foreign diplomats sent RSVPs. I flew in Judge William Branch from Greene County, Alabama, to be the keynote speaker. The judge and I had some kinfolk ties I never could properly pen down. The judge was right out of the fiery pages of America's second civil war, the civil rights movement, which had enabled him to become the first African American probate judge to chair proceedings in Greene County since reconstruction in the old American South. The IMSCO summit opened the night of April 9, 1980, at the Hyatt Hotel on 42nd Street and Lexington Avenue. The opening was a victory for my team with close to sixty foreign state representatives in attendance.

Suddenly we were off into the biggest debate between African representatives with IMSCO sitting in for the PAD and African diaspora community. Judge Branch sprang to his feet and crossed the short space between the podium and the chairs where the guest speakers sat to the front of the room. The judge was a handsome man in his late fifties with a dark complexion standing 5 ft. 7 in. or better with a confident inviting smile. Like James Baldwin, the judge began a slow climb to what turned out to be an unforgettable speech. First, he reminded the African ambassadors and foreign dignitaries of the love and brother- and sisterhood in the room. Then he spoke of the oppression of Africans throughout the diaspora. He also discussed the suffering of the women and children. In the end, the judge reminded the guests of the value of trading with African Americans.

"I urge you all to look to Africans in the diaspora for the solution to many of your economic, trade, developmental, and political problems."

The judge encouraged the foreign dignitaries and ambassadors to sign onto the IMSCO-drafted codevelopment plan being offered. After he sat down, a number of other invited speakers from the community took the podium and addressed the summit guests.

It was my hope that the IMSCO summit would help educate African Americans and others about what I had learned about certain areas of Africa and these men that were selling us out while we blindly supported them and the governments they represented. During my year or so search for business contracts at the African missions to the UN in New York City, I witnessed most worthwhile contracts routinely given to people they saw as whites. One mission gave up a large contract to a white contractor because, as the African ambassador put it to me, the white man had a small camera he dropped down the mission residence's fireplace chimney to let the ambassador witness the clogging of the chimney, the ambassador was more impressed with his magic. I wont comment any further on that. My company lost a number of contracts due to the New York City commission to the United Nations lobbying for white-owned businesses and everywhere the Africans were to live and shop. My company and crew lost out and went hungry, so I went after the Organization of African Union's (OAU) ambassador who headed the African missions and ambassadors at the United Nations. I placed Ambassador Youssoufou (a brainwashed sellout to the black people in New York City) at the top of the IMSCO hit list of corrupt Africans to go after in New York. This ambassador was the worst of the bad African United Nations representatives. IMSCO and its supporters demanded responsible action from all the African representatives who seemed not to respect African Americans at all and readily gave contracts and jobs to anyone but them. Before the IMSCO summit, my team and I often discussed the scale of the madness taking place in Africa and in the diaspora. Mind you, Tamara and a number of the IMSCO team were non-Africans, so the African denials hurt even my non-African friends and allies.

When Ambassador Youssoufou approached the podium, he had a lot to say, but he could not promise or agree to anything and sat down. Then my turn came to speak. The room was buzzing with anxious energy of expectation. Most knew who I was from the many TV, radio, and newspaper articles in which I had featured in an all-out effort to gain cooperation from the United Nations on behalf of the global African community. I squeezed in my gut, taking control of the jitters that once got the best of me in high school, stepped up to the podium, and began to speak. I welcomed the guests and then issued what I thought were facts I had about the lack of cooperation from the diplomat's side. The room tensed up and never relaxed as if they had not expected to hear the remarks being made from the African American community.

"What many of you are doing is leading us all into a deathtrap by not doing business with Africans in the diaspora," I said. "We Africans cannot put trust into the Western system of white male monopoly management to be a friend of African people. It is an insult to all the years we have struggled in America and elsewhere for African and South American embassies to grant all business contracts to whites only," I continued.

The audience was so silent you could hear a feather fall onto stone. I was angry and afraid of what was coming if African men did not act and act fast. Slavery could and would return if we did not get our act together and manage our wealth with black hands and skills. I said, "Only black men would give blacks power." In conclusion, I offered IMSCO as a conduit to help link us all on the road to economic partnership. I demanded that no less than 60 percent of all African contracts awarded by African missions and embassies in the United States be awarded to African American business people.

When I opened the floor to questions, Ambassador Youssoufou was the first to rush to the podium like an Africanized killer bee. It seemed I had pinched a personal nerve in his pride, and he aimed his sting directly at me. Youssoufou rambled on about a number of things, even suggesting the Reverend Jesse Jackson would be damn angry if African representatives onducted business with me or any other member of the black community without Jesse Jackson approval. Youssoufou suggested he had good reason to believe Reverend Jesse Jackson had the right to grant him approval to make the statement. Ambassador Youssoufor sounded as if he was directed to make such a statement as he had. Like the people in the room, I just about fell off my feet. What the hell did Jesse Jackson have to do with our rights to free speech to hold a summit to conduct private business with anyone anywhere in the world? I was tired of seeing black men, women, and children going to jail and wasting their lives on fast-food unemployment links. Boos from the floor chased the ambassador to his seat. Then a businessman name William Parrott from the African American community stood and delivered a passionate speech in favor of IMSCO's aims and demands on the United Nations, African, and Latin diplomatic communities. One IMSCO and community member after the other stood and angrily voiced their outrage toward the diplomats and UN representatives calling for their immediate support and cooperation. I relaxed and let the community speak. Ambassador Youssoufou was now on the defensive. He was trapped. If the IMSCO summit did nothing else, it had forced open a hidden closet of skeletons in the African and Latin communities that would never again be allowed to close.

Ambassador Youssoufou seized the mic again and again, trying to defend his stance, but failed each time. The Arab representative from the Libyan mission took his turn at the mic. He reminded us that Minister Louis Farrakhan, the leader of the Nation of Islam for black Muslims in America, had borrowed a half million dollars from the Libyan government and had not paid it back. He cut into Louis Farrakhan but made no mention of the billions of dollars Libyans, his clan, and other Arab invaders had stolen from Africans and not to mention the land they occupied in North Africa dating back to the ninth century. Was the bad blood debt with black Muslims the reason the Libyan government was not going to do any business at all with the rest of Africans in America? In the end, we all failed to reach each other. I repeated IMSCO's demands, and we all went home.

It seemed most of the representatives that had showed up at the IMSCO summit were only interested in what the white business community could give them. It never dawned on them that they represented the most powerful communities on earth. Somewhere behind the scene the People's Republic of China was watching and planning.

Soon after the summit ended, Ambassador Youssoufou went on the attack against me and sent letters to every ambassador and African country to stop me. Ironically, the very people who worked for the ambassador in his office sent me copies of the letters before they were sent out. I decided to call on a few ambassadors after weeks of noncompliance. I began with the Republic of Niger, which was the country Ambassador Youssoufou was from. I selected them because they were refusing to pay a labor bill to some of my men the ambassador had hired to do some work. I entered the Niger mission on the East Side of Manhattan near the United Nations and refused to leave the mission unless the ambassador paid the debt he had so far refused to pay. The

ambassador's staff asked me to leave when time
came for the mission to close for the night, but I
refused unless the ambassador issued me the $5,000
check on behalf of the men who I had hired to do
work for the missions. The ambassador and his staff
refused, so I spent the night on the sofa in one of the
offices. The next morning, the Niger ambassador
issued me a check so I could pay my workers. I then
went home to get some sleep. In all, I confronted four
African missions to the United Nations to force the
issue of blacks in America. My long struggle landed
me on the front pages of newspapers, the TV, and on
radios. WLIB radio reporter Dominick Carter, who
became a political reporter with CNN on New York 1
TV News, covered most of the news events that came
out of my push at the United Nations in the late
1980s. The diplomatic dispute between the African
missions and me ran as feature stories for a few
years on New York City national radio stations and
then went national in a syndicated column I wrote
for a newspaper in Brooklyn called *Big Red*. My
nationally syndicated column was called "Strategies
for African Codevelopment." My weekly nationally
syndicated articles suggested a major fall for African
Americans if they did not move beyond the present
place most of us were locking ourselves into or worse
yet being locked into by those who were stealing our
future as they had a large part of our recent past.
That was it for me. I needed some African sky. My
brain needed some clean air, so I cleaned up a few
details, said good-bye to friends and Tamara who
split for the West, and I left for Africa.

Chapter 26

Goree Island

I landed in West Africa, this time Dakar, Senegal, where I rented a house for the summer near the beach in a village near Yoff airport. Nobody and nothing could have prepared me for what was to come next. I had only been in Dakar a few weeks when I met Nafi, a lovely dark-skinned Senegalese woman in her twenties, a showstopper. Nafi was so beautiful to me that I found it hard to think of anything else when I first saw her walking on the beach in Yoff Lion, a local village near the national airport. I introduced myself and found her to be open and full of life and love, apart from being knockout stunning in every way. Tamara and had I split up after the Harlem Jazz Festival. She returned to Michigan to be with her family, drifted west Texas, and moved in with some guy in the crude oil exploration and drilling business I learned later on. We remained friends but not in touch during much of this time.

I will never forget the night before Nafi came to visit me at my house on the beach a short hill road walk above her house where she lived with her family. There had been a great thunderstorm in Yoff that dumped more rain in the desert sand than I had ever thought possible. I had not yet bought a bed, so I slept on the floor in my sleeping bag that I had carried with me from New York. The next morning, just at dawn, I awoke slowly suddenly realizing I was not alone. During the night while I slept, the rain and windstorm had driven hundreds of small, gross-looking scorpions into my living room. The unwanted visitors had crawled onto my sleeping bag to take advantage of the warmth from my body heat during the cold desert night. It was the first light of dawn. The large school of scorpions had entered through the many cracks around the floor basin of the four-room house I had rented. At first, I didn't know what to do. I must have been there for an hour trying to decide how to get out of my sleeping bag without getting stung in places that were reserved for Nafi when she arrived later that morning. I checked to see if I had already been bitten and found no signs of discomfort on my body inflicted by those often-aggressive creatures. Lucky for me, my guests were not yet awake. I finally decided ever so slowly to ease my way out of the sleeping bag inch by inch without disturbing the night visitors. Had I disturbed these masters of pain, I could have suffered an agonizing death. Once free of the bag, I then rushed to the bathroom to check myself again. I showered, swept the house, and placed the sleeping bag in the sun so the early morning tropical heat could drive out any remaining scorpions. Nafi arrived later around noon, and we had some of the best sex ever under the African sky. As I lay there with Nafi, I prayed that the scorpions had not remained. Later, Nafi and I were out the door and into a taxi. An hour drive later, we were at the dock where we took a short boat ride over to Goree Island. For centuries, Goree Island in Senegal was a major departure point for enslaved Africans.

Senegal gained its independence in 1960.

Nonetheless in 1982 when I visited, French influence could be seen everywhere, especially in Senegalese business and government. Like most of Africa, Senegal was still struggling far behind the Western world economically and industrially as a result of standing in the shadow of the corrupt French foreigners. Being near Goree Island, the last forced exit point for millions of defenseless Africans sent my blood rocketing to heights never witnessed before. Most Africans in Africa and the diaspora still sleep with one eye open whenever there is a capitalist in the African hood or forest. I am not hating'. I am just missing Africa and home like a billion plus other Africans who want to get on with our short lives and regain our cultural links with self and homeland. That is the reason I was in Senegal: to start the healing.

Senegal is prone to drought since it's located in a desert. Instead of planting trees and pumping water (there is plenty of it under the sand), African leaders are reliant on Western death aid. In the fourteenth century, Zenega Berbers, an ethnic blend of mostly biased Arab people, invaded from the north into Mauritania and Senegal bringing Islam.

Goree Island was a small and isolated outcrop in the sea, far enough out that it would have been very hard for most to escape from it and swim back to shore, though I am certain some of my ancestors did swim back successfully (I hope). As the boat Nafi and I were on approached Goree Island, I could feel a pressure building up in my chest. No one could have ever prepared me for what was to come that day. It was as if I was snatched and taken back in time as we walked through the island's narrow alleyways and small streets, where my ancestors were marched in chains and leg irons out of a green heaven into the European dead hell waiting beyond. To make matters worse, the large fort the French built to serve their evil deeds was now turning into a world tourist attraction, a United Nations World Heritage Site. There were a few European and Asian tourists milling about with cameras taking pictures as if nothing earth shattering in human history had taken place here. A sign of insult I thought. Or maybe it was the planted inner demons getting the better of me. They were just being tourists. For two hours, we drifted about the buildings being restored by the United Nations Educational, Scientific, and Cultural Organization (UNESCO). After the painful tour of Goree Island ended, Nafi and I took the boat back to the mainland and had dinner at this great local beachside Senegalese restaurant. As we sat overlooking the Atlantic Ocean on a laid-back balcony with tropical air softly blowing and music playing in the background, I was in African heaven with the most beautiful African woman on the planet. We talked about a great many things, such as where the world might be in ten or twenty years, and we gave thanks to the ancestors and our living people who made much of what we had possible. While there, I told Nafi I wanted to take some time and visit Bobo-Dioulasso, Burkina Faso, believed to be the birthplace of some of my family members. My grandmother had asked me to perform a small ritual for my family and ancestors. I explained to her that in order for some of us African Americans to keep a focus on who we were and where we came from in Africa, some male members of the family were named after African locations. My cousin Bobo was one person selected to be named after the African area Bobo-Dioulasso. I had been asked by my aunt to try and make it back to Africa and find the place because she could not make it. Nafi wanted to come with me, but I said no because I did not know what to expect during the trip or even if I would make it back to Senegal anytime soon. Nafi suggested I enter Burkina Faso through Abidjan, the capital of Ivory Coast, and take the overnight train into Bobo Dioulasso.

Days later, I closed my rented house on the beach, said good-bye to the villagers and kids I often walked with on the beach, boarded a plane, and flew south down the West Atlantic coast. The small plane danced on the West African trade winds as it hugged the coast line of Guinea with its massive ancient forest, teaming with exotic wildlife and natural riches that blew my mind.

My thoughts drifted back to the time when I had visited Sierra Leone and Liberia to go diamond hunting with an African American friend Bill Walker. We had traveled deep into the bush to purchase diamonds from the locals because the Europeans, Americans, and Arabs had pushed the price of diamonds so high that our money would not buy much in Freetown, the capital. These European and Arab masters of destruction had laid waste to the lives of an entire people, second only to the devil's disciple in the eighteenth and nineteenth century, King Leopold II of Belgium, the mastermind behind the Congo's enslavement, slaughter, and death of tens of millions of Africans in the eighteenth century that last to this very day. To understand the Belgium bloody quest in and across the rest of Africa I strongly suggest researching King Leopold II.

I departed a golden Senegal and headed down the coast to Abidjan, Ivory Coast.

Chapter 27

Journey through Ivory Coast

I spent only a day in Abidjan, Ivory Coast, and got sick to my stomach watching the many French gangs of foreigners, spies, and thieves roving about the struggling city. Felix Houphouet-Boigny was the country's first elected president in 1960, and sadly the same president was still there when I drifted through with my backpack and bed roll in 1982. Because I hurried through the capital, I only got a brief glimpse at Abidjan. I had read extensively, however, about the country before traveling. I knew how wealthy it was in agriculture, timber, coffee, cocoa, crude oil, and an endless assortment of minerals. It was all under the iron fist of the French and white American economic influence carefully watched over by the US Department of State in Washington, DC, that served only the interest of the Western economic system. Little did I know then that economic hit men were being sent in to make certain African men like Felix Houphouet-Boigny, president for life, who would sign just about anything did just that. One could tell this guy was one of the main reasons Africa lost the edge on early development. The not so very wise president of the struggling country had spent $300 million on building a cathedral—not a university, but a cathedral with all the French and other European cultural trimmings. I wondered if one had to bribe his God, then what use is the God. The cathedral having nothing to do with African culture or history built only to please the French and to keep the black broken minds in lockdown was large enough to play American football games seating thousands. The wealth and money should have been used to build universities, factories, and health care centers or to train and employ African people. Instead, the poverty was seen everywhere among the Africans. There were flies everywhere. Billions of flies feasted on the trash lying about uncollected as markets went about their business selling food and other wares. I nearly broke down and panicked. In the end, like others, I had to accept that bad sanitation and poor infrastructure planning were mostly likely to blame. In all my travels in the African bush, never have I seen such poor sanitation. Where was the money made from African wealth? In French banks naturally, where it remains to this very day if it has not been, as I suspect ripped off, used to develop the French Rivera.

I admit you are viewing Africa through the eyes of an angry man, but nonetheless I am being truthful in what I write and what I have witnessed and felt. I write this report as it happened on the scene and some from recorded written documents and memory. To help my memory record this document, I have saved every passport and visa since 1962 when I received my first passport in the military to enter Thailand. I departed the city of Abidjan in time to catch the weekly train headed inland to Burkina Faso, and the sooner the better for me. The flies were getting the best of me. What was happening in Abidjan, one of the largest cities on the West African coast, sickened me to no end.

The only good thing about Abidjan at the time I passed through was the cultural excitement from the crowds at the train station as I departed. It was the best exit entertainment I have ever experienced, at any airport or bus or train station anywhere. The free festive entertainment in this open public space had all kinds of colorful vendors and hawkers milling about and selling goods to the rhythm of life and sound of great African music. That was enough I must admit to get me upbeat in spirits. Everything from fresh food and locally made traveling kits to multicolored cloth was for sale. The hawkers, who were both adults and children, were quick at handling the money as they had to serve many travelers trying to buy their goods before the train departed. I sat onboard the French train built in the 1800s watching the whole show unfold. Once out of the capital, the air was cleaner, the flies had vanished, and nature was starting to take control and clean up the disorder. Once the train was on the move, sales of goods continued, and I settled into my first-class seat, which by Western standards reflected conditions one would have found on a 1930s New York subway during rush hour. They were good seats, but a bit hard on the behind considering the country could well afford to build first-class rail systems and anything else needed to lift a young rich and growing Africa into a future even France could not afford or compete with. A last-minute sale to a passenger caused a vendor to chase after the train with the goods in hand that the person on board had ordered. When the vendor caught up, he quickly handed the passenger her change.

Before long, the train was rumbling alongside newly plowed fields, through the African bush, past local villages and cash-crop farms where

Africans labored freely without European meddling for the first time on their own land in centuries. It was out here, among the poverty-stricken people, that the French and global markets competed for naturally grown tropical woods that most Africans, including me, need better education on; coffee, coco, and fruits are stable foodstuff worth their weight in gold in the Western and Asian world. They now would pay highly for it, but the people are shut off from outside world trade and do not know that. The people did not realize their natural wealth and true international power because the president was just too busy kissing French hands of people who would have kneeled before the African president out of survival had he demanded it. Sadly, it was the other way around.

During our night passage train ride out of Abidjan, I met an African family whose five-year-old son, Mammado, became the center of my attention. They were seated across from me. I could not speak much French, and the family could not speak English, but through the noise and activities taking place on the busy train, we managed to pick up enough of what the other was suggesting to develop a bond that lasted the entire journey. At first, Mammado just sat there focusing on my eyes. He hung on every word I spoke, naturally not understanding the meaning, but something told me he was learning faster than a programmed computer. He was drawn to the unique sound coming from a dark complexion much like his own. I thought he liked me, and I felt he knew the feeling was mutual. On that train, we built a friendly bond that has remained with me till this day. Mammado's family were traders and had gone to Abidjan to purchase goods to sell in their small shop in Ouagadougou, the capital of Burkina Faso meaning "Land of Upright Men." I learned Mammado was their only child, and they worked hard so that he could go to school and one day become a doctor. After a few hours of talking with the parents, Mammado made an effort to get to know me. Mammado left his parents and climbed into my seat even though there was not that much space for him between me and another African businessman who shared the seat with me. I offered him some Western snacks from my pocket, and that sealed our friendship.

Later that night after everyone was asleep, we were suddenly rudely awakened by voices of armed army railroad border inspectors. I awoke to people scrambling about the train. We had to get off to be counted and have our passports and identification documents checked. At first I had no idea what was going on. The father of Mammado was glaring across the aisles at the businessman and me. Suddenly, I felt the strong hand of the businessman pulling me in his direction. We moved to the door of the train and stepped outside to find a nest of badly trained, gun-carrying, government border soldiers. They were holding flashlights, checking documents, and trying to bribe money out of the passengers.

When it was my turn to have my documents checked, the border soldiers noticed I was not from the land and decided I would be an easy mark for quick money. Fortunately, the family of Mammado and the businessman, who was standing next to me, were determined not to let me be shaken down by these legal bandits. The guard pulled at my arm, and the businessman pulled me away. He stepped between the soldier and me, giving him eye-to-eye contact. I could not understand all that was being said, but it was clear the businessman and Mammado's father were protecting me. In the end, the soldier backed off, and we were soon on our way.

I thanked the two men for their help and the rest of the trip was an amazing emotional bonding experience with a family, a stranger, and a small boy who was now fast asleep at my feet. His arm was wrapped around my leg, and his little body rested on a blanket I had pulled from my backpack just for him. The next morning, the parents and I had a hell of a time getting Mammado to remain on the train when I finally departed at Bobo-Dioulasso, the first stop on my journey inland. I had to bribe Mammado with a necklace and what was left of my bag of sweets to remain onboard the train. It was the last I saw or heard of Mammado and his family, but in my thoughts we continue to have a life-long relationship.

Chapter 28

Land of Upright Men

On the train platform, I saw more hawkers, making last-second sales for everything from fruits to STD pills as the aging French-made train on its last legs vanished from view on the uneven railroad tracks. One could tell how much the Europeans respected the Africans by the condition of the roads we had to risk our lives on under foreign mismanagement. Bobo-Dioulasso was a dusty, timeless town. I imagine parts remained much the way they were when my ancestors were stolen or run off. I took a small room in a boarding house owned by a local family who ran the guesthouse at the center of the town. Except for the odd piles of trash waiting for collection, the town was clean.

A day to myself led me one afternoon to a large outdoor market where I decided to try my hand at trading with one of the hawkers, a young boy selling goods at the local market. I thought I would have a bit of fun with the youth selling mixed tourist items and try to put one over on him; you know, beat him at his own game. I pointed to a group of brass gold weights made in the likeness of a mudfish. I had to have it. Well, after five minutes or so the kid had me wrapped around his fingers, and I did not know which end was up. I walked away with much more than I had planned to buy and with less money in my pocket than when I arrived at his stand. How the hell this kid got the best of me, I do not know. After a day in Bobo-Dioulasso, I hired an aging taxi and driver to go to the outskirts of town to find a single baobab tree. If this was the city my ancestors were from and stood upright, I wanted to commemorate my journey by finding this ancient tree. After a short drive out of town, the taxi driver stopped and pointed to a baobab tree. I looked up and was blown away at the massive size of the baobab tree. The baobab was ash gray with huge trunks bulging with enough water to sustain itself for years. The folds of this tree's trunk were like thick steroid muscles, more than twenty to thirty feet around and sixty feet high. I was about to perform an ancient African ritual around a tree that was older than the birth of Christ.

I came prepared with a bottle of water to

memorialize this moment with libations under the baobab tree. I walked about ten yards to the outskirts of the tree, put the bottle down, and pulled off my shoes and socks. I picked up the bottle, poured the water in a circle around the large tree, and then positioned myself to turn toward each direction of the earth. With each step, I called out the names of my grandmother, aunt, mother, and father(s). With each turn, I stopped and looked skyward, raising my arms out and up and repeated the names once more. I then stepped back from the baobab tree and took a handful of earth and tossed it into the circle. That sealed and completed the ceremony. I put my shoes on, picked up the bottle, and walked back to the waiting taxi. As the driver drove away, I looked out the window at the farmers working their fields and wondered what life might have been like had Africa not lost its way two thousand years ago.

Burkina Faso, "Land of Upright Men," is a country that shares a border with six other African nations. The Mossi are the largest tribe in Burkina Faso. The rest is made up of the Gurunsi, Senufo, Lobi, Bobo, and Fulani. The Burkina Faso people earn a living from farming, growing cotton, millet, guinea corn (sorghum), groundnuts, shea nuts, and gold mining. With the adult literacy rate at just 13 percent, it was no wonder that Mammado's parents wanted him to complete school and become a doctor.

After my short visit to the city of Bobo, I departed for Ouagadougou, the capital of the "Land of Upright Men." After I spent a few days checking out what was hoped to become a major film industry location if the French's meddling did not screw it up, I was invited by one of the local film directors to comment on the development of the project.

Journey to Seat of Ancient Knowledge

After Burkina Faso, I took a small plane to Mali, where I visited Timbuktu to view the greatest collections of African historical records and books left over from the golden days of the Mail Empire before it came under Arab influence and later European. It is back to African influence again and not a minute too soon for me, hopefully for good this time, but with Africans leaning to Islam and the Western version of Christianity to teach the young instead of African history, math and science as a way forward who can say just yet where any of us are headed.

Under the widest, bluest sky I have ever seen, the small plane flew low, less than twenty thousand feet, and gave the passengers a chance to see some wonderful golden desert country below. Around forty million years ago, the prevailing climate was wet and warm; geologists suggest this based on fossil evidence that the densely, vegetated mountains trapped substantial amounts of rainfall that still lay under the sand, where both ancient riverbeds and huge reserves of water and canals lay still hosting ancient animal and human remains. Africa is a natural tomb. It consumes all that it creates in time only to rebirth it all over again. I should know. Mud is an excellent medium for the fossilization process. My own studies of geology would teach me much about this subject later in life and set me on my career path. Nearby lay the Niger delta, which is part of the trans-African drainage system of Amazonian proportions, twice as large as the Congo drainage basin and three times the size of the Nile River. To understand the size comparison, the country of Mali is a mere shadow of its former self before the coming of the Arabs and Europeans who made a mess of some of the best human achievements in human and world history.

All of the southern part of the continent rose to a height of eighteen hundred to twenty-five hundred meters above sea level during the Pangaea era. This part of Africa was part of the "southern super continent" or Gondwanaland, which housed most of the world's southern continents. Its thermal climate uplifted the elevation of the continent, and erosion swept away an average of two thousand meters of rock from Africa's surface during the breakup of the continent sixty million years ago. This helps to explain why so much of Africa's mineral wealth is lying exposed on the surface of the earth. East of the Niger delta is East Tanzania, where a complete skeleton of Brachiosaurus was excavated, stolen by the Germans, and moved to the Natural History Museum of Berlin. The Brachiosaurus represents one of the largest land animals that ever lived, weighing an estimated eighty tons. This dinosaur was so big, it outweighed and outate as many as twenty mature elephants. An eighty-foot creature, its height allowed it to see over 12.6 meters above ground.

Adventures in Bamako, Mali

My trip across Niger and Mali is what caused me to become interested in and later study geology at the university level. I was seeking better understanding about the evolutionary process beyond the limited view of the Christian and Islamic belief system that humanity and all other life forms were a divine creation and heaven and earth were made in six days. Ancient Africans, the early Nubians, and Egyptians proved that was not true. Thanks to Charles Darwin's research and theory on the subject, open minds can now freely challenge the lies that we were all created by this myth of a white male that walked on water. I felt like I was traveling back in time, discovering my own evolution and history, a human who was the first to stand upright on planet Earth. Every part of my body was on fire, a kind of thrill-seeking overdrive. I had never felt as good and as free as I did then and after. I was learning faster, wanting to learn, needing to learn more and more than I ever had before about the world around me. I think back about the awful Alabama high school education I had been trashed with. I felt I could survive now and begin to live a quality life. It was all about being motivated. It was a new dawn, a new day, and a new way for me, unfolding like a wild flower among rocks and thorns, but I was at last starting to stand my ground and I loved it. I was free to be, to be me. My life had taken a major turn for the better!

I read later that Mali was once one of the grandest and most productive trading empires in Africa until the arrival of Arab and European invaders. Mali once a great empire sadly Mali today is a landlocked, poor, fenced-in sandy area in the Sahara desert plains. The Mali people are primarily concentrated along the Senegal and Niger Rivers, which provide most of the water for livestock and irrigation and serve as an important communication and travel route. The Niger River and its tributaries support an important food source and fishing industry that export (trade) mostly dried fish to neighboring Ghana, Ivory Coast, and Burkina Faso.

Mali was held as a French colony between 1890 and 1960. Mali won its independence from the oppressive French government in 1960 when all hell was breaking loose on the embattled continent and in the Western world as black people regained their footing and information flowed like the Nile River, bringing life to a once-oppressed area.

When I arrived in Timbuktu, I could see that there was little left of the old empire built on gold and desert trade. The records in the ancient library dating back to the beginning of the written word still held Timbuktu's early and late African history; their arts influenced Europe, East Asia, China, the Middle East, and the Americas. In Timbuktu rested what was likely the only ancient African library the Arabs and Europeans had not burned. This library holds early world history and the history of most of those who came to learn and to plunder; row after row stuffed with dusty pages on shelf after shelf, leaning but still standing, made of wood and stone and holding the priceless documents of knowledge worth researching regardless of your culture because all cultural links and roads lead to Africa. For me, this was truly one of the adventures my life could not have missed. When African Americans and Africans across the globe rediscover this library, this pure spring of knowledge protected by centuries of blood, they too will once more flow with life, knowledge, and power like the great timeless Congo and Nile Rivers. I hear some are starting to come and visit the great Timbuktu library.

Advanced schools should direct tours and classes here and across Africa to enable the students to excel. It not only helped me; it saved what was left of my life. Some feared the unknown, others feared local border crossings, while still others feared ocean crossings. But is it fear or conditioning? Most or many of us suffer from lack of interest or motivation. I get it. I have been there. I have come and gone, and I am here to tell you not to blame yourselves. Better to educate yourself with the power you have, and no one but you can replace that power and manage it. Many, like me, had their cultures all but erased from their minds during and after slavery. The attackers' aim was to play you while stealing all you owned, even your soul. But regardless of the fear or the challenge, it is always best to cross the line. Let no one draw the line for you. For the doubters, it's not too late. Africa is still there, and more than ever the motherland needs her children to take yet another stand and raise her up and show the continent off again from an African global cultural perspective. Some African minds were broken, but the will is not broken; that spirit can never be broken. Africans in the diaspora must speed up the return to their homeland, and Africans in Africa must know or learn their role and better manage that role and use it to beckon and welcome the reunion of family with open minds and arms, not fear for we have much to offer and share with each other. I am here. I am back, and I will stay even while holding on to the land and gains my ancestors captured in the west and the Middle East. So, come on, African brothers and sisters. Let's do this thing. Let's rebuild and take back all that was taken now! I am no savior, but I am here to assist by exposing avenues, hidden paths across the mountains, and through the forest of all fears to serve the ones who would dare to reach and live productive lives that give and keep on giving. That is being African! After visiting the historical library of Timbuktu, I thought I would fly to

Bamako, Mali, and spend a few days relaxing before heading back to Dakar and Nafi, the love of my life now. In Bamako, I found this peaceful little café at the end of a street that had the last big shade tree before turning into the endless desert that reached as far as the eye could see. It was one of those very, very hot Bamako afternoons, so I sat there with a cold drink and listened to the seductive Bamako music while dreaming of Nafi's beautiful sweetness. I fell asleep halfway through the cold drink under the big, green shade tree outside the African-owned and operated café.

"Mr. Rashid! Mr. Rashid!"

The tallest black (black as any timeless female African beauty could be) had come to my table to wake me. The female waiter had gotten to know me as Rashid during my visits to the café in the week since I had drifted into the area. The shade from the big tree had shifted, and I was exposed to the direct midday desert sun.

"You must move your chair back into the shade of the tree. You are not yet ready for the direct sun."

How right she was. As I opened my eyes, I could feel hot sweat on my darkened skin that was starting to glow like new, black velvet. I had been dreaming. My whole experience in this part of my quintessential Africa seemed a dream I could not and did not wish to wake up from.

The waiter placed a chilled glass of well water down and said, "Drink, but slowly."

People, drink from the water of life, but drink slowly. Make it last for as long as possible, from as many directions as possible. A few days later, I flew back to Dakar to see my beloved Nafi.

Chapter 29

Changing Masks in Dakar

Back in Dakar, Senegal, I returned to the house I rented in Yoff Lion and just slept for a few days. After I was rested, Nafi and I began visiting the local village in Yoff Lion mostly during the evenings to feast on lamb and listen to great Senegalese music. Music was indigenous and without Arabian or European influence. The music was as much a part of the Senegalese culture as the timeless beauty of these elegant Senegalese women with their creative fashion. Nafi and I often went shopping in the many fine tailoring shops that lined the graceful tree-lined avenues of downtown Dakar. Nafi was now dressing me in the local fashion, and I felt great, like a whole new person. I was now a new man. In time I adopted the fancy African style of the country's handsome men that the woman gazed upon with endless smiles and greetings.

One evening I was invited to dinner at Nafi sister's home and was finally able to meet her very busy sister Yacine Ba, who was a successful business lawyer. Yacine was slim, warm-spirited, and very beautiful like her sister Nafi. She was another black pearl in the long line of striking black pearls with ancient African features that captured me in a manner that few women have since. Their grace and timeless beauty gave me extra pride and confidence in being an African male. Walking in the streets of Dakar with a graceful, beautiful woman is like being part of a priceless artifact or painting on the wall of a museum sought after by the best society has to offer with people paying respect and standing long hours in line just to get a glimpse. Was this me? The shy boy born in Alabama, now transformed, remolded, and wrapped in silk and fine cotton laced together with gold threads—a culture the Europeans and Western world thought torn from my being, thought distorted forever. And here I was having dinner with not one, but two such priceless African gems in a home in West Africa. I was a guest of honor and welcomed by the man of the house. Yacine's husband was a tall, graceful man a few years older than me and a thousand years wiser I thought; he was a man of vision and just as welcoming as his lovely wife. By this time, I had adopted a more suitable name to reflect my new surroundings and identity: Rashid. I had added and welcomed the name to relieve me from the stress of being called Frank or Weston, a Western name I never cared for. I had always meant to change my name but never settled on an African name I liked yet. Being in such a splendid environment and home in Dakar, Senegal, I wondered what life could have been in all of Africa had the hand of greed, lack of respect, evil, and man's inhumanity toward man not entered Eden.

"Rashid, why don't you stay on here in Senegal?" Yacine asked me during the traditional African dinner that consisted of lamb, fish direct from the sea, dates from the north, and greens, all producing a combination of traditions, food, drink, and people of the finest quality I would never forget.

Their home completely embraced African culture, and it reflected their daily lives, starting with their dress codes right down to the way the table was set and candles were lit and placed for dining served in traditional Senegalese manner full of grace, art, and style reflecting centuries of fine living dating long before the void (the coming of the European invasion).

"I would love to stay, but there are a few things I am afraid I cannot abandon in the West just now," I said with regret and some hesitation. I knew right away based on what I had witnessed in the country there was no way I could earn a living here. I may have looked smart and able, but I knew I had work to do in the area of advancing my education in the Western world much to my regret.

Yacine's husband quickly replied, "You could have a house near our home. We could help you locate a $10,000 loan to get set up here."

Nafi wanted me to stay. She had told me so, but she asked her sister and brother-in-law to back off for a while and let me think about it. The evening turned inward, and we focused on the cultural art of being African and paying respect to our ancestors in a way I had never experienced before.

What man in his right mind would turn down the offer Nafi, Yacine, and her husband made me about settling over in Senegal, especially the part about Nafi and me being future partners and housekeepers? Before I left their home, Yacine picked up a carving made of African teakwood, a prized piece from her coffee table and handed it to me. It had a human face carved on it with a diamond-shaped piece of ivory in the center of the forehead that spoke volumes about its cultural origin. Most of all, it is a gift from a royal African family and friends that is priceless, and I own that art still.

"Whatever you decide, please do not forget us and that you have a home whenever you wish to return to Senegal," Yacine said, hoping I would remain in Senegal.

The next day Nafi and I climbed in a friend's car with a driver in traditional dress and departed for the Muslim holy city of Touba. I learned during the long drive that Islam can and does serve a useful purpose when it's in the right hands. But the verdict was still out as far as I was concerned whether Islam or Christianity would or should stand the test of time and last forever in Africa with Africans never having the opportunity to find their own footing again in their own belief systems.

Touba was a splendid place having been let to stand for centuries by the invading, enslaving French who had made a cultural pact to tolerate Islam if the Arabs would tolerate Christianity and take part in the complete destruction of black African civilization, its cultures, and linking infrastructures. They left only a divided African people who flocked to Touba unaware of the damage they were doing to themselves and the continent just as Christians and Muslims in their bid to grab the land claimed they were African lovers. With the kind of love Africa is receiving from outside, who needs love? Didn't Africans know or wish to know they have far older unique cultures and belief systems of their own that had served Africa and its people since the birth of civilization as witnessed in ancient Egypt, Sudan, and Mali. The list of sights still standing goes on and on for as long as mankind has stood upright and walked with his head held above the elephant grass on the planet. Proof of these achievements was everywhere, but yet everywhere I went in Muslim areas, I was tested, harassed even, by a question: "Are you Muslim?"

"I am still seeking my culture," I would reply.

I must say I was moved by the visit to Touba. I respected all my transformed African Muslim brothers and sisters, but they did not always respect my right to discover who I was and what I think in the end will be best for me to decide. But, still most of us bonded like brothers and sisters as best we could after being so brutally forced apart for centuries. I left Touba feeling sad because I knew in order to correct this unresolved matter of cultural belief and direction, it would take a far greater and bloodier war between Africans, Europeans, and Arabs. In the end, would Africans realize they were fighting a war for Islam and Christianity to try and maintain domination over us Africans? The future of a whole global people and a whole continent was at stake, and foreigners had their greedy eyes on Africa and could care less about the people; they have said so in words and evil deeds for centuries. The wars were bringing change that was already starting to boil over in Africa. I predicted Africa would lose because under Islamic or Christian domination and foreign rule in the land, it would vanish just as much of Native American cultures unless Africa stood together in the development phase of our return struggle as we had in the war on those who would enslave the people, any people.

Nafi and I drove the eight hours back to Dakar, and I remained a few weeks in Senegal, feeling a tug-of-war raging within myself about being African, my directions in life, my need for an advanced education, my undiscovered belief system, and love for Nafi and Africa.

I thought about the offers made by Nafi,

Yacine, and her husband, and it was very tempting, but in the end I declined the generous offer knowing I had a mission that would not yet allow me to remain for long anywhere. Later Nafi and I were driving in downtown Dakar in a taxi continuing the conversation.

"Then why not stay and grow your family here? They do not like you back in America. Wouldn't you rather be home in Africa?" Nafi asked. Her words were direct, well placed, and well meaning, I thought.

"Yes, but we are still at war with Europeans, and then there is the East Indians and some Asians pushing hard against us. As we speak, Arabs are pushing against Senegal from occupied land to the north in Mauritania, Sudan, Libya, and Egypt. Beyond the Europeans are occupying South Africa, Congo, Central Africa, Zimbabwe, and Kenya. I have work to finish before leaving America to live in Africa for good. When I come home to stay, I wish to come a free man to a free land and with something more than just empty hands. Europeans and Arabs stole me and a lot more from Africa, and I aim to get as much of what they stole back with interest and bring it back. Can you understand that, Nafi?" I replied. All the while I knew I only had a high-school education. Like all people, I was at major risk without an advanced university degree.

"Well, come home soon, Rashid," Nafi demanded.

"Now, that I will do," I said.

Nafi smiled, kissed her chocolate fingers, and gently pressed the tips coated with love and respect against my lips. Outside the taxi window, Senegal, like much of Africa, was busy moving forward as the world tried to hold it still, hoping to send Africa and its global people in the wrong economic direction. Directed by the World Bank, IMF, European and Arab cultural influences, and the Cross and the Koran as the weapons of choice, it was anyone's guess to know where the continent or men like me would end up. Little did I know then how deadly the economic attacks and dirty tricks were on Africa, supported by some of the most misdirected African leaders since Nigeria chiefs had sold their own people and gone to hell as enslaved fools. Still today, African leaders are making illegal deals behind closed doors in property and land they do not own, enslaving African people, and ruining any effort to survive and claim final victory.

I doubt Nafi accepted most reasons why I said I could not remain. Our now somewhat different cultures were linked well enough, and we could have made a go of it as a team. I had no doubt about that, but the timing was the problem. I wanted a son, but I wanted my stolen wealth, land, and life back as well. I wanted my complete cultural freedom, whatever it was, and I was not in any way willing to compromise yet and risk sending my DNA into the future ill programmed with power.

Three months had passed, and I was headed back to New York City on Air France via Paris. I had exhaled. It was early when I landed. Nafi remained on my mind during the entire flight back. If there was anything I did not want to do, it was not to leave Africa and Nafi behind. Nafi's questions to me in the taxi rang over and over in my head. "Wouldn't you rather be home in Africa?" Any number of African women and men had asked me the same question. "Wouldn't you rather be home in Africa?" To marry a cultured, beautiful woman like Nafi would have made me personally happy, I felt certain of that, but I would still have to live with the fact that I walked out on myself and the chance to get our land and wealth back under control. I wanted to get a higher university education so I could help my people hold on to the land and our future under our control forever. I departed Senegal sadly back to New York and then drifted out to East Africa for a while visiting Kenya, Tanzania back into Zimbabwe.

Chapter 30

A Journey into Zimbabwe's Hard Land

I was being inviting by my close friend Diniwe, a local Zimbabwean businesswoman, on a trip to Shurugwi to witness Western economic violence being imposed on African people. The trip was an eight-hour drive east of Harare, Zimbabwe, where we planned to establish a branch office of IMSCO. I heard young women were dumping babies, and AIDS was out of control. Africans were saying AIDS was planted, and I believed them knowing what diseases white American medical institutions injected into African American men and women in America in the 1920s. The deadly medical experiments on black men in 1920s Tuskegee, Alabama, is an example that gives me cause to believe what I was hearing here in Zimbabwe. The whites wanted the land and would do anything and were doing it to obtain the rich land in Zimbabwe, so denying medical treatment to black men and women was a weapon. Once called the breadbasket of southern Africa, black kids in Zimbabwe were going hungry; millions were without work or shelter as a direct result of the white settlers refusing to remove themselves from stolen and occupied African land.

Our plan was to cut across government red tape, go to Shurugwi, and sign a coownership land and resources agreement, an IMSCO establishment agreement between Zimbabweans and Africans in the diaspora before we went public on a TV show I had been invited on. Our plan was to use the threat of African diaspora power to help force the land issue into the open with the government. The trip to Shurugwi was our little secret, but there were spies everywhere even from the US embassy in Harare we learned later. I knew I was being watched, but I wouldn't learn why until later on in life. For one thing America and Britain had reneged on large cash amounts promised to the people in Zimbabwe's government after the war if the new black government would lay off the white settlers for ten years, but the United States and Great Britain had no intent of keeping the secret bargain with the black government. United Nations records will support this statement and review the whole truth that later led to major sanctions placed on the Zimbabwean people for a decade on, even though most Americans and English thought their governments were the good guys in Africa (granted some people who work in government do some good). I learned also that in order for the white settlers to hang on to the land they did not own, they went as far as to begin selling the property illegally to their clan members in the West, New York, and Europe undercover. As an NYU student, I would later interview some white Americans in New York City who were in on the corrupt business of buying interest in land in Zimbabwe and other areas in Africa with vast wealth the whites and only the whites knew was there and how to locate it. The black people in Zimbabwe including the new government officials had no idea that satellites in orbit sent imagery back to Earth with a color code telling the user where to locate vital minerals.

The local chiefs and community had agreed to invite their prime minister to witness and make the signing of the IMSCO agreement legal. At the wheel of the American-made Ford truck, Diniwe drove the eight hours down to Shurugwi, listening to African music with me entertaining her by dancing in the passenger seat. Shurugwi is a place of hot, dry, rocky, hard countryside with little or no topsoil or water to grow anything but anger and hunger pains. Here was a place the white settler community had forced the indigenous people to move to with the hope they would all starve to death or die of disease. This was a part of the settlers' dirty little secret that was never fed to CNN, BBC, or the rest of the outside world. But the angry truth was now beginning to rise from the scorched earth policy. It threatened the slender dreams of white settlers that grew tobacco instead of staple food crops, attempting to push starving, already-oppressed Africans into submission. Africans who had yet to witness freedom of any kind even though the United Nations and global white media had said this part of black Africa was the breadbasket of Africa and England and Germany were taking most of the commodities coming from Zimbabwe. However, the Western media did not say the area was free of white domination because it was not. Most Africans who had fought in the bush for liberation for centuries did not even know it was the twentieth century as I had not known when I first ventured out of my own personal hell in Alabama in 1960.

Although Shurugwi was hot, dusty, and dry as hell on the surface, a few feet down you were certain to strike water, platinum, gold, silver, iron ore, rubies, emeralds, and diamonds since it has one of the world's largest diamond fields and a host of other minerals. Ironically because of these minerals and their deposits, no clean safe water could be brought up from the mineral-rich ground. More importantly, there was a platinum vein that drifted across the land called Great Zimbabwe and down into the land of gold in South Africa.

This platinum vein running under Shurugwi is believed to be the largest and richest platinum vein in the world. The agreement codevelopment plan being signed by the people of Shurugwi and myself on behalf of IMSCO was intended to provide me with extra backing and power when I went before the TV cameras a week later in Harare to debate the white settlers over the land issue. The agreement signed at Shurugwi was intended to place part of the wealth and land the whites thought they had under African control. The Jews, Europeans, Asians, East Indians, and Arabs all have such a plan. We knew that if certain government officials got wind of what we were planning before the signing, they would try to block it, so the whole affair was kept well under wraps. The plan was not to try and negate the Zimbabwean government or any official policy but rather to fill in where the government failed or feared to tread. And there was plenty of fear to go around in African governments with so many representatives having sold out the people and land for their own personal interests.

For the historic signing, we all gathered under a large mangrove tree in the center of the small town of Shurugwi, while the people prayed and sang songs. Then we signed the first historical IMSCO codevelopment agreement that had been drafted earlier and amended in Harare. As I stood there in Shurugwi under the big mangrove tree, the culture I was receiving and sharing was an extended mandate being approved by the people of Africa to send an African people's institution (in this case, IMSCO) to the United Nations to represent them. We had no other choice because sure as hell no African government was interested in doing so. The government representatives were too busy grabbing the spoils and crumbs falling from the European, American multinationals, East Indians, and other exploiters at the tables. Did I say East Indian? Yes, because they were here teaming with the Europeans dividing the spoils just as many were doing across the border in apartheid South Africa. Witnessing the signing of the codevelopment agreement were the local chiefs and headmen of the towns and outlining villagers from miles around that we hoped would grant all parties a mandate to work together and codevelop.

I made a speech, a bit too long I expect, as did the long-winded Zimbabwean MP official who had come from Harare to witness the ceremony and no doubt seek a few votes as well for himself. The village elders, chief, and headman called for closer ties between our people all over Africa and in the diaspora. After the speeches and signing the documents, it was time to eat. The food suddenly started to arrive under the big mangrove tree carried by women. I felt a bit uneasy eating because many people were going hungry, so I pretended to be full very early in the dining process and reached for a cool local beer. As Diniwe was passing me, she reached over and pulled the cold beer from my hand, pointing me to natural juice made from local fruits. We sang again and danced in the tradition of the ancestors, and then it was time for the long drive back to Harare.

Driving Deep into the African Night

As we approached the truck, Diniwe tossed me the keys and said, "You drive back. I am tired." There was one problem.

"I do not drive stick shift," I said.

"This is Africa, not America, Rashid."

As I opened the truck's front door of the driver's seat, I saw five extra people seated in the rear. One was a woman near ninety years old. Diniwe and one other person, a young girl of about ten, sat in the front cab leaving me little room to shift the gears I did not know that well to begin with. Diniwe looked across the cab at me and said, "Drive Rashid."

I turned and looked up the street toward the main road. Darkness was rolling in fast from the surrounding countryside and a soon-to-be moonless rainy night. I cranked out the first gear, then the second under the watchful eyes of Diniwe and the town's people, as the Ford jerked and moved slowly forward. The people in the town were strung out across the yard taking a last look at this dark stranger of three centuries removed from them and must have wondered if they would ever see me again just as I wondered about my chances of survival on those African roads at night. We really had no way of knowing one way or the other if this was the end or the beginning. But at least we had each other and the codevelopment plan that would bind us, link us forever, we hoped. In those days in Africa, nearly everything we did was left up to chance just as I knew it was chance I was facing on the road ahead. The townspeople waved. Diniwe and the rest waved back, while I sweated knowing I had hundreds of miles of a very bad two-lane, unlit road ahead. There were potholes as large as basketballs lying in wait like pockets of death. While on the road in Africa, I came to fully realize why flying was safer.

I drove the damn truck out of the village square and headed for the main road. What else was I going to do? Within a span of a few minutes, I had the hang of the gears and a feel of the wheel. It's funny how fast we learn when properly motivated. As I drove, I had to come up with a plan to keep me focused and awake on the narrow road because one slip, any one- or two-inch mistake, and we were all history. We could be dead as quick as the sun had dipped below the horizon. In seconds the dreaded darkness had flooded our view ahead. Worse yet we were not alone as a long trail of cars and oversized lorries flooded the narrow two-lane road carrying billions of US dollars in mineral ore, gold, platinum, silver, and copper all headed our way to South Africa. Many of the trucks were passing on the right (or was it left?) to move ahead of us on roads really not suitable for driving let alone not worth bombing. Driving a stick shift on what was to me the wrong side of the road was bad enough, but when you had speeding mini buses full of people coming at you like rockets in combat, you really needed to be awake, sober, and in control. It's at times like these you hope the drivers are Muslims, since they are not supposed to drink. On the other hand, many Muslims are not supposed to mind dying, but I leave nothing to chance in this world. I knew then why Diniwe took the beer from my hand back in town. Women, what would we do without them?

To reach your intended destination safely on these roads, you had to be either a close friend of God or dating Satan's child. I had no such contacts with either. I just drove and drove, and then sometime during the long night's drive deep into the welcoming arms of Mother Africa, a slow steady rain started to fall. "Mother Africa will welcome you dead or alive, so watch out," I thought to myself. The rain was leaving the road slick as diamonds drenched with crude oil, diesel fuel, and wrecked vehicles on the side of the road. Beyond the road, the moonless night and surrounding countryside was a curtain of blackness, a void. Had I survived America only to end up dead before I could gain my big payoff by reclaiming my wealth and land? The rain began beating against the windshield just as I was now beginning to feel the need to fight off sleep when the headlights from oncoming vehicles lured me toward the peaceful darkness of death. I had to defeat the lure of the hypnotic bright lights many people reportedly see just before entering the other side. Had I drank the beer Diniwe evicted from my hand, I would have been in real trouble trying to keep us alive! I wanted to talk with someone. I thought about food, getting laid, or just taking a walk, anything but sleep. My thoughts drifted into the world of finance. By the time I arrived in Zimbabwe in 1989, the debt forced on Africa and its global people was approaching US$1 trillion and the cost of serving the debt obligations was going to be high in human lives, development cost as in no development if western Banks could help it and then there is the interest charges. It is reported in many independent reports the World Bank and partners were personally pocketing more than US$130 billion in tax payers money. It was impossible to see a light at the end of the tunnel because you would be dead before the end. I glanced over at Diniwe. She was resting her eyes, and I did not want to disturb her in case she was praying for our safety.

I am agnostic. I do not believe in this concept of God as such. I had outgrown the brainwashing I had received of the Western concepts of a God or religion. I felt around in my shirt pocket for half of a toothpick I always kept to dig food particles from a hole in a tooth in my mouth. A tooth I had been having trouble with since the late sixties in Paris and for some reason, mostly budgetary, I never got around to having it fixed properly. I found the half toothpick. I popped the pick in my mouth, which was now as dry as a desert. I used my tongue to flip the toothpick on end and bit hard down on the sharp point, driving it into my gum to produce desired pain to ensure that I would stay awake. I could feel pain and also a bit of blood running from the gum where I jammed the toothpick in. I bit harder and harder for about half an hour until my gum was sore enough to keep me awake. I rolled down the window at one point, spat out the blood, and felt the welcoming cold rain. I rolled the glass up again because the noise and rain was too much for the old woman. We had moved her into the cab from the rain and sent the younger girl to the back of the truck where four other people sat under a large plastic sheeting.

"Are you all right Rashid?"

"I bit my lip."

"Good. It will keep you awake. I want to have your baby in the future, so keep us alive," Diniwe said. She had been watching me all along. I wondered if she saw me place the toothpick in my mouth. African women are strong and always there to back a man up when he needs it most. That was the number one reason why Diniwe and I got along so well. I was there in Africa with them facing the music, on the job day and night regardless of the task before us, and she was doing the same. She even suggested once that I could govern Zimbabwe. Sometimes I think she went too far. As we drove past certain areas along the route, Diniwe reminded me that Ian Smith, the former African butcher and last colonial prime minister of British Rhodesia, controlled all the farm land around as far as the eye could see. She was angry about the fact that now President Robert Mugabe had let this evil Ian Smith remain on the land as the government protected him while millions of African people starved to death and went without food, clothes, shelter, and education. This was a black man's burden if ever there was one. Don't ask me how, but eight hours later I had driven across some of the toughest road I had ever faced in Africa outside the Republic of Liberia. The truck came to a full stop on the side of the sharp-edged road. There were no shoulders for safety margins having been badly constructed by Western contractors and funded by the World Bank. We had reached Harare city limits, and I sat there for a minute frozen, staring out the front window, not thinking, not moving, and barely breathing. The rain had stopped, and judging from the bright glow in the morning sky overhead, it was promising to be a sunny day. Diniwe sat looking at me, smiled, and said, "They don't make them like you anymore."

"I will be asleep before you can take the wheel," I said.

I stepped out of the truck to change places with Diniwe, and as we met and passed in front of the truck, she slapped me on the butt. We climbed in the truck, and she drove off into the future, into the early morning air, and toward the city of a changing Harare. As we drove, I remember Diniwe asking me if I would rather be home in Africa. There it was again. Nafi asked me that same question eight years earlier. Home in Africa is the only place I ever wanted to be. But could I stay? I wanted to, but could I remain and still be the man I had to be? In seconds I fell into a deep sleep and dreamed. Again I heard Diniwe's question. The answer is yes, I would rather be home in Africa.

Chapter-31

Black Hope versus White Hope

The African hit producer of the Zimbabwe Broadcasting Cooperation (ZBC), Masimba, had invited me to come to Zimbabwe to take part in the heated African versus white settler land issue on TV called "Business in Zimbabwe Nine Years After." Most people in the world did not know that ten years earlier the United Nations, under orders from America and Great Britain and dancing to the tune of big business, had placed the nation and people of Zimbabwe back into slavery again even after they had won the centuries-old war for liberation with other African's help including the PAD. The UN was able to do this by using a document called the Lancaster Agreement cooked up in London by Western economic power and hit men that demanded the white settlers remain on the land and in control of all wealth and land for a full ten years without any regard to African rights to the land. Naturally, all African human rights went to hell with the deal. Witness US/EU sanction involvement see ZBC TV letter page 453.

It was now 1989, and the ten years were up. The Western world through the United Nations infamous *"Landcaster Agreement"* demanded the people of Africa give the terrorizing whites more time to a adjust back into the same land now controlled by the very blacks they had been slaughtering and enslaving for centuries. Even though the whites had lost all African wars and having no return tickets were still seeking to retake land the blacks in

Zimbabwe had retaken led by our hero, our African pharaoh, our giant, President Robert Mugabe. As CEO of IMSCO, my United Nations–affiliated NGO at ECOSOC, I had stood with Mr. Masimba against all odds. Even though I was facing extreme danger for doing so from the American government, all of the European Nations, and business, I stood with Zimbabweans on behalf of all the PAD.

Paying all airline and hotel fees out of my own pocket, I had gladly accepted the invitation to debate the whites on ZBC TV and push the whites off the land my people needed so badly to rebuild their lives. The document arrived in New York City from ZBC TV allowing me to fly to Harare and help the black people out of the dry, white season the white settlers were attempting to hold my brothers and sister down in. It was a mess some government officials seemed too afraid to act on, demanding the settlers vacate the land at once. Appearing on ZBC TV would later get me banned from Zimbabwe by the minister of immigration, and then for decades I had to suffer unbelievable attacks from some US government officials. It wasn't the US government, but the white officials who later told me, "We know who you are, Frank Weston!" Even as an American veteran, I was not able to find work linked to any white-owned company in the United States, but I had Africa, and that was all I needed.

The heated TV debate was over, and I had done what was asked of me: take a political bullet for the nations. I had helped make the people's case and faced off with the white land-grabbing terrorists by telling the white settlers that they were remaining in Zimbabwe, indeed all of Africa, on limited time before PAD team with their family members, move in, and force the colonist off the land and "Out Of

Africa!" My playing this role on TV placed every white settler in Africa that witnessed the debate on notice. The once-enslaved now warriors were loose, free of their physical and mental chains, and were coming home pissed! The Zimbabwean government official in the immigration department fearing white backlash sent me a secret letter demanding that I leave Zimbabwe immediately. Fearing for my safety, the producers of ZBC TV along with members of the black community had arranged for Zimbabwe secret service to keep an eye on me around the clock. On the flip side, the TV debate had a major impact on blacks taking direct action to force white settlers off the land. It also caused billions of US dollars invested by foreigners including the World Bank and IMF to fold, fail, and lose their value.

I had no regrets are fear of the losers blood stained minds or hands. I, like millions of other African, lost family and centuries and material items but we still had the land and hope and a future. The settlers did not now have land or a return ticket to a declining Europe that had forced the unwanted settlers out of a Europe that were not invite the settlers and squatters back. The Zimbabwe newspapers gave the story the front page complete with my picture over the settler's angry response calling me every name but a son of my ancestors they and their kin had murdered. The government offices and newspapers were flooded with letters and phone calls from the white community calling me a racist and demanding my head on the chopping block, and for what? The above letter from ZBC-TV Assistant Director at the time sums the feelings of the losers and the scope of our advancing victory in a land rich enough to buy Europe and America. I accepted the white settlers attacks on me as a pleasure.

Frank Weston President CEO IMSCO
Debates Zimbabwe Whites on land ownership

Frank Weston President of IMSCO UN NGO
Debate Zimbabwe white community 1989

Masimba came by my hotel where I was packing to depart for New York. My work was done. For certain, the action and messages sent out in the country would cause a shift in African thinking, and it did since the Zimbabweans did force the white settlers off their land. I was busy finishing up some last-minute details inside my Holiday Inn hotel room with the secret service agents standing by outside my door. My one bag was packed, and I was ready to depart for the airport bound for New York City.

"Has this food been tested?" Masimba asked in a good mood, leaning over to help himself to what was left of my cold uneaten lunch. Masimba took a bite out of one of my bread rolls.

"You would be dead if it wasn't tested brother," one of the agents said. We all laughed.

"We did it, man. We pulled it off and made history. We spoiled the great white hope in the remaining land that they stole," Masimba said. "President Robert Mugabe will have to act sooner or later." I drank the last of my warm South African Castle beer. Programing news and current affairs sent me a letter soon after I departed inviting me back to Zimbabwe for a follow-up taping regarding the same matter, and I accepted. White settlers had to give up their grip on the land.

I picked up the telephone and dialed a New York City number, hoping Molefe, my friend and a member of the Pan Africanist Congress (PAC), would be home and would pick up the phone. The PAC was the militant wing of the struggle for freedom in South Africa, and I was moving money and information for them. Molefe was in exile in Harlem and hated it. It seems the CIA, FBI, and MI-6 were all leaning on the PAC because the wind was blowing in the ANC direction to take control of the new South Africa. Molefe also had good reasons to stay in the shadows because whites in South Africa wanted our heads and you had to know that every telephone and computer (if you could afford one) might be bugged. I supported both the PAC and ANC, and I had carried out a number of missions inside and outside South Africa for both. I was in luck. After a few rings, Molefe picked up the phone.

"Hello! Hello, Molefe, it's Rashid. I am in Zimbabwe—" I said as Masimba from the background cut in, saying, "We had better leave if you are going to make that flight." I waved my hand for Masimba to chill.

"I am on my way back to New York City. See you in two days."

I hung up the phone and grabbed my bag. On the way to the airport, I explained to Masimba and the secret service agents that I had a mission to carry out for the PAC in South Africa, but that I really could not discuss it and left it at that. En route to the airport, I kept looking out at the city of Harare, wondering what the future would be like here in ten years and where I would be. I wanted to remain in Africa, but this was not the place or time to settle. The economy in Zimbabwe and elsewhere in Africa was still under white, East Indian, and World Bank control, and as long as that was the case, Africa was not going anywhere. The drive to the Harare airport was short and with little or no traffic. I was rushed through customs by the secret service as I said good-bye to my friend and producer Masimba, who got all teary eyed just before I boarded the plane. I hid my feelings under my tough guy act. A short time later, the American-made plane was airborne and jetting toward America with me at a window seat looking down at the land I loved and hated to leave. The land quickly vanished from view under some angry storm clouds blowing in from the Indian Ocean over the Mozambique Channel as we headed west for a massive land bridge, Angola, and on to the Atlantic Ocean.

I had been watching the storm clouds gather from the window in my hotel room while waiting for Masimba to arrive with the tapes. An old landless African farmer I ran into standing on the street in the old colonial sector of Harare told me, looking up at the sky and watching the clouds forming, "The monsoon rains will be heavy this season." The old wise farmer said the rains would come early that year as a blessing for my coming. He said he had seen me on the first TV show and liked what I had to say. I could tell he missed digging in his rich African soil, but soon he would have his land back, I thought, I hoped. I was glad I did and said what I had on TV. The clouds had formed as a result of the shifting in the timeless trade winds as they reversed from southeast to northwest in a giant wind tunnel, mixing hot and cold air over the Indian Ocean, just as they had done that time of the year since as far back as mankind could recall. The old African farmer stood there with his weather-beaten face and hands. He knew this land and weather because he was an African man who first stood upright on earth and had been here since the beginning for humankind, and he would be here when the last European and Asian departed from the land like the locusts; he would be on his land in one form or another a million years from now.

Chapter 32

Cut to the Chase

It's 1988. I am putting together a press kit with detailed documents I have been keeping for years of everything that happened in my efforts to openly challenge the African representatives at the United Nations and in Washington, DC, who were in charge of billions of US dollars to cooperate with African American business people seeking work badly needed. In the information press kit, I challenged Ambassador Youssoufou to a live TV debate in response to the debate that took place in 1981 at the IMSCO summit in New York City. They thought no one dared go after them since no one had until I took on the case. "Risk? To hell with the risk." I had nothing to lose. Besides, these guys were helping the enemies of African people steal everything we owned, and they did not seem to care. I sent information kits and documented proof to Tony Brown, a well-known African American journalist, who produced a national weekly program called the *Tony Brown Journal* on current issues in the African American community. The show broadcasted once a week on PBS. At the time, Tony Brown's TV program was one of the most popular black television news journal shows in American television. Tony Brown had apparently been following my work in the community. Dominick Carter, a reporter on WLIB, the black-owned radio station, had been following IMSCO's work for some time.

When Tony Brown received the documented proof I sent him in the mail, he quickly agreed to televise the debate. Ambassador Youssoufou, the worst African representative at the United Nations I have ever met (and I have met some bad ones), accepted much to my surprise. Naturally, everyone expected me to get my butt kicked by this seasoned ambassador during the debate. I was not worried. I knew how to stay alive and keep my cool in a heated pan. After all, America had successfully taught me that. The TV debate was what I needed as training for the United Nations I hoped one day to be able to address. I wanted to tell it like it is and have the power to back up my call.

"Do Africans Boycott Blacks"

The day of the TV show finally came in the summer of 1988. Tony Brown opened the debate—justly named "Do Africans Boycott Blacks?"—by introducing the ambassador and me to the audience. Tony asked me the first question, so I was the first to speak. I repeated what I had been saying all along: that African countries and representatives in America are discriminating against African Americans and people of African descent from Brazil to Mississippi, New York City to Canada, to Europe, and beyond. I was pushing this agenda because I had discovered what was needed was a PAD solution to our problems or put in a more uniting way: "Africans need an African solution." In 1989, PAD were locked out of African development opportunities.

People in the TV studio reacted positively to my opening remarks. I relaxed a bit; I had a good opening. The ambassador's turn came, and he told the audience that Africans in the OAU were in full and complete charge of the continent's wealth and resources.

"Anyone who knows Africans knows we cannot be told what to do."

I told the viewers in the studio the OAU and the African states were selling Africans out by giving all worthwhile development contracts and wealth to the people's enemies, leaving the African community with nothing but hardship and early death. The embattled ambassador shot back complaining to the audience about my earlier protest and actions my team had taken to expose the wrongs done by his office and other African missions to the United Nations.

"Mr. Weston occupied the Kenya mission," Ambassador Youssoufou said.

"No, I did not take over one mission. I took over four missions," I corrected the now angry ambassador. I went on to remind the audience that Africans should feed family first—meaning the descendants of the very people who were stolen and sold from our continent. "It was downright stupid," I told the audience, "to do business with the enemy of Africans in the diaspora and feed someone else's family before you feed your own family."

The audience applauded approvingly. Seeking an escape route, the ambassador held up a little orange booklet, so thin it appeared to be just two covers bounded back to back and suggested this was where black-owned businesses could be found. It was an insult to the proud African community worldwide to suggest that was the sum total of our business culture.

The ambassador continued as he held up the shameful, orange booklet with zero pages. "Whenever we need a doctor or a contractor, all we have to do is pick up this book and call."

The whole studio could see there were not enough pages in the orange booklet the ambassador held to wipe a gnat's behind let alone reflect the number of African American businesses in the whole of the United States of America. He suggested all PAD businesses among the then four hundred million Africans in exile were in the booklet. In fact, the ambassador did not open it to reveal the embarrassing contents. Everyone could see he was lying, and that nothing was in the booklet.

"Weston is a one-man crusade. Nobody knows him," said the ambassador, trying to recover using slander as a weapon. This was a desperate attempt on his part to discredit me on national TV. If I were such a "nobody," what was a big shot ambassador doing on national TV debating such a "nobody?" Surely, if I could see that, the public could also. It was sad; I had hoped to have a more positive debate, but I made the best of it. Tony Brown moved the microphone to the audience and placed it in front of a young African American college student.

"Ambassador, does the OAU have a policy in place to assist Africans in the diaspora to go into business?"

"We have this book." The ambassador held up the pathetic orange book again trying to escape the heat from some four hundred eyeballs staring at him and millions more watching across the nation and world. I called out to protest the booklet the ambassador held, but I could have saved my breath because the people in the audience were smart enough to see the ambassador was a lost cause. The now furious ambassador was on the ropes and about to go down for the count.

"The OAU has no plan in place to do anything with African Americans," I said. "The ambassador has written letters to block me and other Africans in the diaspora from doing business with Africa," I told the audience.

The ambassador grew angrier. He began yelling and sweating as he glared about the room trying to find anyone who might side with him.

"Don't lose your composure, Ambassador," I said.

"I am losing my composure because you won't let me speak!" he cried and everyone laughed.

The ambassador came back at me with, "The only thing my colleague on the left has said that is correct is that Africans in Africa do not own Africa any more than Africans in America, Brazil, or any place else."

There! I had the ambassador where I wanted him, admitting he was wrong from the start, dead wrong about what he and other black men and women, Africans across Africa, our homeland, were doing; how they were managing and mismanaging Africa's vast wealth, our wealth, our future! That being true, what was the plan of these African leaders? Was it their plan, or was it the plan of France, the United States, Brazil, or Germany? To ban just one person of African descent in the diaspora from business ownership, property, contracts, concessions, dual citizenship, or a birthright is committing a human rights crime. It prevents Africa from breaking free of the debt of economic slavery, the Western and Arab nightmare, and the lack of quality education that I still lacked and was determined to get at all cost. Here I was seated on international TV debating the representative of fifty-three African nations with only my bad high-school degree from Alabama. This meant I was actually debating 192 representatives when you factored in the UN member states with their interest and hold on Africa and its people. I had done the same in the TV debate in Zimbabwe and Zambia. I somehow survived it holding my own for the people who supported IMSCO's aim to get back our African land, wealth, and respect. My eyes were open now so I could face and debate, even defeat and win at this game, I thought to myself. So I decided to stay in the struggle regardless of education level or cost!

"Ambassador Youssoufou, you do agree Africa should have a political and business relationship with Africans in the diaspora, don't you?" Tony Brown asked.

The ambassador just about fell out of his chair, choking on his words. "I...I..." the ambassador said, confused and defeated. The man hated my presence. I frankly felt sick but never ashamed of being there, facing down, doing battle single handedly as the "one-man crusader." I had been labeled by my Brother who wanted me politically dead! Why? Because I was exposing how the OAU present day African Union followed foreigners guidance to deny PAD and his own human rights after centuries of mental physical and mental enslavement?

"We have this book," the ambassador stumbled, as he pinched the leaflet repeating his words holding up the disgusting orange book showing signs of defeat and frustration. The ambassador could have won or been a runner-up for an Academy Award for playing such a failure like most of the African leaders, save for one or two. Because of them, the bigger losers are the people. We must run the bad examples out of Africa and demand back every dime over the centuries they and others had stolen and shipped. They let the wealth be shipped out to foreign banks through the IMF who partnered and cooperated with bad African leadership that did not include PAD people, as the OAU Ambassador Youssoufou testifies on the TV program. Here was a man representing at least fifty-two African nations at the time; I am not so certain the people of Africa know they are wealthy, unaware of the land we own, and with bad leadership as evidenced by the ambassador I had just debated, Africans could lose it all if we did not take immediate action.

Ambassador Youssoufou defeated, then pointed to a gold ring on his finger. "We do not even control this gold we produce. What can we do with this gold if we do not give it to the white man?" The embattled ambassador finally conceded on camera.

I had my knockout! What was such an uninformed, unlearned person doing in the OAU representing Africa people? The studio room burned with heat so hot, so extreme the flames were appearing as a black fire. In the end, the ambassador had defeated himself but had not helped our cause at all I feared. He had said in the very beginning that I was a "one-man crusader," and the ambassador was not far from being correct at the time since most people in Africa and in the diaspora were not yet aware of what could be done. Coming out of slavery of the mind is not easy for any people! So African people get off your butts, and start being the kings and queens you know you are. Take full control of your African kingdoms again, not as Muslims or Christians, but as Africans with a collective ownership of the vast land and inheritance Western multinationals are trying to grab. Making this mission worse, many blind Africans are investing in the very multinationals and Wall Street to assist in the Western scams attempting to steal African people's inheritance. The ambassador and his blind unlearned comrades had no approval to represent the land and the wealth, half of which belongs to five hundred million PAD from across the planet.

In the end, Tony Brown thanked us both, and the taping ended. The ambassador and I faced off again backstage, and then went our separate ways. But our paths would cross again and again and keep crossing as this African inheritance war heated up globally. Later I ran across the ambassador at the United Nations, and he discovered I was the founder of IMSCO.

Ambassador Youssoufou and his fellow OAU and AU's mission to save Africa was just plain wrong, and the audience let him know. The production "Do Africans Boycott Blacks" did air and helped educate, still educating blacks and whites across America and the world on current issues relating to the PAD in the Africa diaspora that, to my knowledge, had never been aired or debated in public before anywhere.

Almost since its inception, the OAU has been marred by controversy. A few years after the debate aired, the news leaked out that the OAU and Ambassador Youssoufou had been involved in the failure of the Freedom National Bank in Harlem, once the largest black-owned and operated bank in New York. On behalf of the OAU, the ambassador had gone to Harlem and borrowed US$500,000 to renovate a five-story building on east 52nd Street in Manhattan that housed the OAU mission to the United Nations. At one point during the debate, a supporter of the ambassador lied and said he and the ambassador had received US$66 million and that they had the money to build the Harlem Third World Trade Institution. That was another super lie since there is no Harlem Third World Trade Institution in Harlem or anywhere on earth. It had taken African American PAD business people centuries to obtain enough resources to grow and establish the Freedom National Bank in Harlem, and in a heartbeat, the bank was gone.

Years later in 2011, the debate was uploaded on YouTube by a supporter of IMSCO. This caused quite an international concern among the African Union political leadership and the multinationals, mostly I am certain over the part of the debate where the ambassador admits Africa is owned by all Africans from Brazil to Mississippi to Alabama to across the so-called European Union that cannot feed itself were it not for the exploitation of Africa and its people. It seems in time, the debate developed some powerful enemies with its powerful statements; even more so than it had when it first aired in 1988. The show is both historical and educational and nearly too powerful for the minds and times then and our time now. The African Union and other hidden hands were behind lobbying to have the video taken down from public viewing and naturally contacted Tony Brown. Weakened with age maybe or greed, he sold out the PAD and must have given YouTube the green light to go after me by confronting me with threats and directly accusing me of being behind placing the debate online. I had not done so, but I had no problem with it being up there as that was the original intent. My team had advised me to hang back. The idea was to educate people, mostly African people, about what the real game was behind attempts to reenslave PAD from behind closed doors. Europeans also would have had cause to be alarmed about the video being up online. However, at the top of the list had to be white male fat cats who were lusting for African land and wealth, but this time they had gone a bridge too far with their system fading like a creative lover in a bad love story built on lies. I had clearly won the debate "Do Africans Boycott Blacks?" but not the debate and the struggle to save Africa and ensure PAD a place in the new Africa.

After the taping of the program, the OAU secretary-general H.E. Salim Ahmed Salim in Addis Abbaba, then Ambassador Youssoufou's boss, sent my organization an official OAU document committing my organization to a seat, voice, and vote in the OAU. The secretary-general had made history by invited PAD back into the fold of the continent. The OAU head office had reached out to the extended African family and coowners of Africa and seemed to be welcoming PAD back into the land, not that we needed to be welcomed home. Ambassador Youssoufou and other people's bitterness drove them to the point of madness and wanted to stop at nothing to deny the PAD. The Western world, Asia, our Muslims brothers and sisters, and the whole of the Arab community labeled PAD people as nonbelievers. Even the people of African descent have trouble knowing we are human based on the evil shown us, let alone what God to believe in or pray to.

      After the TV debate, the ambassador began to write the most evil of letters aimed at me and my teams from New York, including the ministers of Zimbabwe, and sent the letters to every African United Nations mission in New York and every embassy on the planet in an all-out effort to ban me and my organization's efforts from the global African community. And for what? Freedom of speech or the right to represent my people in exile. Self-hate can drive a person to the lowest level imaginable. The ambassador had hit the lowest level just as the white settlers had in Kenya, Zimbabwe, Zambia and South Africa, America with its false freedom doctrine, and those across the globe seeking to beat PAD back to Africa in the hope of stealing their birthright and humanity. The ambassador, the white settlers, the evils and greed of the Western world, and all others who had set out to destroy Africa and its people in the end had failed. It turned out to be a new beginning for Africa and its people.

      The family matters between PAD and Africans are now political and must be addressed as such to find and maintain peace. To achieve inclusion for PAD people in exile in the Western world, IMSCO recommends support for the IMSCO Prime Minister's Office established inside the IMSCO office in order for PAD to have control of their lives as they move toward total self-determination. IMSCO have a copy of the letter as proof to let the people of Africa and PAD see for themselves the kind of person the ambassador and African Union are capable of; what some African representatives will do to feed their egos and pockets and in the end ruin the lives of many suffering African people.

The ambassador wrote a letter before at the IMSCO Summit in 1981 and again after the TV debate addressed to all African missions to the UN and African embassies worldwide designed to save his own neck as he had just made a fool of himself and damaged the OAU. The letter was meant to be a death threat to me and a political bullet to anyone who stood for the rights of the PAD. Someone bigger than the OAU wanted PAD to remain enslaved or sent back to prison. Perhaps they wanted mass murder to be committed on the African family that just would not die after their millennia of enslavement horrors. Ambassador Youssoufou knew this or should have known it, but in fact he just did not give a damn.

Ordering a copy of the historic video tape may be near impossible now because Tony Brown Productions is trying to help the African Union today keep the truth and DVD off the market. A bootlegged copy exists of the now disputed copyright ownership between Tony Brown and the author. Contact IMSCO to assist in locating one. Viewing the historic DVD will be an educating experience in PAD and African history on who wins Africa.

Chapter 33

Running Cash to the Struggle

After the debate with the ambassador, I traveled back to Africa to do more research and obtain needed resources I sure as hell was not going to find in America to continue the work my team and I were doing. In Zambia, I was taken to the African National Congress (ANC) underground where I delivered some cash to the ANC representative. I also had the opportunity to meet National Executive Committee members of the ANC who were helping blacks in South Africa fight the evils of apartheid. I met Joe Slovo, the Jewish renegade freedom fighter, and I must say I just never could trust the man. While in Zambia I was invited by the government and given the landing rights and approval to operate the African American airline I was trying to get started that if successful would move cargo between southern Africa and America; sadly the airline never got off the ground. Europeans and South Africans under apartheid were attacking Zambian Airways to close it down out of fear of African competition to European interest. From Zambia I flew into Zimbabwe to wait for the day I was to appear on Zimbabwean TV to debate the white settlers over the heated Zimbabwe land that is one of the richest areas on earth. It was not what was in the ground so much as what could be grown in the ground that was at issue and kept hidden by the white community and international investors. I was met at the airport by Diniwe, who quietly slipped me into the city and put me up at her home for a few days until I found a safe hotel. The reason I was in Zimbabwe made it unsafe for me to stay at a private home.

African Solutions

Arriving back in America, I found New York City at the end of the eighties was becoming a great, oversized, racist bore, with apartheid and Jim Crow up north. New York in the seventies was a sinkhole of greed, political corruption, and blackouts as people of color suffered from lack of cash flow and mental illness. The people in Zimbabwe, Zambia, South Africa, Arab-held Egypt, Libya, Morocco, Brazil, and across the African diaspora faced the same economic burden. In America, black people were facing increasing racist attacks and stop-and-frisk setups all led by New York City and state police in cooperation with New Jersey and beyond, right across America. Local black leaders and the cowardly reverends were doing their things in the church were doing about it was praying and demanding white men to give victimized rich as Africa black men and youth jobs in fast food joints.

Why didn't black men and women fight? Hit back? To tell the truth, many do not know how or where to strike back with any lasting result outside of killing the motherfuckers attacking us. Some including me were doing the best we could to inform the marginalized black community too. I was taught to read more and focus on the riches of Africa to help retake the continent from where we stood for the sake of our own lives! A few entertainers and I wrote and did radio and TV shows and even walked the streets trying to reach out to the millions of homeless Africans across the diaspora. But, most African American leaders like the leaders in Africa did not even consider these options I have discussed to promote institution building as a final solution to the growing problem that would soon bite us all in the asses. Sending black men and women to jails and prisons in Africa and in the African diaspora only pissed us off more. Black men more and more were turning to the gun culture regrettably to kill each other, themselves mostly. By now, the black inmates, including the recent African arrivals from the seemingly "Hopeless Continent," own the jails, and when they are released, they bring the prison culture with AIDS and a host of other diseases back into the black community and spread it across the nation. The system's slogan and final solution was still to lock up black men and now women and children and throw away the key to keep black youth from realizing what Africa held for them: their rich business culture and history. They had to be stopped from being and reaching heights of leadership and empire building, like their ancestor the youthful Pharaoh King Tut in ancient Egypt. This is what the white business and political system feared most: a rise again among the African and African diaspora youth making up the whole of the population in all communities and Africa. And the rise will happen again in a split second. Change is often like an earthquake, quick and sudden! I have but one bit of advice for black youth and African people. Read!

Research what you own, Africa, and every damn thing in her, and every person and nation worldwide having anything at all to do with what the continent and its people produce and buy. Take what you own, and control it. African people own a hell of a lot on this planet, but they just do not yet know how much and how easy it is to have it all back. That is what I have learned so far. To get started, Google "Africa nation resource wealth state by state."

To this end, every black man in America, including myself, now had a price on his head: death or life in prison. We black men were worth more to the white-controlled system dead or as forced labor prisoners of society. Prisoners in private prisons housed and fed like farm animals for profit paid for by the US federal system and taxpayers' dollars. That way the promoters of this human rights crime could work black men for a dollar a day or nothing again after slavery. Meanwhile white youth were busy learning how to fly air planes so they could map Africa from the sky and know what minerals were on African land and then go in and steal the wealth under illegal hundred-year deals that amount to a worthless US buck a year. I tell you, dual citizenship is the return ticket to have and to own. With a dual citizenship ticket, an African person can plant his food in Africa, ship it, finish or process it, eat it, or sell it for a profit and never be in need of a home or employment. The East Indians do it, the Chinese do it, and the Europeans do it, so Africans must now do it as they own what others ship any way.

Back in New York, I was no longer unpacking my bags. Instead I took out the dirty clothes to be cleaned and left the suitcase and shoulder bag in the closet, always at the ready. I had also left clothes and other items like first aid kits, dried foods, and media kits scattered in every African country I visited and lived in. I got in touch with my friend Molefe. He lived in a five- or six-floor Harlem walk-up, but he truly preferred to be in his homeland of South Africa just as much as I did, but a lack of money prevented him from escaping. This was one of the strongest bonds between us. We had been teammates in the struggle ever since the day we carried a coffin through the streets from the United Nations flanked by a group of New York City police officers and sat the coffin down in front of the OAU office, hoping to shame the officials into action, and demanded that the OAU and other African missions and states back home in Africa smarten up. We wanted them to face up to what they had created with the greed, corruption, and just plain bad management that was selling out, killing our dreams, and holding back nearly every African man, woman, and child on the planet. This was just before the bloody Rwandan horror that killed and injured a million plus people, and it was before the slaughter of millions of Africans in the DRC. It was before the United Nations' troops failed peacekeepers, under the not so watchful care of Kofi Annan (then the head of United Nations peacekeeping), and had teamed with American and European troops to assist in grabbing the wealth of Congo over the dead bodies of millions of African people. EU countries invaded Somalia on President Bill Clinton's watch, who was following through on what President George W. Bush (the father) first in the White House had started on behalf of American big business trying to grab Somalian oil and gold fields. It was during this time that I started to focus more on how to get inside the United Nations and work from within to help change things that might improve matters to the extent that my small team and I could.

It was also during this time Molefe introduced me to Dr. Peko, the then Pan Africanist Congress of Azania (PAC) representative to the United Nations. Azania is a historical name given to South Africa, though not all Africans (mostly just members of the ANC) prescribe to the name. Dr. Peko was a man of medium height and dark complexion, middle aged, and sporting a diplomatic style that told you he was not shy of direct contact to face the enemy; he meant business. The PAC rightfully suspected Western capitalists of seeking to maintain total control of South Africa's wealth.

This is why the apartheid supporters treated the PAC and their supporters as the more militant wing of the black South African struggle and favored the ANC with the keys to the outside world. Mr. Peko, like Winnie Mandela, inherited and represented black South Africa's uncompromising stand at the United Nations in New York City that in part caused me to make a bid to enter the United Nations as an NGO. I saw what the PAC and the ANC were doing and tried my best to support both organizations. They both were making a big mistake by not inviting African Americans and other Africans in the diaspora to partner with them at the start and help run the country. The ANC was now under the control of Mr. Nelson Mandela's management who pushed the African diaspora dual citizenship request and objective away as an OAU/African Union issue. I had the feeling from the beginning that the ANC sold out the PAC and African people by lying down and rolling over to the interests of the white settlers and transnationals in South Africa in order to eat first.

China's ugly duckling breakaway, Taiwan,

was also in the mix and totally supportive of the evil apartheid system born out of America's own model of how to treat and control African Americans still economically enslaved in the American police state for black men then and now. It was the PAC that informed me what the Chinese in Taiwan, Europeans, and members of the Jewish community were doing in South Africa to undermine African freedom everywhere. They were selling out African people by grabbing a fast buck as if they were half-priced, low-hanging fruits. It was at this time that Molefe asked me if I would make a run to South Africa to pick up a cash of diamonds in the name of the struggle. I said I wanted to think about it before deciding. I knew I had damn well better plan ahead and plan well before traveling into apartheid South Africa to face off with evil, greedy masters.

Chapter 34

Nelson Mandela's Vision

After twenty-seven years in prison, Nelson Mandela was invited to visit and address the United Nations General Assembly on June 22, 1990. The media event was to enable Mandela to present his new vision for South African people only. It just so happened I would be present at the United Nations that day to learn more about Mr. Mandela's vision, which leaned toward protecting white settlers' interest in South Africa while giving limited concern for the interest of the global African family that had played a bloodletting role in helping free black South Africa.

This was and is a common complaint raised about Nelson Mandela from marginalized Africans in South Africa and the world over, so don't go blaming the messenger. Mandela did speak that day at the United Nations international news conference presenting his "new vision," but it did not include PAD across the global African diaspora. I posed my question for Mr. Mandela through Michael O'Neal. He was the editor of *Big Red*, a newspaper in which I had written a nationwide editorial called "Strategies for African Co-development" in the eighties. Since I knew I was being targeted by the OAU/African Union, Michael and I had arranged for this approach in advance. "How did the Africans in the African diaspora fit into his new plan for Africa?" When the question was placed before Mr. Mandela, he seemed unprepared in front of world media.

Guess who tried and did influence Mr. Mandela's reply to my question. None other than the OAU representative Dr. V.E. D. Toko, acting Secretary General replacing Ambassador Youssoufou. Dr. Toko recognized me from the time I took over his OAU mission when I directed my IMSCO team place a closed casket at the doorsteps of the OAU mission on 52nd Street in Manhattan with the New York City police backing up our right to it. I tell you, my America can be a bitch when she decides to get it right with black people because it's then that America advances the farthest. Dr. Toko rushed across the platform with a note in his hand to warn Mr. Mandela of who I was. To Dr. Toko, I was a threat to the idea of a peace treaty that spelled war on blacks in America and blacks in South Africa's economic advances. I was not alone. Mr. Mandela's own wife Winnie Mandela and close to a billion other African people were not in support of his closed-door policy but kept quiet for now. In my views, the OAU, which was bought and paid for by the Americans and British, faced a harsh reality down the road sooner rather than later. Africans worldwide had all fought for a free South Africa, and the plan Mandela supported was worse than the biased, worthless Lancaster Agreement designed to kill as many African people in Zimbabwe as the Boer War had killed blacks in early South Africa, trying to dislodge the white land grabbers and squatters then and now. Toko's fear was facing in public a fearless black man on the attack, so again when I got the chance I put the heated bullet questions to the African leaders and representatives like I had his predecessor Ambassador Youssoufou who I had grilled with a diamond bit.

Being the statesman he was standing before the world at the United Nations, Mr. Mandela took a stab at answering my question. He was on the spot, and I had not been the one who placed him there. It was Mr. Toko that had jumped the gun on Mr. Mandela. Mr. Mandela's comment fell short of support for African diaspora return to Africa in mass like we had been forced to exit in mass. After Dr. Toko sat down, the room waited for Mr. Mandela to answer the important question.

"That is best left for the OAU," Mr. Mandela said, no doubt repeating what Dr. Toko had quickly written on the scrap of paper and rammed into his palm.

Mr. Mandela's vision was suddenly flawed for five hundred million black exiled family members. He was still very much uninformed about the trappings and workings of hidden deadly foreign political games of the twentieth century. Mandela could not know what many of us Africans knew having been locked away behind bars for twenty-seven years under the evil bootheels of white information control and apartheid. You can only smuggle so much to men behind bars after twenty years. I was not going to attack Mr. Mandela on his record in front of the world media. I wanted him to address the need for all Africans in the diaspora to be able to return home to Africa after apartheid. The way things were going only the whites' biased interest in South Africa was being protected. What Mr. Mandela did not know was that on an August afternoon at the United Nations in 1989 I had sent a letter to the OAU office in Addis Ababa, Ethiopia, requesting the organization respect dual citizenship rights for all oppressed Africans in the diaspora. The question was to Mr. Mandela.

"Mr. Mandela, do you support the rights of people of African descent in the diaspora to be included in these records and treaties?"

I wanted the question to Mr. Mandela to be placed on the records at the United Nations for history and the future to claim and own. I was determined not to have any African denied his or her birthright by anyone.

Following is the letter I sent to the OAU in 1989 spelling out the needs of unity with Africans in the diaspora:

To: His Excellency: OAU Executive Secretary-General of the OAU, SALIM AHMED SALIM (Regarding membership for Africans in the Diaspora) From: Frank Weston Chairman, (African Committee), "The organizations is committed to the goal of reuniting the African Diaspora with our homeland via a Global Economic Co-development Plan," wish to congratulate and welcome you as the new head of the OAU.

Excellency, "The year 1990 will be the year of the African." It will stand as a landmark for our people's return to greatness. So to this end African Americans via the African Committee call upon you, your good office, the African Heads of States and government and the people in our homeland to help reunite our family by fully supporting the effort of the African Committee as did wise former Executive Secretary-General, IDE OUMAROU in his commitment to our centuries of efforts to reunite and become a total part of our homeland during its good times as well as its bad. Excellency, our homeland has for years called upon African Americans for help in its time of need and we have always said yes. Now we need our homelands help. We need you to understand that we are oppressed in America and the only way to total freedom for us is to re-unite with our African homeland via a signed Co-Development Plan and full membership in our homeland via membership in the our) OAU (now African Union). In 1990 we seek observer status and by 1991 full membership. Please review the African Committee's file and letter sent to me from the OAU office by the OAU Secretary-General IDE OUMAROU; reference PL/GM/13 (VII) 77.89 Date 23 May 1989. Excellency, This is also, an official request to meet face to face with you on this pressing matter before our community. Yours Sincerely, Frank Weston Chairman, African Committee 17/8/89.

      The OAU Executive Secretary General Salim Ahmed Salim sent his official telex letter to me as a representative of the PAD's human rights to share our birthright and wealth in Africa on October 25, 1989, nine months after the OAU discredited Ambassador Youssoufou sent out the above biased letter that was sent to me for approval in New York City by members of Youssoufou's own office staff who were supporters of my organization's aims. I received a copy of the insulting letter to Africa people before it was posted. The staff member had asked if I wished the document sent out. I said, "Send the document out." Even after copies of the letter were sent to African missions and embassies, some of their staff informed me and sent copies of the ambassador's letter to me as a show of support.

      This is the telex sent by Executive Secretary General Salim Ahmed Salim confirming he

was Ambassador Youssoufou's OAU boss:
TELEX: 254971-ACUNDC 4 Park Avenue, New York, N.Y. 10016. Full stop.
Secretary-General SALIM AHMED SALIM of the OAU responded to my letter in a Telex letter addressed to me on October 25, 1989:
ETAT Mr. Frank Weston African Committee ACUNDC, 4 Park Avenue, New
     York NY 10016 MESG ID: WCB 275 UWNX From;
     ETHIOPA ETAD Addis Ababa
     1156/111 24/10 1702 P1/50 Mr. Frank Weston
African Committee ACUNDC, 4 Park Avenue, New York NY 10016, TX 0254971
SG2853 I thank you for your message of congratulations on election as SECGEN of the OAU stop like my predecessor comma I committed to your cause and will extend all possible cooperation stop as regards your desire for observer status and eventually full membership of OAU comma I wish to reiterate what SECGEN IDE OUMAROU told you in his letter PL/GM/13 (VII) 77.89 of 23.5.89 namely the criteria for such status stop I remain ready to meet you and extend on p3/11 this dialogue stop highest consideration full stop. SALIM AHMED SALIM OAU SECGEN COL CKD WCB257 ETW792 OAUC151.

13105 Northwest Freeway Suite 770
Houston, TX 77040

MCI WORLD MESSAGE SERVICE

Telegram · Cablegram · Postal Dispatch · Fax Dispatch

October 25, 1989

ETAT
MR FRANK WESTON
AFRICA COMMITTEE ACUNDC
4 PARK AVENUE
NEW YORK NY 10016

MESG ID : WCB257 UWNX
FROM :ETHIOPIA ETAD
ADDISABBA 115/111 24/10 1702 P1/50
ETAT
MR FRANK WESTON
AFRICA COMMITTEE ACUNDC
4 PARK AVENUE
NEW YORK NY 10016

TX 0254971
SG2853 I THANK YOU FOR YOU MESSGE OF CONGRATULATIONS
ON MY ELECTION AS SECGEN OF THE OAU STOP LIKE MY PREDECESSOR
COMMA I AM COMMITTED TO YOU CAUSE AND WILL EXTEND ALL
POSSIBLE COOPERATION
P2/50

STOP AS REGARDS YOUR DESIRE FOR OBSERVER
STATUS AND EVENTUALLY FULL MEMBERSHIP OF THE OAU COMMA I WISH
TO REITERATE WHAT SECGEN IDE OUMAROU TOLD YOU IN HIS LETTER
PL/GM/13 (VII) 77.89 OF 23.5.89 NAMELY THE CRITERIA FOR SUCH
STATUS STOP I REMAIN READY TO MEET YOU AND EXTEND ON
P3/11

THIS DIALOGUE STOP HIGHEST CONSIDERATION FULLSTOP
  SALIM AHMED SALIM
OAU SECGEN

COL CKD

WCB257 ETW792 OAUC151

MCII Cable Dispatch: 800-876-4471 (713-462-5900 from Texas)
Or to reply via telegram/cablegram call 201-585-3195

It may sound like the OAU secretary-general was cooperating, and I wanted very much to think so, trust me, but that was not the case. Though he was the representative of fifty-three African states as secretary-general, the e-mail, as good as it sounded, turned out to be a powerless political reply. The United States of America and the European Union's dirty hands and slander were behind the blinds calling the shots I was to learn later. It was all about the money the OAU was giving away to the enemy, the foreigners. You see, Africans in the Western world were no longer on the farms; we had jumped the ditch and the fence and headed for the cities worldwide leaving farming and heavy lifting to the former masters with now near-empty pockets and bankbooks that China was day by day taking control of. Never was I invited to sit at the table and discuss any of the issues I sent the OAU to address. You have to remember this was 1988, a few seconds in the run of the deer from the date of most African states' freedom. My team and I tried our best to turn the tides to cast some light on the subject, but in the end, we were shut out. The OAU representatives were all behaving like fools blind to the realities of managing the power Africans have. Mr. Mandela did his best, but he had no idea what the world was like when he came out of that hole he had been held in for twenty-seven years. But the people around him did or should have known, and they had a binding obligation to do something, but did nothing. The foundation for corruption, the foreign monopoly democracy, infests Africa. Needless to say, the OAU Secretary-General Salim Ahmed Salim or the African Union never implemented the written commitments, at least not at the writing of this book, but they will see to it that the commitment is carried out, or the people will carry them out. After nearly thirty years, one must conclude that it is force that is required to move on the African leaders to change the actions of the African Union (AU) to include and welcome PAD and Africans in the diaspora into our black continent's fold. We all know power, real power, is taken and never given, and only black men can give power to black men in African global affairs. Foreign-controlled and foreign-owned democracy in Africa challenges Africans in the diaspora and their rite of passage, having never given up anything based on how their ancestors left Africa.

In the letter above, the then Secretary-General Salim Ahmed Salim said the OAU was committed to the cause of the African American community to be reunited back into the continent and family fold. He kept his word that things would be a whole lot better in Africa to this day. The African Union would have power, African diaspora power, and respect in Africa. However, the matter of full dual citizenship in Africa and membership representation for Africans in the diaspora have yet to be fully carried forward. On December 2, 2002, Africans all over the diaspora were invited to meet in Washington to discuss the future role Africans in the diaspora will play in Africa's future. The event was funded by the African Union, and I was invited under the banner of IMSCO and the Global African Diaspora Union, founded to represent Africans in the diaspora. However, the outcome of the four-day meeting, called "The Foundation for Democracy in Africa," turned out to be a less than satisfactory attempt by the African Union to destroy the African diaspora's attempts to enter and share their African homeland. But be that as it may, African Americans and all Africans in the diaspora have a legal human and birthright to demand and hold dual citizenship and full membership in the now African Union regardless of what any person or government does or says. When African Americans take their right to vote, to dual citizenship, and to full membership in Africa, the world will fast become a great place to live. A free and all-inclusive African people means endless opportunities for the people of the planet. The 1 percent of the white males or Europeans who control 99 percent of the wealth can only hold on to this economic and development control by enslavement of a set percentage of the people, like 99 percent of the population. Africa is the wealth base for those who would continue to oppress humans, animals, and nature. These are deadly facts most of us live and breathe each painful day of our lives. Out here in this big universe, wherever we are, there is enough space and resources for all humans and animals to be free to live quality lives.

It is unthinkable that Africans depend on poor white males in America and Europe, or Asia even, to do the thinking, taking, stealing, and managing African wealth while they become rich and interfere with Africa's economic and political development. This is unthinkable and unacceptable.

Denmark was the first European country to abolish slavery in 1803, followed by the not so Great Britain in 1807. The United States of America claims to have abolished the trade in 1808, when in fact actual economic and political slavery did not start to crack in African Americans' favor until 1964 when African Americans trashed much of their enslavement using brute force and economic and global political weapons. Africans were never given anything, which is the reason for countless millions of Africans being victimized economically and politically by Chinese and Europeans today who are out to grab African land wealth and future. Now Africans must realize freedom is not free. Freedom will cost money and lots of it, and this freedom will need education and advanced weapons to protect that freedom especially as African Americans have witnessed in a democracy. In 1990, millions of African men, women, and children were in prison in America for life twice: once for being uneducated and black in America and twice for being forced to live without a culture that can restart their ruined lives and link with lost family or a free will needed to enable them to play by their terms on a level playing field. They need the proper motivation to obtain a quality education, have a business culture, and develop their own employment to guide them in the fight to survive. The final solution for the poor and uneducated in America still seems to be prison or death by neglect. It can get better, but it will take time. I am not at all certain America or the EU has time.

I am not suggesting African Americans or any PAD living in the Western diaspora should give up their Western or European citizenship. Africans have made more of a contribution in America than the former slave masters or many of their descendants, beginning with the late Harriet Tubman, the bedrock for the African American revolutionary foundation in America. The final solution for Africans in the diaspora and in Africa is linking through culture, economics, and dual citizenship now. This was the question and the issue Dr. Toko wanted to prevent Mr. Mandela addressing before the world. Toko knew I had been in contact with the OAU head office in Addis Ababa, and he knew I was committed to staying the course. He understood the power of the question being put to Mr. Mandela.

But did Mr. Mandela understand? What type of blindness were their African men suffering from? Around that time I had requested and received a signed, supported document for African codevelopment, coownership, and comanagement on a fifty-fifty basis from Archbishop Desmond Tutu of South Africa. Nelson Mandela's own wife had been onboard with the idea since before Nelson was released, and she had invited me to visit her in South Africa to present me with a pending cable TV license as a form of support to help link the people of South Africa and Africans in the diaspora. It was clear Mr. Mandela had not been properly briefed or debriefed at all since his twenty-seven years of confinement. Debriefing and briefing African representatives properly on where their collective power bases are is one of the most important things to be done in the global African community, but who has the time to wait for dead men to rise? There it is again: the black man's burden of being trapped between the Cross and the Koran. Africans were carrying the white man's burden; all his failures and our wealth were paying most of the world's bills with Africa receiving aid taken from African Americans and their community today to the tune of trillions of dollars a year if not month in some cases.

While most of the people in black Africa welcome or would welcome their exiled family's return to Africa, some African leaders see the African diaspora as a political and economic threat to their corrupt games with foreigners. Watch the white and Asian hands that are greasing southern black Africans' hands and witness the crumbs from the tables of the African land occupied by Arabs; the

Cross and the Koran are the main stumbling blocks for all PAD returning to Africa's bountiful table, which is able to feed the entire African family. Has President Nelson Mandela's leadership and those who follow in the ANC dashed Africans' hope and promoted white dreams of conquest in Africa? Every multinational organization under white control in the world, including every country in Europe and the United States of America, pretended to rejoice in the release of Nelson Mandela from his years in prison as a great white hope and moral trophy reflecting white bigheartedness. Thanks to Nelson Mandela, the white settlers' illegal claim on Africa's wealth will remain in their hands and banks for the moment. Now the white men in South Africa and their profit-sharing stockholders and allies in the west could continue to walk (work) black dogs, a metaphor for black men used in a classic doomsday prediction song about America in "A Hard Rain's Gonna Fall." The white jackals it seems are being watched by more than just Africans or the poor in developing countries. Europeans and their African clones continue to defraud Africans on both sides of the Atlantic out of their cultural birthright, land, wealth, human rights, and educational needs. To rid Africa and it people of lagging colonialism and sleazebag imperialists afraid of fair trade, even the most uneducated African Africans must take full ownership control and move away from the European abyss as China has done. China has not come close to educating its full work force. Chinese people are learning as they go the way we Africans have done in the past and must continue to do today. All one needs is a brain and the resources, and in Africa, we have the best of both.

We must protect children from future

capitalist pitfalls, economic hit men and women, and imported killer diseases. HIV/AIDS is a disease many Africans have the right to feel is a doomsday weapon imported from Europe and America that wishes Africans dead! Africans don't date monkeys, so the disease had to get into the population somehow. IMSCO was told by an employee in the eighties at Doctors Without Borders not to trust them and to warn Africans. I did inform as many health departments in a number of African nations and even spoke with African representatives at the United Nations for what it was worth. Still African people are dying of just about everything imaginable, and why? Africans have looked after themselves since mankind first stood upright on our planet and gave birth to humankind. Could all this and more be happening because Africans are rich, maybe too rich to have friends? Equality is clearly linked to education.

Chapter 35

Meeting Warrior Winnie Mandela

I returned to South Africa, rented a house in Jo'burg, near fashionable Sandton City, chilled, and went to meet confidentially with Winnie Mandela, who like sister Rosa Parks in America was on steroids against racism! Winnie was at the time Nelson Mandela's devoted, stand-by-your-man wife whose decades of struggle and leadership of a people had forced the ungrateful ANC her way into a position in the ailing black South African government. I needed inspiration and partnership after the depressing lack of vision from Nelson Mandela at the UN press conference earlier. Winnie had heard about my work and life quest, and she offered to help. During that visit to Johannesburg, Winnie offered guidance and agreed to support me in obtaining a license to open a cable TV station to broadcast African international voices and cultural events. Winnie had been given a post as Deputy Minister of Art, Culture, Science, and Technology and wanted to use her new post to help shed some much needed light on the suffering people in South Africa. She was also under attack from blacks and whites that feared her. Winnie and I worked hard at gaining final government approval, but the forces around her were just too strong and too numerous, so time ran out, and I had to return to New York City to wait out the process. Back in New York, I made contact with the United States Agency for International Development (USAID) in Washington, DC, and sent them a written request for cooperation and funding for the media project Winnie had offered. I was received and held talks that seemed to suggest I would receive the funding once approval was granted to operate the cable TV station in Johannesburg, South Africa. It was the first hint of a possible fix. Winnie was the voice, and she had the power to grant the right and approval, which is why I was requesting the money from USAID. Winnie was the voice and one of the most important voices and in that lay the problem: hidden forces in Washington and beyond wanted Winnie fenced in, muzzled, or dead as did most whites in South Africa and still do in fact! The word "approval" went right over my head. Approval for whom? Hell, Winnie was then the power of the people, still are in fact.

The first multicultural elections included the voting rights for all white settlers and no African Americans or Africans in the diaspora. Suddenly, it was Christmas for every white person in South Africa. This is how white settlers got their groove back. We hit it off! Winnie could have ruled that country and would have done a much better job in healing the people and moving the country for Africans in the right direction. Instead all the black people of South Africa got was a flood of foreign direct economic hit men and women who were bent on taking the black people back to the abyss or back of the bus. After running into yet more roadblocks from foreigner interference, I longed for historical cultural meaning, renewal, relaxation, and truthful mental stimulation, so I flew back to Cairo, Egypt, the former capital of ancient Africa where civilization began. Winnie, to me, was Queen Hatshepsut, and I felt like King Tutankhamen at war. In spite of the dark Arab madness shroud hanging over Egypt, for now it seemed just the place to help me get my groove back, focus, and get a grip on the next stage of advancing my plan to find a way to help get my land and wealth back for all the people even those who thought they were doomed forever in the West or Africa.

Chapter 36

Rise of Civilization in Egypt

The large door between first class and coach swung open on Trans World Airline, soon to suffer the same fate as the late Pan Am Airways, Air Afrique, and Zambia Airways: go bust and go out of business. The fifteen-hour journey from New York to Cairo, Egypt, was filled with excitement and wonder. Each time I return to Egypt, I find a part of myself carved in ten thousand years of granite. Egypt was the cultural payoff for me.

I was seated close to the door when it was pulled open by the hostess. The smell of the musty, dry desert air rushed into the cabin and entered both my nostrils and lungs, reminding me of some long-lost ancient part of myself. Including this time, I will have visited Egypt more often than any other country in the world. All was not well in Egypt, however. Long before I was born, Asian, Arab, and European looters crawled into Egypt and desecrated ancient African temples and holy tombs of pharaohs, even before Alexander the Great plundered the country. Then there were the Arab invaders starting in the eleventh century, followed by the British and French, not always in that order, who entered and continued the beastly illegal plundering of mankind's greatest ancient achievements in law, religion, science, astrology, engineering, technology, medicines, and culture to name a few giant steps for mankind. Even with all this, Egypt still held fast to much of its greatness and splendor. As the aging, British-made taxi crept like the dying empire it had become through the maze of Cairo traffic and people, clogging every inch of space on the roads, streets, and walkways, my heart was pumping so much dust and filthy air polluting my blood and flowing to my brain that I felt a dizziness. If I were a religious believer, I could have easily been confused with a feeling of the Holy Spirit. After departing the airport and passing the once holy city of Eliopoulos, I forgot about the dangerous dust and poisonous air circulating inside the taxi produced by the sixteen million Cairo inhabitants' frantic efforts to stay alive that made this part of the beautiful Nile River undrinkable unlike the clean Congo River, the last clean river on earth. After a few days in a dying Cairo visiting the Pyramids of Giza, I boarded an overnight train to Aswan, Upper Egypt, to catch some fresh air. The aging British train the Arabs were too religious or disinterested in to improve somehow made it through the African starry night. During the night, I was seated in what was seen as a very shabby first-class coach: no bed, no water, and a hole to piss and dump in that fell on to the moving rails. You bring food or do without. The rattling eighteenth century train followed the Nile River south toward Sudan for twelve hours to Aswan where the largest population of the Nubians, our descendants still lived.

Nubians and pharaohs of the holy land were still holding on to as much of our original culture in the face of the continual Arab attacks failing to uproot them. The Nubian people are the original people who built Egypt, and like the indestructible civilization we Africans built, they clung on still waiting for backup: African descent backup from the Western world. At real risk were the priceless artifacts, ruins, and tombs still holding the remains of ancient pharaohs, queens, and kings. Boy King Tutankhamen (King Tut) and Queen Hatshepsut ruled here a few trillion hours ago and their ghosts still wait for the day when the Nubian rule would return, drive the invaders out forever, retake the throne of power, and rebuild the empire of Egypt as the capital of Africa.

It was early morning when I stepped from the belly of the rusting tin and steel beast into the hundred-degree heat blowing in with the sands from the Nubian Desert. I fought my way through a thick crowd of Arabs and a few tourists milling about seemingly aimlessly. Most of the people were dressed in long gray robes dragging in the dirt. Not a country for fashion I can tell you that. I made my way to the Aswan Hotel and checked into a local hand-built hotel with flooring that cried out with each step. It totally fit into the rest of Egypt's fading infrastructure and buildings that the Arabs had not lifted a hammer or board to improve since their eleventh century exile from the Middle East desert. The Chinese were here starting their construction at the Aswan Nile River bank to install a boat landing dock. In the outer areas, the foreign gravediggers and thieves were busy searching for scraps to patch up the holes in their budgets back home or steal for European and American museums. During my one-week stay in Aswan, I would be invited into the Nubians' royal circle and receive what amounted to the title of Nubian Prince. I was given a three-thousand-year old scarab belonging to Queen Hatshepsut for safe keeping. The queen's name is carved inside the royal cartouche, which was no doubt buried at one time with her in her royal tomb. There was an image of the Pharaoh Hatshepsut seated inside the royal cartouche still in mint condition, where her name is spelled out in Egyptian hieroglyphs. She is holding a royal scepter with the head and half body of a lion carved over her head. The jackal stood at the top among the finely carved hieroglyphs with a loaf of bread and what could be a boat (solar bark). At the bottom of the cartouche are three strokes and what seems to be a half-moon.

For certain, the 3500 BC scarab bearing Hatshepsut's name was very old and genuine. The gift was to honor my return and for assisting the Nubians in their struggle against the oppressive Arabs and Islamists demanding that they abandon their African cultures and adopt Arab culture instead. The unwelcome European version is of Christianity forced into the African mindset while enslaved, which ruined many a man, woman, and child. This was done by descendants of those who did harm in the name of God and now wish the victims to believe that God has called them to heal the victims with the lies told in God's name. Salman Rushdie's book *The Satanic Verses* does a much better study than I could ever do. I mention Salman Rushdie's book because it seems unwelcome foreign belief systems, religion, and the Western system have had more negative effects on my life, my development, and my community than any other invading force. Working with and bonding with the Nubian population among hostile Arabs that hate everyone was not the kind of North African homecoming I wanted, so like the rest of the rational world, I turned a blind eye and let live. The Nubians told me it was very hard for Africans under an Arab system. It was fine for me to visit and travel to Egypt because I carried an American passport and spoke differently from my black brothers, most who had been forced deeper south to the border of Sudan in a place called Aswan. Nubians were not the only ones caught in this cultural warp. Most Egyptians were forced to accept being a Muslim, face a fate worse than death, or total banishment. Nubians chose to be banished to keep their own culture. There, they suffered the fate of every black African in Arab-occupied areas in North Africa since the eleventh century.

Without a doubt, it was the Nubians who build the once-great ancient empire that lived still among splendid ruins and once-golden temples. For centuries, the world outside would be hard-pressed to learn of this wonder the Africans built. Then darkness fell, and Arab and European thieves rushed in calling themselves historians, reducing African culture and history into the abyss of horror. To me, the Nubians are the most important clan in the African community because they gave mankind its first civilization. That can never be hidden or changed. How demented are the thieves who plundered Egypt. How proud I was to walk among the Nubians. I promised the Nubian elders that African Americans would continue to assist them until they were returned to power in Egypt and could unite once more Upper and Lower Egypt, indeed unite all of Africa from Cape Town to Cairo. You think I am tripping, smoking something, or drinking too much palm wine. We will see. I predict African unity will come, and it will come as a direct result of actions taken by people in South Africa and the African diaspora. I predict Egypt will be retaken.

Egypt was not the only African state faced with such ills. It became clear to me that a secret war brought on by Arabs, Europeans, and American corporations was forcing the Nubians in Sudan's southern and western region, boarding the nation of Chad called Darfur, further and further south into the desert to face certain death if the Arab-controlled army did not slaughter the unarmed women, children, and old men first. The war between their forces had been ongoing for some fifteen hundred years or more, and the Nubians, like many Africans globally including yours, truly were still refusing to submit to Islam, Christianity, or Arabian Western rule over them and their cultures. Over the centuries, millions of Nubians had died but still they stood and fought like those of us in America and across the African diaspora. But the Nubians had done something very special. The Nubians had somehow maintained their cultural dignity and self-respect even though their cities, towns, and villages had been often burned, still they stood and fought. I made up my mind then and there I would travel south into Sudan. This was before the Nubian big split from the Arab-held North Sudan that controlled all resources, selling all to the Europeans who could take the heat and lazy Americans who wanted everything for nothing, leaving the Africans as they had left African Americans and South Africans with not even a place to take a Nat nap. It was time now to take the fight back to the invaders and oppressors. Yes, I would team with the Nubians and join the fight just as soon as I could arrange it. Later, I went sailing on the Nile River and drowned myself in thoughts of a grander Egypt and Sudan. I imagined myself being there dressed in the entire fashion and splendor of an earlier African culture, and I loved being here in this land called Egypt and Sudan. And nothing, nothing would ever cause that love of self to be abandoned or to disrespect African cultural belief systems. It was saving my life.

Chapter 37

Harlem, Black Soul of America

Years later while visiting Harlem, I came across some written words bolted to a wall inside the 110 Street West subway station. The words stopped me in my tracks and held me still until I had finished reading them. Placed there by the city in honor of the African American community, the words suggested I was not alone in my yearning to be back in Africa from where I came. The unforgettable timeless words taken from ancient writings in Egypt read: "I lived in Egypt. I stayed in Egypt, and I was among brothers and I felt the spirit of brotherhood." This was the case for me everywhere I set foot in my golden Africa land.

As I walked up the near half mile long ramp leading to the holy temple of Queen Hatshepsut, I knew then that I, like all Africans, was invincible. All that the Western world had tried to take from me and my spirit amounted to no more than what harm a feather could do falling on to the granite pillars in the Great Gallery of Khufu's Pyramid. As an African man, no enemy of my people would ever have more power, never stand more erect than I.

The great obelisks commissioned by Queen Hatshepsut would from that day forward represent where my spine and my manhood would come from and stand as the foundation on which my providence would stand; the Great Sphinx would serve as the symbol of wisdom I sought, and the Nile River would represent my lifeblood, veins, and renewed culture. Why would any African, particularly after being held captive for centuries, continue to turn against his or her ancestors' culture and belief systems? Africans must never abandon their culture; to do so means abandoning African blood and land. In Egypt I came to realize that it is better to stand against all mankind rather than turn against my ancestors' belief systems and the rich powerful timeless cultures they developed. I made an oath that I would willingly give my life before I ever strayed from my culture for any foreign culture or belief used to steal African land and wealth. After that visit, I would return to Egypt often. Each time I visited this part of North Africa, I was interested in looking closer, much closer at the history of this area south of Aswan, the great land called Nubia, the land of the blacks, Sudan. Here, the blacks are still fighting a two-thousand-year-old war with the Arabs armed with European super weapons, tanks, and the so-called sword of Islam. The European-armed nukes, jet fighters, and the sword of a biased Western brand of Christianity are all floating in lakes of blood drained from slaughtered Africans down through the centuries leaving Africans like me who survived and left with nothing more than the sun-kissed skin on our bones.

The foreigners were pushing hard against the near defenseless Africans crippled with useless death aid promoted by European rock stars and movie superstars, most of whom were more interested in selling box office tickets. Then there is the biased media control by corporate-sponsored commercials at $50,000,000 a minute and the mind-altering political pimps using the people's United Nations to cook up resolutions to rip Sudan apart in order to divide it and the spoils so as to patch up holes in their failed system's budget while calling this crime against humanity protection for black people. Just look at where 5,055 million other African diaspora people in the world were stashed. Now Africa resembles what it did in the nineteenth century. I was there to witness much of this in the field, on the ground in Sudan, and at the United Nations. Yes, I was there to witness the Western system and Arab insults claiming to partner to solve an age-old African problem they created by using the United Nations soon after the colonial powers founded the world body by granting independency to illegal Arab squatters in North Africa. They knowingly aimed to create yet another African cultural-unity miscarriage by cutting the rich, black Sudanese baby in half (Arab North and black South), creating a trillion nightmares in order to get at black mother Africa's umbilical cord linked to the young, independent, black nation full of rich mineral resources such as gum arabic, crude oil, and gold. Hell, Sudan was ancient Egypt's bank if you did not know this. The wealth found in north and south Sudan today is the main reason Western member states refused to grant black African states independence in the fifties until a deal was cut at the United Nations with the invading Arabs into North Africa to secure the north for themselves. Now that deal was falling apart, and a new shady scheme had to replace the old deal. Also, this was a fight between the Christians, Jews, Chinese Americans, Europeans, and the Arabs to grab as much of Africa as possible before the likes of me return. This would soon be proven, not that more proof was needed, through documents leaked to me from the American embassy in Arab-held Khartoum, Sudan. US Department of State e-mails, dated and stamped detailing such human right violations aimed at Africans, will be provided later on in this book. First, let's take a look at the spoils the band of human and cultural death angels had grabbed in South Africa in 1992 (the evil years) and now were in the process of looting ever so slowly like the sand draining through an hourglass or a too tightly held fist.

Chapter 38

Date with Apartheid South Africa

In 1992, political apartheid went down for the count, not economics.

Postapartheid South Africa: 2005

Republic of South Africa Area: 1,219,916 sq. km (470,566 sq. mi)

Population: 43,586,000

Capital (population): Cape Town (legislative, 2,350,000), Pretoria (administrative, 1,080,000), Bloemfontein (judiciary, 300,000)

Government: African controlled as a multiparty republic with a bicameral legislature (1994). The first multiparty election was held in April 1994, and after that all internal boundaries were changed and the separate homelands abolished. The bank, land, and mineral resources remained under white control.

Ethnic Groups: blacks 76 percent, white 13 percent, mixed race 9 percent, Asians 2 percent

Languages: Ndebele, Sotho, Swazi, Tosonga, Tswana, Vanda, Xhosa, Zulu, Afrikaans, English, and Mandarin

Religions: Christian 68 percent, Islam 2 percent, and Hinduism 1 percent

What's missing here is the African belief system before Christian, Muslim, and Hindu, so who is in control?

Currency: Rand = 100 cents

Annual Income: Per non-African person $2,560.00

Main Primary Product: Gold, iron ore, copper, uranium, diamonds, coal, tin, phosphates, and 100 percent cheap black labor

Main Industries: Mining, iron and steel, vehicles, food processing, oil refining, agriculture, clothing, and 80 percent cheap African labor. Foreigners from the European Union, Eastern and Western Asia, and white Americans mostly own these industries all using black gold energy

Main Exports: Gold 39 percent, base metals 14 percent, mineral products 10 percent, pearls, chemical products, and African youth

Main Imports: Mechanical equipment 31 percent, transport equipment 14 percent, chemical products 11 percent, and 100 percent cheap African labor

Tourism: 2,892,000 visitors per year, mostly whites from Europe and America

At the time of this writing, the ANC was in power, and no visas were required for Americans to enter South Africa, but to remain for long periods a temporary residence permit was required. They had it all. British, Germans, Dutch, a cross section of the whole of Europe, white Americans, Jews, Chinese from Taiwan, Arabs (excluding Libya), and a select group of Asians were all supporters of apartheid. They were all trying to grab African land and wealth and prevent Africans in the diaspora from returning home to link with their people and take part in the rebuilding, the very African culture these foreigners spent centuries trying to destroy. The black man and woman in Africa and in the Western world are under attack because of their vast wealth, not the tone of their skin. Europeans, Arabs, and Asians are all promoting racism within their ranks and societies as a weapon and to hide their poverty. To that end, the battle for South Africa and the rest of the continent is far from over.

The flight I was on to Johannesburg, South Africa, took about eighteen hours from New York. Molefe had assured me that the diamonds would be there and that a member of the PAC would meet me at the airport, a man a few years younger than me by the name of Sweetboy.

South Africa is a land of rich rolling plateaus within a mountainous range that rims its territory on the seaward side and separates the coastal cities of Cape Town and Durban from the inland centers of Pretoria and Johannesburg, where I was now headed. Each time I fly back to South Africa, I am rendered speechless by the grandness and beauty of the four billion-year-old landscape. As the plane I was on approached South Africa, I imagined my distant ancestor on his first hunt of the season for food seeking his first kill so the clan could eat and remain strong. My hunt for all manner of freedom had taken me from Alabama to New York, Europe, and now back home to Africa and for the same reason. Sweetboy would be waiting for me at Johannesburg International Airport, and he and I would travel by car to the northern part of the country where mineral-rich Zimbabwe shares the border with South Africa and the world's largest vein of platinum, about 98 percent of the important mineral to reach the area where the diamonds were supposed to be held for us. En route to South Africa,

I thought about how rich Africa was and how cash poor our people were in Africa and in the African diaspora. I thought about how a few Europeans and Arabs had held all the land and wealth since the Boer War and World War II, but we Africans were now fighting our way back. Apartheid may have been kicked out of the "Matrix," but we were now facing economic apartheid war and the whites, like those in Zimbabwe, were dug in deep in South Africa. I had not yet entered university, but I had developed a wide range of knowledge about my Africa, its people, wealth, and land. Knowledge is power, and flying in I could not help thinking about the power of my vastly wealthy Africa and African people.

If you think I am talking through my hat about African power, that I am dreaming, check out some of these carefully researched mineral facts and numbers below. In short, Africans hold the winning hands and always have. Southern black Africa and Russia control 80 percent of the cotton and 89 percent to 99 percent of the world's supply of strategic minerals; 96 percent of the chrome; 99 percent of the platinum group metals; 98 percent of the manganese; 89 percent of the diamonds; 68 percent of the gold; 25 uranium; and 40 percent of the vanadium, to name just a few. But look closer at what's in Africa when it comes to understanding the power of strategic mineral management, usage, and values. As political economic apartheid in America, South Africa, and Europe bites the dust, a new force of power, PAD, rise to the challenge as a winning hand for restoring organized united African power. The power is already here if only the people will open their eyes to this reality of vast wealth they own, is hidden under the biased press type dictated by multinational companies and media. But watch out!

The black family smell, total victory! It's here baby. Refined the above name minerals are found under ever hood of every automobile, in every computer, inside cell phones, airplane engines and trains, the cargo the train carries and the rails they travel over, and every copper wire. It's all done with the use of African mineral wealth. Africa is the foundation of America, Europe, China, and the whole industrial world. I agree with the saying "The hands that control the ores of the earth will control the earth itself." When the minerals and value-added finished goods are moving out of Africa through African hands and industries to African links in the diaspora, Africans worldwide will be the super power brokers their rite of passage demands. Africans have the tools to turn poverty and intimidation into vast wealth and power. Africans and people of goodwill around the world, look at what is in our hands.

Chapter 39

African / PAD Vast Wealth & Power

The study of science and the physical world is the key to understanding Africa's landmass. Three times the size of America, China, or parts of all of Europe, Africa holds the largest cultivable landmass on earth.

Copper
Africa holds a reported 14 percent of the world's supply of copper. I say reported because no European or Asian will provide Africans with the true available amounts of vital resources in Africa. The only way Africans will know is for African Americans to use their right to the Western-held mineral knowledge bank to know for certain, and even then more and more of Africa's wealth is being discovered daily. Copper is one of the most essential metals, and its annual world consumption exceeds that of any other nonferrous metal. The main properties making it such a desired commodity are its high electric and anticorrosion, its ductility, malleability, and high strength, and its attractive appearance. It can readily be alloyed with other metals to form various brasses, bronzes, and gold. Some of the more important uses are in the manufacture of electrical equipment, home appliances, and materials used in communication, transportation, construction, and

decoration. The largest single consumption is in the electrical industry, which accounts for approximately 50 percent of the demand. Aluminum, plastic, steel, glass, and various other materials can be used as substitutes, but in some instances copper is irreplaceable, and when in adequate supply, it is preferred for many purposes. Copper is an excellent investment. Africans should do what they have always done. Invest in the land and in the people that own the land and wealth not the goats on Wall Street and other economic traps that have sprung up around the globe and Africa. These economic traps are just that, and they will steal you blind if you trust them.

Uranium

Africa's share is 25 percent. Once Russia is added, it's 40 percent of the world supply. The demand for enriched uranium used in the production of nuclear warheads has in recent decades been far outstripped by the requirement of a growing number of uranium-fuelled electrical power plants. Naturally occurring uranium is composed of a mixture of three isotopes: 99.3 percent U238, 0.7 percent U-235, and trace amounts of U-234. Most commercial power reactors require uranium containing about 3 percent of the U-235 isotope. This is produced through an enrichment process, which leaves a uranium component correspondingly depleted in U-235. Owing to its high density and pyrophoric properties, this mildly radioactive depleted uranium is much used in armour-piercing projectiles with smaller quantities being consumed in the manufacture of counterweights in aircraft, radiation shielding for medical applications, and catalysts in specialized chemical processes. Africa has full capabilities to develop advanced weapons for protection.

Uranium is rare and commands high prices. It is found in mass in the DRC, once totally under the control of the bloodsucking King Leopold II of Belgium who claimed the territory the size of America at gun point and machete blade for himself as the rest of the European powers were squatting and planting their blood-soaked flags around our beloved Africa during the 1870s. The horror visited on Africans was just the beginning of the inhumanness. During World War II, European plunderers took control of Africa's, Congo DRC vast supply of deadly radioactive uranium contents and dropped the atomic bomb on Hiroshima, Japan. Still uranium is an excellent investment. Its also good, bad, and ugly all at once The world's largest mine for uranium is located in Shinkolobwe, where the powerful deadly ore is found. It is located in a region of the DRC called Katanga.

The power is yours to make them come to you. Make those who need the minerals and resources come to you. You take the investment money and invest it near you in your country, land, and people. Why must China ship raw materials to China? Why not keep the factory at home and even in the bush where you can relax after work over a traditional fire and make love to your woman or man near the easy flowing river? This is what the exporters do.

Vanadium
Africa's share combined with Russia's makes up 100 percent of the world supply. The main use of vanadium is as a hardening agent in steel. It forms hard, stable, heat-resistant carbides used in high-speed tools, steels, and rotors. It is also important in

catalysts of certain chemical reactions, notably as vanadium pentoxide in the production of sulfuric acid. Vanadium is most commonly produced as a byproduct or coproduct from the mining of other elements such as uranium, phosphorus, or iron, and it is also recovered from crude oil residues and tar sands. In igneous rocks, it is relatively abundant in titaniferous magnetite and other magnetic iron ores. Vanadium commands high prices. Again, this is an excellent investment. Africans must partner with Africans in the diaspora to control the economics of the business and ensure the finished products get into the overseas markets.

Bauxite

Africa's share of bauxite is 36 percent. It is a common residual or transported constituent of clay deposits in tropical and subtropical regions and occurs in concretionary, compact, earthy, or pisolitic forms. Bauxite is the principal commercial source of aluminum. It was bauxite that the West was most afraid to let African people control, even to make their own cooking pots and pans. Africans must make their own daily household and industrial items.

Gold

Africa's share of gold is 54 percent, and it's 68 percent of world supply when Russia's share is added. Gold is widely used in industries and accepted as the most stable monetary item in the world. Gold is widely used in dentistry and medicine and has long been used in articles of jewelry, where its value, strength, and workability make it an attractive mount for gemstones. The metal is rare and commands high prices. Gold is an excellent investment. Africans must move to nationalize every mine in Africa, the Caribbean, and South America as community property and enlist boards of governors to oversee the management of the global community gold reserves. Put Africa on the gold standard, and keep it there regardless of what the World Bank and IMF say because these Western agencies don't have a clue what the hell they are doing mainly because they have nothing to base their advice on but failure in Africa and the Western world pays in the end. China tossed the West out of China, and the rest is history. Africans do not need Western credit; the Western world needs African credit. Why would you sell it? Sell the paper to the foreigners stating how much your gold is worth, and keep the mineral at home in the ground for the future generations.

Cobalt
Africa's share of cobalt is 68 percent. It is indispensable for the production of mining, machine tools, and long, sustained magnets. Its resistance to high temperature and terrific stress makes cobalt a basic necessity in the function of jet engines. The metal is rare and commands high prices. This is an excellent investment.

Coltan
Coltan (short for columbite-tantalite) is a rare metal that conducts heat unusually brilliantly. It is the metal contained in global community cell phones, your laptop, and your child's PlayStation. Of the world's supply of coltan, 80 percent rests beneath the muck and mud in the DRC. Coltan has to be one of the world's top investments, and it can be controlled easily by Africans on both sides of the Atlantic as

well as throughout Asia. With coltan and tin alone, Africans control the modern world supply. Africans are fools to let the unrefined minerals leave the continent. Manufacture the finished product in the Congo and other locations in Africa and the global African diaspora community, or at least keep it under African ownership and tight controls. It's easy to do this. The investments will come from China alone when Africans in the diaspora demand it on behalf of Africans. Just establish an African coltan and tin club for members only, and the world would be ours. Apple and Silicon Valley wouldn't operate without coltan. Many people know, but most do not realize that it's the mineral that mostly comes from the DRC and other remote areas of the plant. This is the mineral that makes the modern computer and electronic world of ours work. African people own a controlling share of this vital mineral, and that means one important thing: black people own a controlling stake and interest in what makes the world and Silicon Valley work.

Tin

Tin was found in abundance in eastern Congo and a few other places on earth. It fuels the world cell phone and computer industry as a conductor, and without this African resource, the electronics of the world would not operate as well if at all for modern demands to drive jet engines and the space industry. Since this metal is rare and commands high prices, it is an excellent investment.

Tantalum

Africa's share of tantalum is 70 percent. Tantalum is an easily fabricated ductile metal with a high melting point and strong resistance to corrosion by most acids. Although tough and durable, it is easier to work with and weld than most refractory metals. Over half the world's tantalum production is consumed in capacitors and other electronic components. It is also used in machine tools as a carbide often blended with other carbides, in corrosion-resistant chemical processing ware, and in refractory super alloys for the aerospace industry. The metal is rare and commands high prices. Tantalum is an excellent investment.

Platinum

Africa's share of platinum is 85 percent. With Russia's share, it's 99 percent of the world's supply. The value of platinum to modern industry lies in its exceptional catalytic activity, chemical inertness over a wide temperature range, and high melting point. The largest single application is in platinum-palladium catalytic reactions used to reduce the emission of carbon monoxide and hydrocarbons from light-duty vehicles. Another catalytic use is in the manufacture of nitric acid, mainly for fertilizer production. Its chemical inertness makes it a valuable material for laboratory equipment, such as crucibles, exposed to highly corrosive conditions. Platinum is widely used in dentistry and medicine and has long been used in articles of jewelry, where its value, strength, and workability make it an attractive mount for gemstones. The metal is rare and commands high prices. This is an excellent investment.

Chromium

Africa's share of chromium is 99 percent. With

Russia's share, you corner the market. The metal is rare and commands high prices. Chromium is one of industry's essential and most versatile elements. Mainly used in stainless steel, to which it imparts excellent corrosion and oxidation resistance, it is also a constituent of a variety of alloy steels, cast irons, and nonferrous alloys in which it enhances mechanical properties and produces special properties of electrical, abrasion, corrosion, and oxidation resistance. Some is consumed in the refractory industry as chromite bricks. Green, orange, and yellow pigments of chromium represent its largest use in the chemical industry. The chromium plating on vehicles and other consumer goods is also derived from chromium chemicals. The metal commands high prices and is an excellent investment.

Diamond

Africa's share of diamonds combined with Russia's is 89 percent of the world's supply. Diamond is the high-pressure form of carbon. It surpasses all other minerals in hardness and is highly prized as a gemstone. Industrial- quality material is used for cutting, grinding, and drilling and is particularly adaptable to automated cutting and grinding processes where the capacity to operate unattended for long periods is necessary. Diamonds formed in pipes of dikes of an ultramafic rock are called kimberlitic. They rose explosively toward the surface from great depths in the earth as a volatile, rich magma carrying fragmented blocks of the wall rocks. Both kimberlitic and secondary alluvial or marine placer deposits are exploited. Diamond gemstones are rare and command high prices. Diamond is an excellent investment. So important was the diamond that it was DRC diamonds that single-handedly won World War II by insuring the so-called Western allies the toolmaking ability over the Germans after the allies outbid them to obtain this pure carbon. It was the diamonds that drilled and cut the gun barrels and steel to make the tanks and other equipment needed to fight and win World War II.

Manganese

Africa's share of manganese of about 65 percent combined with Russia's share is 99 percent of the world supply. About 95 percent of manganese ore mined worldwide is used in iron and steel production. It fulfills a variety of functions: improving strength, toughness, hardness, and workability of the steel and acts as a deoxidizer and desulfurizer. Manganese is an excellent investment.

Crude Oil and Gas

There are seven countries in sub-Saharan Africa to name a few that produce substantial quantities of crude oil: Gabon, Angola, Nigeria, Sudan, Ivory Coast, Equatorial Guinea, and Congo. The crude oil in Libya, Algeria, and Sudan are also a part of the African wealth belt, and the fact that Arab culture is there must not in any way stop Africans in the diaspora from moving in and demanding a fair share of the wealth and opportunities in those areas. Most African leaders and countries continue to give African wealth, power, and future away to nations, clans, and people who insult Africans daily with our own resources that we can and must develop and refine to make our economy grow so we can do for ourselves just as we are now growing degrees from

BAs to PhDs in science and physics. With the amount of resource power that Africans own, they can now team up and supply the world with credit, not beg for credit from resource-poor Western and Asian blocks. It's not hard to do. African men and women just need to focus on what our community needs and work as a team to supply those needs instead of standing by and letting others supply us with outdated technologies that will take years to catch up with the rest of the world. The Arabs in much of Saudi Arabia did not have much education after the British departed, and they have done all right so far. The global Africa that can say no must now just say no!

Gum Arabic before Invasion "Natural Gum" Now

Invading Arabs pushing into North Africa in the ninth century stole and forced the name change from gum Nubian to gum arabic, and they nearly destroyed African traditional cultures in the area. An early African scientist first discovered and cultivated the natural resin and used the gum as a natural stabilizer in foods, medicines, beer, wine, and makeup that women and men used as a nonirritating eye shadow to protect the eyes from disease and flies. African youth the world over had better listen up, get focused, and start circling the resources wagons because this world is entering the abyss of economic horror from the lack of enough resources to maintain quality of life. Be in control, and be the ones to manage and sell to the world, as history teaches us. By far, gum arabic, as we will call it here, is one of the most important natural products on earth to modern industries, such as pharmaceutical companies and soft drink companies.

There would not be any safe soft drinks or cold glasses of wine but for the gum arabic that dissolves in cold water. The food and health product manufacturing industry would be using chemicals in our medicines and food supply. Women's beauty products would be chemical based and unsafe for use. Much of the world is totally dependent on gum arabic. If Africans in the diaspora and in Africa teamed up just to control the gum arabic market, they would end up controlling the world. There is African people power. There above is black power, Africa's PAD power. This is what money and power is made from, Africans own it the land and the water!

Beverages such as soda, beer, and wine all could not exist without it. The usage of gum arabic in the confectionary industry is one of the most important applications. It is the recognized preferred natural ingredient for the production of vital life-sustaining items and life-taking explosives. In high-quality soft candies, the gum is mainly used (and gives the best possible reported performance) in the raw form, enabling the manufacture of a soft, chewy candy. It renders the product soft but firm, long lasting in the mouth, and with a clean, nonsticky chew. Gum arabic is the natural gummy exudate obtained by tapping the branches of the *Acacia senegal* tree that only produce in Africa, largely the Republic of Sudan. In peace times, this area produces up to 80 percent of the seasonal crops with the Republic of Chad, Niger, and Nigeria producing lesser but important crops. Gum arabic is said to be so important to the modern world that it is seen as the economic stabilizer in American, Asian, African and European economies. Here is another natural resource produced only in

Africa that Africans and African diaspora stakeholders must immediately claim, nationalize as a worldwide African community industry, and control the trillions of dollars a year the gum arabic generates as a codevelopment tool for Africans. Gum arabic is seen by many to be the holy grail of all investments. Like clean WATER it's a life giver.

A note of caution to the public and African natural gum producers: Western and Asian scientists have developed a synthetic brand of gum arabic laced with harmful chemicals to try and escape the safe pure gum arabic green gum belt of Senegal trees. This area stretches across the Republic of Sudan from the Red Sea in the east reaching as far north as El Fasher and as far south as Malaki, ending its east to west journey only after a near-exhaustive run through the fertile flat plains of Sudan, which are as large as the United States of America or much of Western Europe. The gum belt finally gives way to the national northern border of the Republic of Nigeria to the Republic of Chad. Gum arabic is without a doubt one of the best examples Africans can point to as a reason for protecting and managing their natural treasures. (Sources, The gum arabic Company Limited, Republic of Sudan). So important is this product that Americans and Europeans, indeed the whole of the modern industrial world, cannot do without for a day, so when sanctions are imposed in the Republic of Sudan or on any African country, gum arabic is always exempt.

Arabs have culturally dominated and oppressed the Nubian kingdom since the Arab invasion in 969 AD. Finally in 2011, the Nubians won the support of a number of their former enemies, the Europeans and

Americans headed by the United Nations, and accepted for now the inappropriate broadening split-up of Sudan, indeed all of Africa that favors Africa's development enemies. The Arabs would hold North Sudan, and the African Nubians would establish independence in South Sudan. The deadly grip on Arab-held African land was failing like a corrupt hand of cards.

Chapter 40

Do You Have A Return Ticket?

People of African descent own the right to an official seat at the African Union table or must now establish a PAD diaspora seat complete with dual citizenship for all. It is vital to African development and survival.

As the American Airline plane dipped beneath the gathering rain clouds forming over the southern part of the continent, the view of the City of Gold (Johannesburg) at sunset from my window seat was truly hard to handle: the approach to the brutal apartheid white regime in South Africa in 1994. I had been here before. I could handle the racism shit being slung around by American- and European-sponsored apartheid lowlifes; that was not the problem. It was the raw suffering of the people. By now, Nelson Mandela had taken office once more.

The apartheid system was still sort of running things. The plane landed and taxied down the runway. A few minutes later, I was standing in line at passport control waiting to clear customs. My turn came to clear, and I stepped up to the counter and placed my passport before the sad-eyed, thirty-something male German customs officer, trapped in a quicksand time clock, who took one look at me, profiled me, and demanded I show him a return ticket before letting me enter my homeland. No way was I submitting to this insult, mind fuck, of a strip search.

"Do you have a return ticket?" The descendaent of the worste horror-committing tribe on earth serving as Africa's gatekeeper demanded.

His tone was ice cold like I imagined the image I had of him engraved on 90 percent of my brain. I knew his history in Africa, and without a doubt his present deeds reflected in his eyes scanning me and causing my stress level to rise. It rose and then quickly dipped, which meant I was ready to engage in whatever warfare the German man wanted to lose at. I was not going to be profiled on African soil or anywhere.

"No man, the question is this: 'Do you have a return ticket?'" I quickly shot back. The customs clerk stamped my dark blue American passport, letting the rubber and wooden stamp fall hard on the document and metal desk he was seated at as if swatting a fly. Then he pushed my passport back toward me with such force that it slid to the edge of the counter and landed on the floor at my feet. I could have caught the passport before it fell, but chose not to.

I looked at him, smiled, and said, "Now get up, come around, pick it up, and give it to me."

The officer's eyes suggested to me that I should pick up my passport and stick it you know where, but instead he exited his booth, picked up my passport, and lightly laid it on the counter.

"Next!" His eyes scanned beyond me. I thought, ok that would work.

I took my much-valued American passport from the counter; a passport I knew for him to process would cost him dearly, and he no doubt wished he owned. I stepped past the red-faced customs officer and continued walking past the "Nothing to Declare" section. A minute later fresh air rushed at me from the open area ahead. Sweetboy who had come to pick me up stood behind the airport public barrier waiting for me at the front of the wall of people standing eagerly awaiting their visitors. I worked my way through the crowd of mostly whites to reach Sweetboy. He was married, had two children, and his wife was expecting a third child. Sweetboy was a salesman for some Indian Cash-N-Carry supermarket.

Sweetboy and I cut short our greetings in public and walked to the waiting car in the airport parking lot. The waiting driver was an older man of about forty but looked sixty. His graying face reflected as many aging lines as found on the African map centuries after the arrival of the Europeans, detailing the life and hard times of black men and women in apartheid South Africa, albeit on the eve of apartheid's destruction.

"How was your trip?" Sweetboy asked me.

"Not as confining and long as the ships that carried me away centuries ago," I said, recalling just how much I hated being confined when I was not in control of my movements. Being stuck in the Western world was the worst for me and five hundred million other PAD whether they realized it or not; not having any option.

At that moment, a car with two white South African Dutch-looking males drove into a tight space near our car and side swiped the side of it. One of the two white males jumped out of the car and raced around the side to inspect his BMW, no doubt made in South Africa.

"Hey, watch it, you have damaged my car," the blond male called to me, his eyes glaring from a face more pink than white and dotting between me and Sweetboy.

I turned and looked at the blond man in the eyes as the second white male joined him in the planned intimidation threat. Sweetboy and our driver saw I was not moving away from the men and moved into position to back my play as the event unfolded.

"What's your problem? You are the one who can't fucking see or drive," I said.

The two men froze. A sound that was foreign and coming from a face more brown than black had entered their world, a world no longer theirs. It was the sound of my deep foreign to them voice that intimated the two men, and I could see and feel it in their eyes and action. It was the sound of my American accent. I assume it wasn't my good looks that had stopped the two white males in their tracks. The two men suddenly made an about face and left the area. Sweetboy told me later they looked like members of the feared undercover police, the death squad. The car did not have a mark on it. Whoever they were, they wanted no part of me, and that was a good thing because I was in no mood to discuss their fucking apartheid point of view. We

climbed in our car and drove off laughing, realizing
as did the two foreigners in our Africa that we black
men had pooled our power to defeat them just with
our presence. Through the rearview window, I could
see the two white men at the crosswalk. As we
departed the airport, Sweetboy laughed and then the
driver. They enjoyed seeing the two white men
retreat in the manner they had.

"I wish I had your brain," the driver said to
me.

Last Kick of the Dying White Buffalo

Sweetboy was now focused out the car
window at his European- invaded South African land
and paradise. Foreign jackals had dug in deep here
and were planning to stay regardless of the crimes
they had committed against humanity. And they had
plenty of help from some greedy, blind Africans.
Poorly dressed, sad-eyed, undernourished African
deliverymen made their rounds as ragged underpaid
gardeners labored under the hot sun in the yards.
Later we drove past German, Dutch, French, Italian,
Indian, American, and Chinese from Taiwan who
were about to be replaced by a more aggressive and
larger number of Chinese from the mainland and
equally biased Japanese-owned companies, all
flaunting their insults in Africans' faces as a group.
They were flanked by office buildings standing
proudly next to large international and
multinational companies, suggesting they would not
be moved while competing for African slave labor to

please the mindless millions of stockholders in America and Europe. Not one of these white businesses would partner with me or Sweetboy or any other black man in or outside of Africa.

"I want to drive up to the houses and office buildings and start shooting and not stop until every last one of the motherfuckers are dead," Sweetboy said.

We were economic outcasts in our own land. We had lost everything but our courage and will to fight.

"We should kill them all and get it over with," the sad-eyed driver said. Why bother I thought. The dying white buffalo's last kick was in motion. As if to prove it in his own small way, our driver then passed a white driver on the road, releasing his anger at the same time. There is no denying that there is and will remain for a long, long time very dangerous and hard times between different cultural brothers in the human race on this planet.

Last Man Standing in Soweto, No Legs

Later the driver pulled off the main road from the airport and headed to the hills toward the sprawling area called Soweto. The population then was roughly 1,690,000. I tell you this was a sight to remember. The people were as tough as they came here. They had to be. They were the backbone of the struggle. It was these people and the area that invited and took the brute force of the white buffalo's death kick. Though some houses were well kept, seated under a deadly dark shroud of ash and killer gray smoke, most were shanties made of cardboard paper, rusting tin, and aging wooden planks that resembled the shacks next door where the boards may have been stolen from the night before that. The previous owner may have lifted them from some person who had carried it from somewhere else. Here again, the invaders' guns had pushed the once-proud, deeply cultured native to the point of zero. I had seen this kind of housing belonging to the poor in Jamaica and South America dotting the hillsides and entering city slums. Here in apartheid South Africa, the shanties grew wild like roadside flowers all burdened with dust, dirt, grime, and millions of bits of scraps of plastic and paper blown into the mix in all directions by passing vehicles. All was coated with black coal dust from stovepipes on rooftops or no roofs, continually spitting out gray and black smoke that clung to human lungs and skin and hung just over the roofs of tens of thousands of homes of breadwinners who could not earn enough money for the undependable, overcrowded bus let alone be able to pay for proper health care white and Indian doctors often overcharged for or refused all together to provide even if the Africans could afford to pay. Shabby-looking, near-starving dogs and kids dotted about, with ribs poking out of rags hung on bodies as thin as a human hair or the hard-to-locate electric wires overhead of the dirty wretched streets, which author Frantz Fanon wrote about in his book *The Wretched of the Earth*. I cannot read enough to better understand the streets of Africa, but from Algeria to Cape Town no one wrote about it better, though my wretched world in Alabama in the fifties was not mentioned due to the banning of free speech in America at the time and sadly still now.

The stench of the open sewers and unpaved roads, rabies dogs and sex predators, sidewalks clogged with filth and unmanaged waste from dogs and humans deposited under the fading street lights competed with the golden setting sun's rays for attention. Dim, sputtering electric lights that tried to stand guard against darkness and crime few could escape or use to warn against the brutal apartheid state police paid for by the willing white businesses and general foreign public calling themselves citizens of this land, forever relentless stalking and profiling African men and woman, heroes to the struggle for freedom of all oppressed peoples.

The grim light representing human suffering hung from loose, decaying electric wires on concrete and steel posts that were cracked, bent, and broken. Some lights were busted, out of order as a result of gun shots and rocks thrown by vandals or street kids. Then there were the extra demands on the lampposts from the thousands of state-posted, illegal electric hookups the poor and wretched black and colored people in South Africa needed from white-controlled, state-imposed wire taps. This energy borrowing to avoid the high price of electric current was needed to keep the electric fans turning to cool a sick child's fever. The light may have been busted to aid the wayward freedom fighters seeking the cover of darkness to escape from the evil death squad, the life line of apartheid. The effect of all this pollution, political stress, and survival violence had taken its toll on the people's souls and health. But still black and colored people in South Africa clung to the dream, a claim on a bright future as I had in my unannounced arrival regardless of the dangers or stench of the moment.

The driver drove the car to a slow halt in front of a run-down shack, and Sweetboy exited the car like a stray cat in a strange alleyway, went around the back of the car, and popped open the boot. Through the rearview mirror, I could see him take out a few boxes of candy from the boot of the car. The apartheid system allowed East Indian shop owners who remained operating in South Africa to play the Indian monopoly Cash-N-Carry game apartheid bosses let them play to drain South African currency from blacks using unhealthy food the Indians label forbidden for Indians to eat. Sweetboy used deadly sweets as a cover to sometimes supply weapons hidden in the car boot to the freedom fighters that awaited him as he made his day-night job rounds. Watching Sweetboy, the tall slender youthful black father of a son, I could see a lot of myself in him. We were both black men, warriors without funding or field guidance, fighting a global millennium war with only the image of leaders like Nelson Mandela; it was the same courage I witnessed in Sweetboy, myself, and countless other men, women, and yes, the youth. Like Nelson Mandela, Sweetboy hated the lingering apartheid economic white European Western system spread out across the globe, more deadly to people like me and our development than the dreaded Ebola taking the lives and future of the people of the Congo spread there by do-gooders who in truth wanted the black man demanding his wealth and power back and totally under African black control.

The relentless attacks on the mind and body and finding ways to feed and grow a family drove some of the best of us, like Sweetboy, to drink a little more than he should and he hated that in himself too. Sweetboy closed the boot, telling me to go into the bar and wait. He released the driver who said good-bye and vanished into the smog and shadows of the dark crowds of Africans returning home from work as miners, maids in the houses the driver wanted to blow up, and street hawkers fighting the ongoing struggle for life. Some people just milled about jobless at the end of the day in the gray grubby Soweto streets. The outside walls of the bar called Shebean were made of the same materials many of the surrounding buildings were made from, and not until you entered did you realize the shack was an undercover, rundown illegal bar under apartheid laws.

I stepped to the door of the Shebean and waited a bit looking up and down the street at the surreal strange scene and near lifeless people, some dressed in what could be called Oliver Twist English rags fashion hanging on a proud people. Growing uneasy at the people watching me and catching a few suspicious eyes in return, I entered and found three middle-aged African men inside. The dimly lit rundown Shebean had a puff of recently exhaled gray cigarette smoke hanging in the small room just overhead like a halo over death, enveloping a gross-looking, yellowish, smoke-stained, aging flycatcher choking with dead flies and bugs that had succumbed to the poison glue that embraced them like the evils of apartheid does to the people even in death. The choking smoke and coal dust in the street drifted in from outside and not just through the door and windows, but from the holes and cracks in the walls as well. The bartender and two other men were seated about the dark spine-chilling setting.

One man seemingly elderly, graying at forty with a life expectancy of forty-two, had his head lying on his folded arms, maybe sleeping off a few beers or holding a gun aimed at the heart of apartheid in a favorite spot in the Shebean he no doubt had claimed as a personal space long before my chance passing this way. The third man sat upright smoking a fag, clocking my every move with his beaming, bloodshot eyes looking right through me that reminded me of black men suffering the same mood back in Alabama after they had been drinking local homemade moonshine. The man seated upright was checking me from head to toe. I knew he had a million questions dangling in his head like the killer smoke that hunted the room and competed with the smell of beer and extra strong smell of human piss coming from the WC. The toilet was choking with partly unflushed human excrement due to a clogged sewer or a near miss by the depositor and the lack of running water to flush the human waste, leaving the job to be completed by the force of male piss streams if aimed directly into the narrow opening that may not have been connected to the city sewer system due to the Shebean's illegal status. There was also a smell coming from the aging scavenged floor tiles that gave off hidden poison vapors along with the decaying asbestos ceiling dust that fell to the titles, combing to produce harmful chemical compounds that helped reduced life expectancy. Infant mortality rates were the highest here, and this was after the "if" in the African male's ability to produce enough healthy sperm to seed undernourished female eggs. More often than not miscarriages accounted for the already-alarming high numbers that were right where most white settlers wished the African deaths were even without HIV/AIDS numbers, which were off the scale.

      During one of my many unannounced trips avoiding apartheid customs into South Africa, I was invited to visit a hospital for blacks and colored people only. A white female friend sickened by being called white, by apartheid insults on humanity, and by the lack of medical care and service to the black community here in so-called postapartheid Johannesburg offered to smuggle me into Baragwaneth Hospital to witness the horror for myself. She did so in the hope I would inform the outside world about the horror taking place in their death wards. What I witnessed was appalling. The hospital I was told by my white South African friend (who I would love to name here but sadly will not for her safety) may as well have been called a slaughterhouse for killing animals. In the Shebean I was reminded of a smell from the hospital I cannot get out of my head even today.

The smell was this faint smell of dried year-old likely illegally killed endangered bush meat that had been smuggled in through the Soweto underground black market and now was hanging on a rack in the Shebean. The competing smell turned out to be drying pig feet; fatback pork that one had to be high on the glue from the flytraps that hung over head to consume. All this and more had added to the harmful environment competing with the aging flycatcher, spotted with gnats, ants, bugs, and black and green flies hanging just overhead inside the Shebean. If the visitor entering were six feet as I was and not careful, he would walk smack into the flytrap fully loaded with dead, decaying flies and bugs, some still trying to escape or give birth. I ducked just in time, only just seeing the fucking gummy flytrap caked with the disgusting flies. Imagine the horror of being hit in the face with that filth with no running water or soap in the Shebean. No wonder beer was sold here in bottles only. You would need an emergency injection of some kind after drinking from one of the bar glasses. Walking into the filth or coming too close to the filthy flytrap was a dead giveaway to the bar patrons that you were a stranger. Still the place had its own style provided mostly by music from Shebean's music box.

"Where are you coming from my brother?" asked the fifty-something-year-old black man. The seated man called to me half in, half out of the gloomy Shebean shadows, just as a barefoot boy of about ten ran in from the dirty street and slapped a few South African rand coins on the makeshift bar counter. All the while, I was casting an uneasy eye on the bartender resting on a stool at the far end of the wooden bar as he was doing the same to me. To reply to the man without words over the music, I pointed with my thumb behind me over my right shoulder, indicating I was from some shithole back in the lost forgettable past, the same as him. I did not know who he was. Besides, apartheid South Africa was still full of spies and broken men and women looking to make a quick buck off anyone's blood to survive in some areas. I was here to do a job. Let's keep that out of the introduction! Some things are best left unsaid in this part of the world. I was a spy. Survival was a bitch here as it was and still is in America for poor black men. With the murder of Steve Biko, the bodies of the students still warm from the Sharpeville massacre in 1960, and the smell of blood still in the air due to white insecurity, guilt, panic, and facing an uncertain future fenced in by justified black rage, anything could and did happen.

The small boy grabbed a small package and slapped a rand, a South African coin six times weaker than the American dollar, on the bar. The walls were pasted with old, apartheid, Nazi-dictated magazines and newspaper stories of hate and greed (white Nazi ideas so evil even some Jews supported them in Africa and abroad, and the proof is there). Infectious ideas of greed and race as a solution to rid the planet of earth's first human ancestors that stood upright on the planet and gave all mankind its glory and civilization as humans. The hate- and greed-filled magazines and newspapers also carried stories about the good life for white settlers. Looking in the direction of the ten-year-old, if that, African boy and then past him, I could see a large-framed African woman outside through the small window, partly covered with a dusty sheet of plastic and rusting iron bars but no glass. The boy ran past me and out again into the near darkness so many depended on during those dark days in Africa to survive. I was hoping to be a survivor among them.

The woman outside the Shebean was taking in her clothes from the recycled wire and string combination that had seen better days and now functioned as a clothing line draped across the alleyway. Attached to a cement light pole and connected to the back wall of the bar, it carried many responsibilities, like most of the black community. I could hear children playing somewhere in the background and a dog barking in the mix of sounds beyond my understanding and view.

"You bring any Oscar Peterson tapes with you, man?" asked the man seated at the table in deep shadows. I had been pegged as a jazz music lover. Sweetboy entered the room smoking a fag and stepped up to the bar.

"Castle. What are you having Rashid?" asked Sweetboy, using my code name Molefe had passed on. Sweetboy took note of the fact I was engaged in distant conversation with the man across the room.

"Castle," I said without looking in Sweetboy's direction. "No, I am sorry. No, Oscar Peterson this trip." I replied to the seated black man.

"We don't have shit now here in terms of outside black culture man. I mean you cats in America are advanced in so many ways, and these backward fucking Boers and mother-sucking, British, invading bastards murdered the soul of life that is still itself blocking anything black entering and leaving this country," the man said.

"You cats have not done so badly I thought." The bartender dropped a coin in the music box, and African music flowed out. I turned and joined Sweetboy just as his lips were about to kiss a bottle of cold Castle beer and leaned back against the bar facing the room.

"What are you drinking?" I asked the man in the shadows. The soft African music played, while his face and body slowly left the deep shadow as the sunlight faded, leaving the single electric light above hanging like a lynched man from the ceiling near the stained, yellowish flytrap, and straining to supply enough illumination for the room. The single light blub suggested isolating the bar all be it just barely from the blanket of apartheid death and darkness that covered every inch of South Africa. The man's bloodshot eyes glanced over at Sweetboy and then at me, the wayward stranger, the lost son of Africa who had to create the blues and gospel songs to survive US apartheid in the goddamn Mississippi Delta and the red clay hills of Alabama.

"Scotch, and I keep my mouth shut," the man said.

"Wise man," said Sweetboy, gulping down his beer while holding up two fingers to the bartender for Scotch with his eyes still on the man. The bartender poured the Scotch in a glass and walked it over to the seated man. When the seated man reached out for the glass in the bartender's hand, I could see for the first time he had no legs. The man in the chair held up his glass of Scotch over the sound of the music offering a voiceless toast at first and then said, "Here is to the bravest and finest man I ever knew, Steve Biko, and the best jazz man I ever heard, Oscar Peterson." All the bottles and glasses were raised, even the bartender grabbed a beer bottle left by the kid, and for a moment all sounds were gone from the room except the African music that seemed a fitting salute to the dead African hero Steve Biko as we gulped down our drinks.

After a short silence, the bartender said with a crooked smile, "Here's to kicking Bota's ass." We all laughed. The bartender bought a round. This time I stepped in and handed the legless man his Scotch. Sweetboy and I departed.

Chapter 41

A Dry Black Season

The one road Sweetboy and I are driving on headed to Drakenberg in South Africa was a hell of a lot better than most all of the roads in Zimbabwe. White lives mattered so investments in roads here were a priority suggesting whites here were attempting to stay. Later, I was searching the car radio dial for African music that the man in the Shebean had warned me just weren't there. Sweetboy started to snore, and I slapped his arm to make him stop. It seems the beer had taken him out. The cars and lorries on the road got fewer and fewer as I drove into the night. I was hoping the diamond connection we were traveling north to meet would be there. I checked the fuel gauge, and the tank was full, so I relaxed knowing we should reach our destination near Drakenberg by dawn.

As I drove, my thoughts drifted back to places I had been: Europe, North, South Central, and East Asia, and Africa. I did not wish to think about the present. I just wanted to escape to some place I had never been and stay there if it was warm and peaceful. I wondered how long it would take Africa to catch up and pass the Western world and peoples that had fucked with the Africans and their continent for so long. As I drove and looked ahead, I knew I was driving head on into a future of uncertainty, bloodshed, and good times, and I welcomed it. Sweetboy turned in his seat next to me, and for a moment I thought he would wake from the beer drunk, but he continued to sleep and dream. I drove into the night with only a dead calm and the sound of the car tires on the pavement to keep me company and awake.

Dawn came and the morning sun rose up over the four billion-year-old South African countryside with my hope for Africa's rebirth and future. The sun came up with a bang, flooding a land full of green hills and rioting yellow flowers and kissing the powerful rays of light that would wake the dead, and it did. Sweetboy closed his mouth, opened his eyes, and asked where we were. While he was at it, he demanded coffee. Later, we were seated at a roadside lunch stand operated by a middle-aged Dutch woman and her man who had got lost out here. The Dutch, as poor as they are, were now the ones trapped and decaying like the flies and bugs, collecting coins still trying to escape before the new nation gave birth to a new dawn that all African people were fighting for. We bought black coffee and bread roles to go, and Sweetboy, awake now, took the wheel. One thing is for certain: most black men in South Africa can't handle the booze unless they immediate snooze. A few hours later at about 10:00 a.m. in the morning, we saw the sign that read "Drakenberg." Africa is indeed big, very big. The United States of America, China, or much of Western Europe each would fit inside the continent three times over. A little later, we pulled up to a small house and stopped. We could see a certain movement at the window as we drove up and got out. We walked to the door and knocked, but no one answered. A car was in the yard. Sweetboy checked the address to be certain it was the right house, and it was. We knocked and knocked for ten minutes and went around to all the windows and doors, but no one appeared.

"Fuck it! We could get shot banging on walls out here," Sweetboy said.

We decided it was a lost cause and left. The person Molefe had counted on to deliver the diamonds had let us down. Nearly every business attempt a black man or woman here tried to do seemed to run into a brick wall, but that was pretty much anywhere for a black man in the day. I coined this kind of failure "a dry black season." But that was going to change, and my team and a billion other black men, women, and children were going to make certain sure of it. I stepped out into the yard of the house and said, "I might know a good diamond connection that will deliver the goods." Sweetboy and I drove back to Johannesburg.

Chapter 42

Diamonds, Chocolate and Sex

I had been waiting a day at the Parktoning Hotel in Jo'burg where Sweetboy had arranged for me to stay before vanishing into his shadowy world in postapartheid. I hoped he was not drinking because most black men in South Africa cannot hold their drinks down. The spirit goes directly to many of their heads, and then all falls downhill. Anyway, so here I am in downtown gritty Johannesburg, where I was staying while waiting for my contact to show. When he did, he showed up as a waiter named Maso working for the hotel knocking at my room that afternoon to deliver a food tray with all the trimmings. Once inside my hotel room, he placed his finger to his lip looking me in the eye. Not a word was spoken. Maso pulled a bit of paper from his pocket and pressed it into my palm with a loaded pistol. Here I was again reduced to having to help my people smuggle, you may as well say, steal our own wealth to survive. The weapon Maso handed me reminded me of the pistol my friend Solomon, who had come through for me more than once here, placed in my hand when I arrived in South Africa during apartheid in the transition. After placing the pistol in my hand, the waiter's eyes scanned my eyes suggesting "Say nothing!" The message from my eyes received, the waiter turned and left the room. A moment later, I looked over the note. An hour after the waiter had departed, I followed the instructions on the note and drifted downstairs. I entered the bar on the main floor that had a handful of people and enough food wasting on the counters to feed half the hungry people in Soweto, a fraction of the millions of black South Africans who were homeless, jobless, and starving. It reminded me of the food wasting in America; it sickened me! All the people here were white tourists and fortune seekers nesting about with plenty of food and cheap African help standing in wait. The whites had fared far better here than they had in Nigeria when I arrived in Lagos in 1974.

In the far corner playing a piano was this tall attractive white South African female, a brunette named Sam, just as the note had said. Sam was in her midtwenties and playing with no one listening. After ordering a drink from a sleepy-eyed African bartender, I crossed the lobby and mostly empty dining room to the piano and stood enjoying the music and admiring Sam's revealing fashion and musical skill. According to the note left by the waiter, my instructions were to approach Sam and ask her to play some jazz; I thought it not cool at the time being we were in a very recent postapartheid South Africa, but that was the strategy. Keep them guessing and my intentions hidden. Sam was a Dutch Boer, a relative of famous artist Vincent van Gogh (born 1853) who tried in vain to warn, in my view, the world in his paintings of the touched souls from this part of Europe. The signs are here if one looks closely at indigenous cultures and in this case Vincent van Gogh's painting especially in "Starry Night" shows signs of twisted minds, a painting to me depicting deep roots, seeds of DNA carrying a history of madness based on the horror visited on Africans introduced by the Dutch camp and its true of most in the Dutch community. A country in trouble, a Dutch homeland that honored Hitler actions that had a twin brother; the butcher King Leopold of Belgium that later gave Hitler a bad name by the slaughter he ordered be carried out in his name in the Congo, still reeling from the horror as I arrived in 1998. Boers's disrespect for African culture caused me to believe that most Dutch felt the same way. But I was wrong. Sam proved me wrong. Generalizing about a whole people is an anti-uncivilized state of mind in which I do not wish to partake. There is hope for humanity, or I would not be doing what I am doing; the way I went about it.

Sam!

"Hello, Sam. How about a little jazz?"
"Anything for you, Rashid."
There it was again. Rashid. How the hell did she know that name? The name came in handy as a code. Shit, Sam was a code herself I later found out. I hated the Western-imposed name Frank Weston, but on the other hand, I was not fond of Rashid either being that it carried a hint of Arab culture. Boy, was I screwed in the name category. I was still suffering from cultural rape. Sam was the diamond contact that paid off. The deal was set to move to the final stage, and I was very pleased about

it because it meant I could now get the hell out of South Africa for a while.

"Oscar Peterson is my favorite composer," Sam said. I remembered the African man's complaint in the Shebean in Soweto a few miles away with no legs. Just like that, Sam delivered! Black culture was getting through to South Africa; it was just not reaching all the right people.

This white chick knows Oscar's music? She can play it and not give a damn now that apartheid seems to be falling apart. Who the hell is this girl? I would soon find out.

"Meet me at 7:10 on the nose on the avenue in front of the Parktoning Hotel. I will be driving a blue 1994 BMW," Sam said, fingering the keys not looking up.

I dropped twenty South African rand in to her tip jar on the piano. Sam frowned disapprovingly, and I left the bar and went back to my hotel room wondering how many white women drove blue 1994 BMWs in Jo'burg. In the hotel room, I downed a cold beer from the minibar and pissed it out again to pass time. It was now 5:00 p.m., so I turned on the TV and flipped through the channels until I found CNN and watched the world news flash by in forty minutes. About 6:50 p.m., I went downstairs carrying the diamonds in the small airline carry-on bag and left the hotel for the avenue in front of the hotel where I was to meet Sam. At 7:10 p.m. sharp, Sam drove up in a blue BMW and stopped on a dime inches from my feet and the bag. She stopped just long enough for me to get in.

"Where to Sam?" I asked.

"You come highly recommended. People say you can be trusted all the way to the finish line,"

Sam said, as my eyes settled on the muscles of her
upper legs that were reacting to the message sent by
her brain to help shift gears in the BMW.

"There is some truth to that," I said.

Sam kept smiling, knowing where my eyes
were focused, paying less attention to the road and
cross sections than I preferred. But what the hell?
Live fast, die young and happy I always say in a
situation one cannot control. We turned off the
avenue that had few cars at that time of day and
headed across town in the direction of Santon City, a
new wealthy city built for Europeans during their
stay to escape Johannesburg's growing crime waves
sweeping the City of Gold, as the Africans took the
war to the front doors of white oppressors and
economic slavery in a postapartheid south. My riding
with Sam in the City of Gold was the telltale sign
that the ground the white empire was built on (black
wealth and labor) was shifting fast. It seemed
destiny was setting in for the Europeans. Sam, like a
few other whites, wanted to help and did so by
placing her life in harm's way. Sam was stunning,
wearing one of those famous little black dresses, a
weapon women kept in their closets to wear when
they were out to kill or drive most men nuts. Sam's
long tan legs shot out from under her short black
dress out over the BMW's black leather seat as I
struggled in vain to escape the inescapable tender
trap. So much for the great divide in race, sex, and
cultural wars. What that little black dress hid my
imagination more than made up for. I took a deep
breath. Sam hit the accelerator, and I fastened my
seat belt and hung on for dear life. The lady knew
how to handle a gear and, no doubt, control, even
wreck a man's psyche fingering the BMW's gear. I
could tell the girl loved busting state laws, any law

in South Africa, and her fashion strongly suggested she hated confinement and control. She showed it in open defiance to the oppression and fading European power around her.

"Should I put on the AC?" asked Sam, pretending not to know her legs and short dress were fucking with my heads. A man has two, you know, heads, I mean.

"It wouldn't help," I said. Sam laughed knowingly as I suffered and sweated. I was doing everything I could to survive the mental rush. Watching Sam's eyes dot back and forth from the road back to me and her hand working the single black gear standing erect out of the gearbox. Life can be so cruel! I double-checked my seat belt just in time for Sam to do her Road Runner parking contest, stopping on a tick of a second in front of an upscale, six-star hotel where we left her car blocking another. As we entered the hotel lobby, Sam tossed her car keys to a young black man who was all smiles on our way to a bank of elevators in the swanky lobby.

As we neared the elevators, I thought "Was this a set up?" I fingered the handgun in my pocket and played along. We got off the elevator on the twentieth floor and entered a large well-kept dining room decked out with wall-to-wall carpet with the latest trends in European dining comforts. This was certainly a far cry in comfort from the bar where I met the black man with no legs.

The bar sat off from the main dining room divided by frosted glass paneling and fine embroidered drapes insuring deal making and social privacy. There was hardly anyone in the dining room except Africans waiters all standing at attention. Sam and I walked into the empty barroom and sat in one of the four tall back booths that lined the wall.

We were all alone. A handsome African male bartender in his thirties came over and greeted Sam who introduced me.

"Teto, say hello to Rashid from New York."

"Pleased to meet you. Sam, Maso is ready if you are," Teto said.

Teto was dressed as a typical bartender, had a medium build, about five feet seven or so, tall for a South African native, and he spoke English with clear British diction that you had to wonder about his role there. Molefe back in New York City murdered English for the hell of it, I think, because he truly hated what the Dutch, Germans, Americans, Jews, and British had done to the people and the country. Hey, you can't blame the truth for uncovering a lie. Teto and Sam were all business when they dealt with each other, but a special cultural tilt suggested a bonding, a much closer community friendship. I could tell. I had that kind of bonding with many women all over the world. A woman would be there for a guy if you didn't fuck her over. Teto and Sam's relationship was not personal in a sexy way, I did not think. Their relationship was all about survival and cause.

"Follow me please," Teto said, moving away from the bar and down the hall.

We followed Teto back into the massive, well-kept kitchen the size of a small African village where we found Maso from the hotel and two African men in their twenties working over a large pot of boiling hot brown chocolate. The hot chocolate gave off a most delightful smell that assaulted the senses imposing sexual desires. On the side tables were a number of trays with hundreds of small pots to hold the contents of the hot chocolate. Sam stuck her finger in the tray and pulled it out laced with a layer of chocolate and sucked her finger clean. She pointed to the carry-on bag I was holding and suggested I open it. How did she know I was carrying diamonds? I pulled the few small bags of diamonds out and placed them on the table, opening them all one by one. Just then, Maso slipped me a folded note. I glanced at the small bit of paper and put it away. The two men dropped the two and three carat diamonds in the pots and then poured molten hot chocolate over the sexy gemstones.

"Why don't you two go into the bar and get to know each other better? We can take it from here," Maso said. "Come on, I will fix you a drink unless you want to watch diamonds make it with chocolate," said Teto with a smile, walking away with Sam on his arm, while I followed them glancing back at the table and workers.

Chapter 43

Downtime

In the bar, Teto went behind the bar and put on some soft music, the first mistake. Sam and I had returned to the same booth. Teto came over, and we placed our orders for drinks, a second mistake. Sam requested a side order of light snacks from the kitchen, and Teto went out to fill the order.

"You been here before," Sam asked, relaxing her head back on the high leather seat.

"South Africa? Yes, once or twice. Where do you live?" I asked. I wanted to change the subject.

"Rose Bank, would you like to see my place later?"

"For you, Sam, anything," I said. We laughed, and the bartender returned with the food and drinks. We relaxed, ate, and talked some more.

"Can I speak freely here?" I asked.

"It's not safe to speak freely anywhere in South Africa these days."

"Who is your father?"

"I wish the God I knew anymore!" Sam replied. "Are we ok with the airport tomorrow?" Sam asked.

"Yes.

You leave the diamonds here over night.

You get them back at the airport tomorrow after you clear customs."

Sam said taking a long sip of her drink. When we finished eating, Teto came back and took away the empty food plates and said, "Sam, just turn out the lights for me when you leave. My wife is expecting, and I want to get home." Teto turned to me, took my hand, and said, "Good meeting you, Rashid. Thank you for what you do. Travel safe, brother."

"Teto, early congrats to you and the missus for the baby."

"Thanks brother," Teto said with a big smile as he turned and walked away.

Near the door, he paused and lowered the lights in the barroom and gently closed the door. Sam and I spent the night at her place, and the next morning we woke up, had what amounted to Sunday morning sex, and fell asleep again. Waking around 1:00 p.m., I found Sam out on the terrace making calls on her cell phone. I checked my pocket and came up with the folded note Maso had given me the night before. I studied the note, ripped it up, and walking into the bathroom flushed the bits of the paper down the toilet and took a shower. I said good-bye to Sam around 4:00 p.m. and took a taxi back to the hotel where I found a message waiting for me from Sweetboy. I called Maso's cell phone.

"Hello Rashid." Maso's voice shot back to me. "I see you did not make it back to your hotel last night." His voice came into the phone receiver from somewhere in South Africa.

"There were no complaints all around. I am leaving in half hour," I said.

"Everything is in place at the airport, and Sweetboy says hello. Have a safe trip, and come back soon to stay," Maso said. I hung up the phone, went down to pay the hotel bill, and was told the hotel bill had been paid.

Later I departed the hotel and found a prepaid car and driver waiting to take me to the airport where I was processed through customs after presenting my return ticket to international airline employees with the rest of the mostly white passengers, all waiting to get the hell out of what was becoming a black paradise. They were all lined up in front and behind me; many of them no doubt fleeing a failing white apartheid empire, a ghostly past most, if not all of them, will carry to their graves like Adolf Hitler, full of guilt, but with no shame, forced to depart and mix with a global humanity, a rite of passage long denied Africans. The Europeans trying to put on a brave mask all looked ghostly and defeated; they had gone a bridge too far. Having cleared customs, I reached the area in which Sam had instructed me to wait. A few minutes later, I saw an airport employee of about thirty pushing a luggage cart into my section.

He dropped a carry-on bag near my feet and said, "Sam, Sweetboy, Maso, and Solomon wish you a pleasant flight."

Just as quick as the black man came from out of nowhere, he vanished into a sea of ghostly humanity and faces in the crowd as if he was never there. When he wrote The Invisible Man, author Ralph Ellison was right when he described the black man trapped in a temporary darkness of white, male-dominated Western madness I call the "System of African Terror," where the black man was indeed invisible. He was prevented from producing or providing for his family or developing for centuries. Now, in a twist of fate, we are witnessing the white world system become invisible in a sea of blackness, vanishing in a sea of black energy. Winnie Mandela was right when she said, "When they lose, they will lose forever. When we win, we win forever." Seated there in the airport, I watched a group flood past who once thought themselves privileged and were now facing a dry white season for the rest of their lives and the future of their offspring being blown back to a dying Europe as South Africa shed the heat of a long hot bloody summer. I felt strangely at ease as a section of a long war was coming to an end for African people all over the world. It was a kind of sad pleasure to witness a broken group of Dutch, French, Germans, Americans, Europeans, and a few Asians fight each other for return tickets and seats out of my Eden, on the coach run back across the bridge too far, across the ocean my ancestors were once forced to go in chains to an uncertain life and future. For these Europeans in South Africa and Zimbabwe, they had to face a doom Africans once knew: no place to return. The alternative was returning as broke as they were when many were forced to leave Europe by their own people to search for fulfillment or money, an empty quest that in the end had cost many whites in South Africa and Zimbabwe everything but their remorseless guilt. One had to ask what it had gotten them.

Later when I opened the outer layers of the carry-on case the invisible black man had placed near my feet, I found four commercially wrapped boxes of chocolates. I relaxed and waited for the time to board the plane and started thinking about the future, a future I could now plan, as could all African people for the first time in a millennium. I watched the South African summer give way to a cooling fall wind blowing in far from the south, cooling an African land and people that could use a bit of a rest, a new wet black season. I got to thinking about things and how I would manage my life. First I would get that much needed advanced university education. Being an honorably discharged American veteran, I had my mind set on New York University as I was ready now.

I knew I would not have a future worth visiting if I did not do something about getting the advanced knowledge needed to help me manage all that I had gained knowledge of: land, wealth opportunity, and things I had learned about Africa and the world at last. No more economic insecurities and intimidation from the Western world I could not defend against. I was ready; I had the motivation, the focus at long last needed to work toward and finish a university degree reload what the Western world acts of enslavement and horrors inflicted on my people, humanity. Being in Africa working and learning with the people Ms. Winnie Mandela, Mr. Nelson Mandela, Arch Bishop Desmond Tutu, Diniwe and her family, Nafi and her family, Sweetboy, Molefe, Maso, Sam, Aranud, and Mr. Vital Balla, Rock and my late buddy Jules from Cameroon in the Congo, Bill Tender in Harlem, James Baldwin and countless children, mothers, and fathers most still in the struggle fighting for our reintroduction and rite of passage back into African culture and land. The ZBC TV producers in Zimbabwe, ambassadors, secretaries, drivers, and countless others in countries at airports and along the roadsides in Egypt and Sudan and across America into Canada and in the Caribbean, South America,

Europe, and Asia. Strengthening friendships, education and the important of taking control of PAD shares of African land, wealth and power for the all the African people, the community, collective economic power, sharing and holding down conflicts is now the mission.

Chapter 44

Reloading A Stolen Brain

It is reported that a visiting British minister said, "It is not likely we will ever defeat these blacks on the battle field. We will have to do it in the schools." For an in-depth past and present review of the extent Western crimes against humanity went on stripping Africans and PAD people went read – "A History of South Africa by Leonard Thompson, Yale University Press 1990," a book on step by step foreign invasions and details on education denial as weapons. That then helps explain why I entered university; it's never too late. Others could not enter at all, and those who do or can have a binding obligation to lead, serve, and help rebuild. That summer in South Africa was the last time I saw many of the millennium warriors. We talk over the phone and fight on, but events and a new

Africa and life we helped birth keep us linked and apart as we rebuild after centuries of delay and decay. Yes, some forms of colonialism, economic apartheid, corruption, and imperialism still need to be dealt with in Africa and in the Western world. They still exist in Africa and will as long as the Europeans remain claiming success where the exploiters have truly failed. The land, wealth, and business culture in South Africa is still being influenced negatively by whites and Asians. Don't get me wrong. Most Africans would have no problem with open trade with foreigners and such, but respect African ownership. We Africans have had it up to our noses with outsiders meddling and using foreign methods to butt into our African affairs. The land is still sick and the health of the people will be at risk as long as black leaders' petty corruption holds the European, Jewish, Arab, and Asian interests over African people. A whole new way of African business culture is required from the youth and the people. Unqualified big man or women Africans, foreigners and self appointed and Coups linked dreamers are now a thing of the past, and they know it is time to retire or just leave. Africa must now be united with one African including dual citizenship holding PAD head of state not fifty-four.

As the big American Airline jet I was on lifted off and headed out over the continent where humans first stood upright and looked out over the ten-foot elephant grass raising civilization to the level we witness today, the jet leveled off at a cruising speed of thirty-two thousand feet and headed for New York City. My thoughts settled as I had a business class seat and drifted into the new world, the new life. I felt I had a place to belong. I felt I was becoming African again. Africa had saved me. I was thinking, eating, drinking, even dancing like an African. I was made of the stuff the continent was made of, and I was damn proud of it. I felt my life had jumped to light speed.

Graduating New York University

In the fall of 1995, the same year my team and I nongovernmental organization IMSCO was inducted into the ECOSOC at the United Nations, I entered New York University Gallatin Division and graduated with top grades, on the dean's list with 3.8. Rounded out, that represents a 4.0 in every class. My main studies were and still are in geology, history, politics, economics, and communication. In fact, I excelled in every course I entered in at university.

Looking back, I was on the A train, the subway in New York City, seated next to Professor Kurp, my geology professor. The train was returning my class from geology field research in the rock bed, the billion plus years old granite rocks foundation of the George Washington Bridge, when Professor Kurp turned to me, smiled, and said, "Frank, out of all the students I have taught, you are the one most likely to do the most with the knowledge of the geology I have taught and I hope you will take it much further."

"I will give it my best shot," I said.

"I believe you will. I believe you will," Professor Kurp said. What he did not know is that I had already been where he dreamed of going but never did. It was my love for nature and geology that helped to save my life, and now I planned to use geology in Africa to help enrich and save my people from a life of want and poverty. I had learned in class that Africa is the Silicon Valley engine of the world future. Things "Confessions of an Economic Hit Man," John Perkins, author, book did not wish

In 1998, I was out of the university reprogrammed in organized thinking after having regained some of the education direction taken stolen opportunity, power from me and my people for centuries I was now equipped with a brain weapon, with a whole new perspective on life and the world. Bring it on! I was starting to love the warrior war game. Having taken all those trips home to Africa, I had witnessed what I owned and was made of in a continent of vast riches and opportunities. I had made the world less of a threat to me and my community. I could now openly challenge the world on nearly every level of thinking. Reading, writing, and math at the university level and beyond had provided me the basis I needed to advance. The fear and embarrassment of hiding the fact that I had only a high school education, and a somewhat bad one at that, gave way to sheer joy. Not bad, not bad. I had achieved a 4.0 in every class. Not bad for a guy whose family members had been stolen from Africa and shipped into a hellhole called Alabama to have his life slaughtered and fed to the ages.

To me, the UN accreditation was equal to a PHD in social development. The UN labeled me and other founders as specialists. With this UN degree together with the undergraduate degree and time earned in graduate school at Robert Wagner School of Social Studies from NYU, I was now reloaded and armed with many of the tools stolen by Europeans. I was in control of my life and headed for economic control of what had been stolen. I would take it back if it meant centuries of warfare. Like millions more like me, I was reloaded! My French teacher, a Haitian woman who gave me a crash course in beginners French, once told me education is a tool (echoing my father, and grandmother), a weapon no one can ever take from me.

Chapter 45

African Queen Winnie Mandela

During the tour at the university, I had been working with Winnie Mandela, who was now the Deputy Minister of Arts, Culture, Science, and Technology of South Africa. Winnie had offered to help me obtain a license to establish a cable TV station in South Africa, and we were close to having approval, or so I thought and hoped. Winnie invited me to come back to South Africa and help her push the matter through, much to the disappointment of the dean and some professors at NYU who wanted to see me in cap and gown at graduation. Instead, I took the first plane out back to South Africa with my IMSCO NGO badge in my pocket feeling like a black James Bond reloaded on a mission.

I had sent Ms. Mandela a letter acknowledging that I would accept to undertake the terms and conditions of an agreement presented as Deputy Minister of Arts, Culture, Science, and Technology of South Africa. This was a post given Winnie just to shut her up. But Winnie did not shut up, but she did try to make the best of it. Her aim was to assist me in establishing a private voice, a cable television station in South Africa. I had partnered with Lunga William, a relative of Mrs.

Mandela who was now the ex-wife of South African President Nelson Mandela. Ms. Mandela was, and still is, hunted daily in the press by the dogs of greed who still ran the apartheid system as other kiss-ass ANC black men stood by and did nothing to protect her or the advancement of real education and economic gain for black people everywhere, but black people everywhere paid a price did support ANC entering a leadership role. The only way to survive for most of us was to smuggle, kill, even die for the survival of family.

They were afraid of Winnie. She was bringing diamonds into South Africa, it was reported, from Angola to fight for her life and to feed the hungry people who supported her. It seems the Europeans, Dutch, Jews, British, East Indians, Chinese, all South African blood diamond warlords, and land-grabbing business carpetbaggers were none too pleased to see diamonds in the hands of the African queen Winnie Mandela who spat dirt and fire at their greed and in their faces. I tried but only received half-assed interest from the USAID office in South Africa and Washington, DC. I was an honorably discharged veteran businessman, and I did not qualify and was not eligible in USAID's limited view of a black man to receive taxpayer funding that would be needed to start up and operate the private cable TV network even with a communication and film history degree; if not me than who was? There it was again: the sting of the white clan impeding American citizens using a US-biased global system.

My contacts in the US Department of State in Washington, DC, were not truthful about being pumped up to assist me in the South African cable TV project. Black veterans' freedom of speech is only

free when it came to white speech. I had been in
South Africa earlier and met Winnie a number of
times with her staff watched by American spies as I
tried to sort out all details of the document being
developed to lead up to the meeting with Pallo
Jordan, the duly appointed Minister of Post,
Telecommunication, and Broadcasting, who would
not in the end support the deal but instead gave
support for the TV station license to local Dutch and
a Jewish lawyer that played a role sabotaging me
and Winnie.

When Winnie was forced from her post, the
TV deal was lost to a white South African group, who
received the license from Pallo Jordan to build and
operate the station. It was here that I decided to
start taking on those African representatives who
sold out African men, women, and children to the
business culture of foreigners. Today, South Africa
has all but banned African Americans and other
Africans in the diaspora seeking to link in business
culture with the black people of South Africa. I tried
and failed to open a company there with a South
African name Solomon. The black people of South
Africa are smart, hardworking, and open to African
Americans, but the ANC government was not
working in terms of business cooperation, not even
with their own people at the time. It was easy to
understand why bribes, kickbacks, and tribalism
used by the black and white representatives of the
ANC and foreign government were rampant. When I
say it was a dry black season for black business in
South Africa, I mean it. It was like being in a black
hole; there was no end to the corruption,
impediment, and racism. Winnie was doing her very
best for the people in this postracial war with
millions of white wretched Europeans who hated our

humanity it seemed, and I wanted to assist Winnie and the people and do all I could. Even America's dirty hands were involved naturally with President R. Reagan heading the American government. Like so many black representatives working under the thumb of white presidents in Africa, the black ambassador to South Africa was little more than a yes-man for an oppressive white system in South Africa, America, and Europe. Something had to be done to put an end to human rights violations so blatant in black people's faces and lives.

I spent the next year or so researching a path into much needed business links and was lucky enough to have made some true friends at the United Nations among the African missions.

Chapter 46

9/11, Wake-Up Call!

I crossed the floor to the ringing landline telephone I truly wanted to toss out the bloody window. Was this call from Mr. Balla making one of his usual 911 calls to me from the Congo Heart of Darkness needing money? I picked up the landline.

A panicky female voice laced with U-235 uranium exploded in my ear.

"Frank! Frank, look out your window...turn on your TV. Someone just crashed an airline into one of the Twin Towers. It's deliberate." I sensed fear gripping Ana's high-pitched voice way over from east 86 Street in Manhattan as she spoke into the phone on the other end, sucking needed air into her stressed-out, struggling, trembling lungs.

I could hardly hear Ana's voice on the phone as seemingly an unlimited number of fire trucks with foghorns blaring, nearly breaking the sound barrier, passed under my window a little after 9:00 a.m. on the morning of September 11, 2001, all heading south. I switched on the TV as the symbols of an economic empire crumbled before my eyes in flames engulfing the Twin Towers and burning them to a ghostly crispy white with thousands of people of all nations trapped inside. The horror, the horror was there for the world to witness as people, only having just left home and loved ones, found themselves jumping and falling to their death on that ill-fated unforgettable morning with most not realizing how much western world attacks on African people liberty had to with 911.

A gross-looking black hole resembling a toothless dragon was in the side of the South Tower where the first jet plane had entered, leaving a blazing, angry, red and yellow U-235 afterglow with flames racing out of control. The human mind was not yet wired for this horror, leaving the people with no way to escape from the intense heat already melting imported steel from Asia within the South Tower. Then, as if seeing a repeated exact copy coming out of a Xerox copier, a second plane struck. The name American Airlines could be clearly seen as the plane circled the North Tower, banking for its final approach to a death landing, just above where the recently discovered old no longer abandon, enslaved African burial grounds of the sixteenth and seventeenth centuries deceased disrespected Africans were. This surreal, live TV show was only minutes old but had already reached historic ratings as the most watched show on earth, and not a single US dollar could be earned by the greedy investors' commercials banned by the horror the greed hounds had created. The second big American jetliner carrying passengers picked up speed suddenly reaching what the terrorist inside must have seen as a "death rush" as the jet buried its silvery nose into the side of the outer skin steel frame of the Twin Tower. The one man's terrorist another man's freedom fighter saw Americans as the terrorists and wanted to take as many as possible that fateful day to meet their God Allah and did in a atomic flash. Then suddenly it was as if dust was falling from the feathers of angels' wings cremated from burning human flesh, skin, and bone mixing with the same likeness already falling from the South Tower to the panicked streets and avenues below covering and mingling with human bodies that had already jumped seconds earlier. Those charred, blackened, bloodied, lifeless bodies in ash rain continued to fall from the sky like snowflakes purified by fire. Joseph Conrad wrote in his mid-1850s classic *Heart of Darkness* the thrilling words "The Horror the Horror!" Conrad's book had warned of these "All Fall Down" days of reckoning during his working tour up the Congo River of horror in the eighteenth century where he witnessed slaughter on a scale of horror that pales the details happening at the East River here and now. Conrad's writings mourning the dead of this era and the past telling the reader about his 1800s Euro/Africa nightmare? Conrad informing about a premonition uttered by African victims dead or the living voices my own now so powerful after centuries of forced silence, the hushed voices of horrors will now be heard over the hidden human rights crimes of centuries echoing, "The Horror, the Horror." Most people, except the other man's freedom fighters, were stunned by the surreal events unfolding on the most powerful nation's doorstep the morning 9/11 challenged and defeated every 911 emergency call. Suddenly white America's untouchable system of secured insured dreams and privileged realities had become a void. Nothing in America or the Western world would ever be the same again.

Then just as suddenly the news flash reached the world that the Pentagon, the US Department of Defense, had been attacked and was on fire, and suddenly we all knew it was only the beginning! The mighty empire's global image had been taken down by its own planes. How far the fall would take the global empire was anyone's guess. All hell had broken loose on the too-big-to-fail, unsinkable, capitalist grid still resting on former enslaved labor. Was this only the first stage to set off the final stage of the Western world's apocalypse? If so, where were Jesus and Allah? Were the gods now at war, and if so, why am I led to believe we have maybe only one God? Earth, our planet, is to be shared by all living things, is it not?

The symbol of the almighty state of nations, the Twin Towers, had been brought down by Arab youth flying crop dusters. Beginner pilots had hijacked four American Airlines passenger jets with training granted to Arab students instead of African Americans or Spanish youth posing as crop dusters. It was a privilege not afforded to the hands of African Americans or Spanish that tilled the fields and picked the cotton and fruits for the tables of America and the Western world. I stood there watching with the rest of America and the world in horror as the two planes entered the glass and concrete. Steel beams that made up the frame and foundation buckled the world's mightiest economic system and superpower. Was this "it?" Was this the defining moment in American history many in the world thought could never come to this as it did, in a flash?

I was so stunned I could hardly believe what I was witnessing. In my travels, I had seen a lot, but never anything like this. Mind you, I live two blocks from the Empire State Building that made 34 Street and the all-mighty safe Park Avenue, safe but now suddenly I feel unsafe. Is any place in the United States safe? From the TV screen across the room running red with blood, I could hear one of the female reporters say in a shaky voice, "This is surreal!" Then a quick cut to lower Manhattan's normally gray streets, now bloody, known today as Ground Zero. Suddenly the revolution was being televised. I could see and judge that the whole nation was in a near state of panic and disbelief. People were racing about while everything seem to stand frozen; yet everything in Lower Manhattan was on the move. A woman in one high heel shoe, ripped torn clothes, dust, gray ash, and dirt and covered every part of the bodies moving like ghosts in broad daylight on the streets. Policemen ran too as fast as they could, some ahead of helpless women and injured people. Many people were covered in powered glass, gray white killer ash, penetrating deep into the lungs and being driven by every breath into lungs that were being poisoned by all that remained of human bodies and debris. The killer ash clouded the view of humans, the camera, and the cityscape. Some did in fact assist others where and only if possible. It was a silent, dead mental cram, a silent panic of the masses in slow motion. At my window, I stood looking down from the sixteenth floor, facing New York's fashionable East Side on 33rd Street and Park Avenue. I saw the first of a human tidal wave of ash-covered ghostly humanity appearing as if they were extras in some Hollywood horror movie like *War of the World*. A reminder of African Americans fleeing the American Jim Crow South to the North seeking a way out to safety. In fact, they were only jumping from the frying pan into the fire for African Americans then and now as well as for Africans fleeing Africa. For better or less in America and Europe, the questions for them now are "Is New York burning?" and "Is Paris burning?"

A small number of people passed at first. Then the numbers grew steady, the streets empty of cars or the subway, all moving north to Uptown away from Ground Zero. Then the wind came, carrying the smell of poison, smoke, and gas, smells of human remains that clung to the dead air particles, now invisible, and falling ever so gently unseen by the naked eye. Killing many like my next door neighbor, Mary Kelly, who would later painfully suffocate to death at a body weight of eighty pounds. Mary Kelly had been working near the Twin Towers on that fateful day, and years later the deathly ash would kill her of lung disease clogged with cement ash. Gasping from the ash fallout horror and exhausted from fighting for each breath, Mary signed away her own life (jumped to her death) to escape the horror of not knowing if her next breath would come or end in midair.

On that fateful day in New York, the air had a kind of sad dullness to it, a grayish ghostly look about it on that cloudless day, as death angels with no wings paid New York, New Jersey every city and person in America a visit. The smell was such I have never witnessed before or after. Not in the Congo or any other war-torn areas I had traveled to had I witnessed evolving human suffering.

Still holding the telephone, I heard Ana's voice narrating the horror as I strained to look southward out my window. I saw smoke, a death storm of clouds, flowing across lower Manhattan's skyline as it drifted upward from the moving bodies of the running horrified humanity in the streets. Suddenly I began to hear the sound of powerful fighter jets just a few hundred meters above the New York skyline and wondered if they were ours. New York City and America had entered the "Twilight

Zone" at light speed. I thought, "Fasten your seat belt! This is just the beginning and what a jump to light speed it is." Drawn to the fire and smoke, I had forgotten that I had Ana, a focused investor from Jamaica hanging on the line. Ana was like so many women I owe much of our success to: smart and a lovely mother of one.

"Ana, are you still there?"

"You cannot travel to the Congo." Ana's voice faded back into the present from the void my burning brain had placed her in. I turned back to watch the horror on the color TV screen where all the images were now dripping in gray ash and blood, falling bodies suspended like supermen and women in midair with no sound and no angels with wings to catch them. Where was the almighty? Just send a just Christian God, or Allah will do; I wondered which the stricken would accept or reject. Had the Karan defeated the Cross in dogma? If ever there was a time Jesus was needed to make a comeback, this was it!

"My next trip to Congo is two weeks away. Why can't I travel? Life must go on," I said.

Ana was a small but willing investor, but then that was all I had: small investors in my mineral trade business. She had one child separated like 65 percent of the rest of America losing the American dream.

I closed the window a bit too late because the smell from the reality outside had already entered the apartment with other unseen elements. 9/11 ghosts had already invaded my apartment.

"I am going to keep my travel arrangements. I will call you later, Ana." I hung up the telephone, got dressed, and prepared a cup of tea.

The telephone started to ring again and kept ringing with calls from around the city, country, and world with friends and family wanting to be close to someone, anyone, they thought would be strong enough to help them get through the longest day of their lives.

What had created 9/11? Greed, control, insults of someone's culture? Arabs, Jews, Europeans, white American males, the Cross, the Koran? They were all clan members in the business culture of exploiting people one way or the other. They were partners in crime against humanity. We all know this but will not admit it openly and I wondered why. What were we witnessing?

Congo Crossing

I was back in the Congo to regain the stolen African inheritance and working out problems or trying to with my sabotaged crude oil allotment in limbo with France, America, and the World Bank meddling. The wars were still raging, the raping of women young and old, some by the very soldiers the United Nations sent to protect them. The same attacks on women and children were occurring in Somalia. Crimes by Canadian peace-keepers were made famous by a group of Canadian soldiers holding a Somali boy over a steel drum with flames shooting out of the opening in the nineties, and the foreign economic raiders still on UN payroll were among them; most were East Indians and Pakistanis slithering about, some with not a word of French or

English, stealing impeded African people's only way to fund food, education, health, diamond, gold, and the all-important tin and coltan used to produce and operate cell phones and computers worldwide. Not one African American or African businessperson from the diaspora was among the so-called peace-keepers, oil companies, and major mining companies. It was as if Africans and PAD in the diaspora did not exist. It was as if black life did not matter!

The Chinese were just beginning the big push into Africa in 1998 funded by the government of the People's Republic of China. They came into the continent smiling, and although welcomed by the misguided African governments willing to sign ninety-nine-year or even thousand-year contracts in backroom deals, they did not and do not own or have rights to sign away or grant without the written consent and approval of all players including PAD. The African leaders, if one can call some of them that, have no idea what is on the land just as they did with Westerners for decades before. This madness unchecked was grabbing large hectares of the people's land and vast wealth all illegally done, and the foreigners knew this was illegal to do with African dictators. Still the urging and crimes continued using the prolonging of the theft by Britain's divide and rule policy. Meanwhile in Eastern Congo, displaced people from blood-soaked Rwanda were still moving in and struggling to find much needed food, shelter, and medicines. In the mix of all this was both foreign men working for multinational companies and local African men being shot or should have been for crimes against humanity. The white businessmen and nongovernmental organizations working for these multinationals, often operating as if they were dictators or the agents thereof and above all rights of world citizens, were not on trial here even though many were promoting the horror in their quest for African treasure before the next 9/11 visits. The very ones who set the killing fields in motion were the only ones who really profited from the slaughter. I was here hoping this time I would depart with my lifting agreement to move 0.5 million barrels per month of sweet crude oil. I had requested cooperation from the American ambassador and embassy in both Congos, but so far my request had yielded nothing, and this was a few years after I had made the deal. How much money had my team and I lost?

I met with Congo government officials again and was told I would receive my crude oil soon. When the deal was signed, crude oil was around US$23 per barrel. In a few years, the price of oil had climbed to US$90, then US$119 per barrel. With Africa back and on the move upward, who knows where the price will end with the world depending on the commodity. You do the math on what my team was losing and still is. There I was standing in the Congo on my own land, now a millionaire a million times over in assets, property land to build cities on, and all I had to do was get the crude oil to the market, any market. When the day of reckoning comes, and it will come, a 9/11 moment in our time that will end all these rogue companies, CEOs will be charged with receiving stolen property. Africans worldwide will have their day in court, but whose court?

I predict it will be out of court via a resources war that will lead to the printing of an African global stable currency, not Chinese, to be involved as the leading currency in international banking and trade. In fact plans for a currency for Africans and other developing nations, like China's ability to assist, based on their wealth values is underway, so stay tuned. While the talks went on between government officials regarding the crude oil, I crossed the Congo River back to Kinshasa, DRC. I had been to Kinshasa before with Mr. Balla and Jules, my late Cameroonian friend who died in 2000 at the age of forty-two, which is the limit for most African men; something the foreigners count on when signing long-term illegal land and wealth-grabbing leases. If you recall, when I signed our deal, it was done on open TV as a news event. It was for life for African people as we are the real owners of all Africa is and will ever be. Never do you witness this type of business action being done openly between foreign companies and African officials.

Jules had come to live and work in Brazzaville hoping to find a better life for his family because his native Cameroon was so corrupted. I had no idea just how corrupt some African governments and representatives were until I visited Cameroon in 2004 and 2005. This is not to say America and other nations and representatives are not as corrupt as Africa. Each time I crossed the mighty Congo River, I could not help but be humbled by its power and astonishing beauty that had cradled my ancestors' birth. The great river runs without making a sound until it becomes rapids later on before reaching the Atlantic Ocean. During the crossing to Kinshasa, I left Mr. Balla seated among the two hundred or so colorful Africans with their goods to be sold in the dusty streets of Kinshasa. I moved to stand on deck and watch the big river roll by between the boat and the city of Kinshasa. In 2005, most buildings in Kinshasa still resembled the old colonial 1600s and 1800s era of Africa, in some ways the mineral-rich country, but not the people, was still stuck in that time: rusting tin roofs, moss-stained sidewalks, and bent railings and walls slowly decaying and giving way to a few postcolonial buildings. American and European embassies are walled in for protections from ground level 9/11s that were imminent. Some walls of embassies and foreign homes were so high one could not see the buildings behind them. The Chinese embassies could have been an exception as the Chinese saw the need for much less protection.

The big boat was built somewhere back in the 1900s. I walked to the railing and looked out over the rolling Congo River toward the approaching city of Kinshasa, frozen in the time of the horrors of King Leopold's blood quest for the Congo's riches using mainly human beings to serve the so-called privileged people of Europe with rubber to run these emerging failures, their wars, factories, and global apartheid economy doomed to collapse later, as they all have. The Congo River for a time seemed blood red in my mind and made me think of the many lynching's of black men and women on both the Mississippi and Black Warrior River back in America's south. But don't mind me. I am a disabled American veteran suffering from anxiety still. I sometimes see things in my mind. Anxiety? I wonder what some of my readers suffer from facing all the shit hitting the fan in their lives these days. Better to let it hang out from time to time. It's safer.

In DRC with the help of Mr. Balla, I purchased a few quality diamonds for the cause of business development among us Africans. Mostly French, Belgians, Arabs, Asians, and Indians were milling about the place grabbing what they could before the next blood uranium and diamond war began. Mr. Balla and I quickly returned to Brazzaville to finish talks with the minister of oil and the officials of SNPC who were dragging their feet mainly because they did not have the power to move the deal ahead and did not wish to let on they were powerless. They could not see the advanced power our team was offering them. But we Africans did have the power to override these insults and trappings of postslavery imperialism; after all, it is our property and future. By now Balla and I were truly fed up with the lack of some family members understanding that we all were owners of the vast wealth and limitless future for Africans, the land, and its people. I got sick to the point of kicking butt, so I boarded the Air France to Paris and then New York City where I had plans of calling some guys in the US Department of State to ask for their help in freeing up the crude oil that was being kept from me by some very powerful and hidden hands, people who ran the multinational oil companies, namely France and Belgium. Trailing was Britain, weak, all biased as hell, like Italy and much of the United States, and driven by a few plotting economic terrorism on PAD's right to return to their homeland and codevelop with family. What was my chance of getting help from Washington? Even being a veteran and having served the United States and the people, I had no idea if Washington would assist, but it was one of the few chances I had left to get the oil before accepting the fact that nothing short of an all-out cultural and economic revolution would work.

Back in New York City, I wrote a letter to the Office of Commercial and Business Affairs asking for cooperation to obtain the 0.5 million barrels of sweet crude oil that the government of the Republic of the Congo had granted my team but had not delivered on for hidden reasons. A few weeks later, I had a letter in my hands stating the US Department of State Senior Business Advisor Office of Commercial and Business Affairs would look into my case regarding crude oil lifting in the Congo. My contact in the State Department did contact the US ambassador stationed in Kinshasa to look into the matter in the Republic of the Congo. The ambassador was in the DRC across the Congo River because it was not safe anywhere in Africa for most foreigners, so the US government closed the embassy in Brazzaville and sent all American personnel to live and work in the DRC, where they might have better protection from terrorists who had already blown up embassies in Nairobi, Kenya, and Dar es Salaam, Tanzania. They had killed hundreds for the very reason my team and I were being denied and sabotaged in our efforts: to obtain our birthright and rite of passage to self-determination. So my team and I understood the actions being taken in Nairobi, Kenya, Somalia, Sudan, and Dar es Salaam. The US ambassador to the Republic of the Congo did call on the minister of oil to follow through on my crude oil deal. Weeks dragged into months, and then a year had passed and still no oil lifting agreement. What the hell was holding it up? The deal had been signed in 1998, so what the fuck was the holdup?

Chapter 47

WikiLeaks / The World Takes Notice

The major oil companies were not about to listen to my team without the right amount of force leveled at them or their international interest. Mr. Balla and I were not the only African men caught in this freeze, squeezed between thieves stealing Africans' wealth and waging war on anyone or nation that stood and faced them. They blocked (even at the point of guns) any profits from reaching the global African community. Now we Africans are faced with taking on the multinationals. Time after time, I went back to the US Department of State and asked my contact in the business department to assist me. This time a contact in the business affairs department in Washington, DC, suggested that we use the US Congo bilateral trade agreement and investment treaty to protect my written agreement with the Republic of the Congo. Again letters, phone calls, and faxes were sent out to the ministers in the Congo as well as copies sent to the American ambassador in the DRC.

Still nothing seemed to break the logjam holding up the flow of our allotted crude oil. The Senior Business Advisor, Mr. Dennis A. Winstead, at the Office of Commercial and Business Affairs in Washington, DC, suggested in a letter to me that I review the bilateral trade agreement treaty between the US and the Republic of the Congo to assist in the effort. I had my New York attorney read the bilateral trade agreement with me, and my attorney sent the letter to the State Department's lawyers asking for guidance, but the response was less than what was expected, leaving me to believe there was some kind of conspiracy against such dealings and me. I had no proof of this, but actions do speak louder than words in this world where money talks. I had little money despite owning a share in trillions of dollars in African assets, but no way was I going to let white males and Europeans grab and hold onto African wealth as if it were off-limits to the true owners: Africans everywhere. As far as I was concerned, we had the oil.

In 2005, a letter from Mr. Dennis A. Winstead, at the Office of Commercial and Business Affairs suggested I fly back to the Republic of the Congo and meet with the minister of justice to discuss the matter and press the law to comply. Mr. Winstead even provided a list of US-approved Republic of the Congo attorneys for me to select from in the hope that this might improve my ability to obtain the promised crude oil lifting agreement. My team and I began to suspect something much bigger was blocking our path.

I was armed with the State Department's support such as it was and had just received a negative reply from the World Bank. I had sent a letter to the World Bank CEO demanding transparency on why they were interfering with my crude oil deal we had signed with the Republic of the Congo. We demanded that the Congo government pay off its debts to the World Bank and its clients. I was led to believe they would do so before supplying crude oil to any outsider like my team and I. The

World Bank's reply came from their Washington DC office. During the same time, reports were floating around that the French government officials in the Congo were interfering with our crude oil deal as well. Why? They had their deals with the Republic of the Congo, and we had our deal. The government had agreed to supply us the crude oil from its allotment received from the companies pumping the crude and had the right to sell it to whoever they wished. In this case, it was announced on Congo State TV that they wished to sell the crude to AMRE Trade Oil now established in the Republic of the Congo as a US company linked to IMSCO, an African American and Congolese partnership. What did the World Bank letter say? In a few words, the letter from the World Bank said, "The Bank is all for transparency but do not wish to do business with your company." Hell, my company and my business partners, Mr. Balla and the rest of the team are Africans who are coowners of the African continent and everything in it, and the World Bank is there with the French and other carpetbagger clients promoting terrorizing methods that keep Africa and its people's human rights to self-determination down. The government of the Republic of the Congo and the representatives came through. They signed the deal, and now it was up to me and the team to see the oil deal through to completion. Yes, sure as hell, there was more to all this than met the eye, and the matter was not closed.

In 2005, I landed in Yaoundé, the Republic of Cameroon, to appear on national TV and was received by Prime Minister Ephraim Inoni of Cameroon. He would later be imprisoned with two other officials for, we are told, purchasing and then leasing a faulted plane to the president of the country, who had engine trouble while in flight with his family onboard. It was widely believed the prime minister was in line to become the president of Cameroon. When I met Prime Minister Ephraim Inoni at his office in 2005, I was announcing the proposed establishment of IMSCO in Cameroon. I flew to a number of cities in the country and was so happily received I was presented keys to the city in the far north. A few years later I would finally establish IMSCO in Cameroon where it remains.

It was a hot Thursday afternoon nearing the end of 2005 when I reached Brazzaville, Congo, to keep my appointment with the Minister of Justice Mr. Entcha Ebia. Few if any modern buildings were rising among rusting tin-topped residences and offices with windows blown out, and the strong friendly eager people were moving about, never ever giving up. I met Mr. Balla, and we hired a local Congolese attractive female attorney who was about forty years of age at the going rate of US$400, who arranged to take us directly to Mr. Ebia's home. Our attorney called the minister of justice and got him to agree to meet us the next day. I had come to meet him to help break the logjam to free our oil and see what was holding up the final approval of the lifting agreement needed to start moving the crude oil to AMRE Trade Oil control.

As we drove the streets of Brazzaville in the dry heat, the trees and vegetation were dry, but the sweat was popping off Mr. Balla and I like drops of water dancing on the eye of a hot stove. The steamy sticky African heat was the kind that made 110 degrees feel more like the 120 degrees one receives with a blast in Sudan. The attorney, who was driving us, seemed cool, as most women are.

The attorney parked her car across the

street from an aging colonial-style house that turned out to be the minister's private home. The three of us crossed the street and were invited through the gate by one of two armed Congolese soldiers guarding the home. The guards looked us over, recognizing the lawyer, and waved her through as she turned to Mr. Balla and me and pulled us past the armed guards with a single glance of an eye. The minister's wooden home on this lazy street in Brazzaville left over from the Dutch and French colonial era had wide wooden steps that led up to a veranda and the screen door. A maid greeted us at the door, and as we entered, we could see the late sixties-something minister as he rose from his European-made armchair and crossed the room to greet us in his bare feet. A cold drink in a floral-designed glass right out of the 1950s sat still sweating from the chilled contents inside. The home of the minister was modest in its appearance. The drapes were drawn even though the house sat behind one of the hundreds of cement walls that rested around most homes and offices in Brazzaville. After we were seated and a few jokes tossed about regarding the heat to relax the air, I thanked the minister for receiving us and cut to the discussion. I told the minister my side of the story about the delay, showed him the State Department's letter sent to me regarding the appointment, and asked for his help to receive the final oil lifting agreement to move our allotted crude oil.

"Mr. Weston, welcome to Brazzaville. I understand you have been here before?" the minister asked.

"Many times," I replied, sipping the refreshing water handed us by the maidservant.

"We Africans have made some big mistakes

in African development by not turning sooner to our African brothers in the US as business partners, which would have presented the people of Congo better and more secure development I think."

I was not all that surprised about the minister's view since the government of the Republic of the Congo had already granted cooperation via an IMSCO Establishment Agreement (albeit a half century late with both sides partly to blame). While I was gathering my composure from the minister's remarks, the phone rang for a second time interrupting the meeting. The first call the minister had received was short, but the second call lingered on as he carefully listened to the long-winded caller. At the end of the call, the minister sat for a beat or two, then looked up, and began informing us what the call was about. The minister said the caller was an African man complaining about some Lebanese businessmen who had been given a license to cut timber deep in the forest of the Congo. Immediately, the horrors and terror the Lebanese inflicted on Africa flashed across my brain as I recalled my visit to the Republic of Liberia, Sierra Leone, and Cote d'Ivoire in 1982. Liberia and Sierra Leone had been the hardest exploited by these terrorists. In the end, President Charles Taylor went to prison for teaming with theses human rights crimes violators. The hands of the Lebanese, English, and Americans were dirty and stained with African blood dating back to the days of slavery and the present-continuing terror. My brain was swelling from anger and disbelief that the timber raid and horrors were happening here as well. Africans in the diaspora were truly needed in here if this mess were ever to end. We were needed as trading partners though some in the Republic of the Congo (not just the whites) did not see this need or understand since they had history totally removed from their lives, as did many of us in the Western world and beyond. If that was not bad enough, the minister said the Lebanese were refusing to pay the men for the months of hard labor.

The way the scam worked was a group of Lebanese would illegally obtain or buy Congo passports and citizenship from some corrupt Congo official for a few US dollars and then promise marginalized African men living in the bush who could not read or write slave wages to cut the trees. Then after refusing to pay the men, the Lebanese would depart the area or the country. A second Lebanese would enter claiming to be a new owner having no knowledge of the old deal with the African workers. Mind you, the Africans in the bush or jungle would have no contact with the official policy of the government, so all they had was the word of the foreigners ripping them, their families, and the country off. The second group of Lebanese, cut-rate business owners buy from the first, the contract owner, and then tell the Africans that if they carry on working, they will indeed honor their contract with the men but never do. So the workers have no choice but to work or walk, and if they walk, another group of desperate African men will come and get swindled. Now we know why war breaks out here so often and Europeans get hacked to death. There was one event where a corrupt, disrespectful Korean business man was beheaded in the jungle, and his head was brought back to the city and dumped at the door of the house he was living in.

In this case, the minister said the second Lebanese businessman had refused to pay the man as well. No news as to what happened to the

Lebanese in this case. Africans are now ridding the areas of these types of foreign elements. I asked the minister why he was allowing this to happen in a free Africa.

"We are letting it happen. The government officials in charge of the forest accept bribes and kickbacks from the foreigners to make up for the little pay the government pays its officials if they get paid," he said. "It's not an accepted policy of the government," he added. "But in the end the buck does stop with the government. We condoned this kind of behavior. There is no excuse I know, but we have so little money and control with such a poor infrastructure to properly police these kinds of matters so far from our sight."

Money? I could not help but wonder if the minister knew what money was made of and that Africa and the Congo were the world's bank for the minerals, resources, and people that gave money its value worldwide? Mind you, this very same horror was taking place all over my homeland. Corrupt Europeans, Arabs, East Indians, Asians, and even African officials too, who claim they love Africa by preaching it on TV and at the United Nations as if they gave a damn when all they really care about is the money the foreigners provide them, with the understanding that the money remain in foreign banks. Our project, demands, and shares of African vast wealth and land for the people represented a major threat to many. In the end, the minister of justice agreed to assist.

WikiLeaks to the Rescue

There is no well-managed African legal system to enforce and protect crucial cultural law in Africa explained the seemingly near powerless Congo minister of justice that summer afternoon in Brazzaville.

It was time for PAD in the diaspora from the EU to Brazil to across the Americas and Africa to bring justice and law to the global African village. So what are the newcomers to Africa like me really facing? An African inheritance war with foreigners. However, the best place to fight and win this war is from US soil as we were doing. Not in a thousand years could I have guessed where my team's success in obtaining this important business dealing would lead to. It is so powerful and rewarding that my journey led to our 1999 Republic of the Congo oil deal. I had no way of knowing at the time that the status of the deal would end up in such important files of the US Department of State as a part of the American economy and the quarrel and interactions that would come with the world famous WikiLeaks cops as a historic review case.

WikiLeaks is an online police squad, a kind of poor man's James Bond, where important documents were leaked to the media and world about nations and major corruption, alleged spying, and dirty dealings aimed at citizens in our Republic of the Congo oil deal. In 2014, I learned our Congo oil was smack in the middle of WikiLeaks cops' hands as a historic case to review with my name among the cases.

Mr. Winstead's name along with my own were published as the main players. Why was this case placed in the WikiLeaks files? Simple. It was big oil, and fifty million barrels of Congo Light Crude oil supply revolving was big business in America's global economy. My United Nations NGO IMSCO and I had the listing of dealing in big oil.

The US department file on me and the Congo oil deal WikiLeaks lifted from US government and Congo government files and published on the WikiLeaks website as a document worth the world's time to review read as follows:

UNCLAS KINSHASA 000819 SIPDIS DEPT FOR EB/IFD/OIA/JPROSELI, L/CID/JNICOL AND AF/C FROM BRAZZAVILLE EMBASSY OFFICE E.O.12958: N/A TAGS: CASC, EFIN, EINV, KIDE, PGOV, CF, OPIC SUBJECT: CONGO/B: 2005 REPORT ON INVESTMENT DISPUTES AND EXPROPRIATION CLAIMS REF: A) STATE 070014; B) Kinshasa 0769 C) State 61595; "Winstead email of February 2005 1. In reply to Reftel A, Embassy Brazzaville reports the following investment disputes in Republic of the Congo Claimant B Year When Dispute Arose: 2004 Case History: Claimant alleges that Societe National des Petroles du Congo (SNPC), the state-owned national oil company of Congo, reneged on a letter of intent to supply 5 million barrels of crude oil that was signed by the Congolese Minister of Hydrocarbon in July 1999. The dispute involves the specified quantity of crude oil; the dollar amount is unspecified. Claimant visited Brazzaville (Congo) in February 2005. Meetings took place between claimant, claimant's Congolese lawyer, the president of SNPC, and the Minister of Justice. Before departing, claimant reported that the claims had been addressed during the meetings and that the results were satisfactory, but did not specify what the results were. Prior to the February visit, the Embassy furnished a list of Brazzaville lawyers to the claimant through the Department. 4. Claimant A: Af-Cap Claimant is a U.S. company. The Embassy does not have a signed privacy act waiver. 5. Claimant B: Frank Weston President International Multiracial Shared Cultural Organization (IMSCO) Claimant is a U.S. citizen and U.S. resident. The Embassy does not have a signed privacy act waiver. 6. Brazzaville Embassy Office— Sanders. DOUGHERTY" END.

As Africans in Africa and PAD in the diaspora begin to now take control of their vast wealth, will you, the reader, understand just how important this move is and will be to the world's political and economic survival? By far, it is of the greatest important to African's survival and the world. How will we manage in Africa and beyond in the wider world? For certain, an African cultural war is upon the world over African people's vast land and wealth, and we are not likely to have much cooperation from a world gone mad with greed. Just as it took a cultural war to change and unite China and make it stronger, it will now take the same and more for Africa, which is three times the size of America and China. China by the way is only as strong as Africans, including PAD, allow it to become. Allow? Are Africans that powerful now? Yes, Africa and its people are that powerful and WikiLeaks investigation into America, the US Department of State documents helps prove Africa rise and the PAD place in that rise is no myth. The biased arrogant Western world now at economic odds, some say war, with the People's Republic of China is starting to expose a chapter of the African and PAD role and their entrance into our modern world to design a new future our planet never saw coming. PAD and Africans are now major players, and China and the Western world realize they should never have attempted to write Africans and most especially PAD out of history.

In the face of ignorance and arrogance, something very big is now upon us all, and that something is change, major change for us and the planet, as we all realize black life and economic culture and political contributions matter. The African have-nots have become the haves.

In the end, we thanked the minister of justice and said good-bye, realizing that the future and success we sought was recognized by the African people worldwide, WikiLeaks, and the US Department of State's historical documents. The future is in our hands and our hands alone as African people, regardless of where we live or our income.

Economic power will have to be taken just as African people have taken freedom and political power witnessed by placing a black man and his First Lady in the American White House for two terms. Africa will need big time and big money protection from greedy outsiders that in the future will attempt to sabotage, delay, and ruin African people's success as we team together as we have here in this epic historical story. Big money will only come about when Africans demand that all its people be educated. Minerals and resources must be processed into completed products, not only in Africa but where PAD reside, live, work, and play and with the cooperation in the hands of true and proven allies and partners who do not fear Africa and its people's success. That success involves PAD and Africans is witnessed by the partnership formed between Mr. Vital Balla and I through IMSCO, AMRE, and his

ONG (NGO), and that is the reason major oil and commodities deals can now only be safely, properly, and successfully carried out when Africans are in control; this book report will be filed with the United Nations in the records in the hope that a large part of humanity will take note of the epic story from an African prospective. I have attempted to tell the story to present and future generations to know that attempts were made to record a part of the African story as they rose, stood upright, and took their well-earned place at the head of society where they rightly belong, and that the biased world did not want this story witnessed.

Power and Bad Influence

One did not have to be a rocket scientist to figure out what was happening. African men and women were being used as slaves in the forest just as most black people in America and across the African diaspora are robbed of African links and held in economic slavery with the US style of apartheid and banning in employment, education, business development, and culture. They were still attempting and getting away with it so far, just like the minister of justice in the Congo and Ambassador Youssoufou Bamba, who I had debated on TV in 1988. They were both powerless at first and lied, but while the Congo minister of justice was up front, the ambassador tried to hide his shame and cover up his ignorance. Here in the Congo and across the African continent, the norm was African officials' greed, lack of wisdom in business, and political power. African leaders often used tribalism games, local and international, preferring to trade with the foreigners. Often, it was with African people's enemies instead of their own well-placed people to gain for profits, leverage, and promote ethnic cleansing.

Nigerian greed and Islam versus Christianity, Rwanda and DRC Congo machete justice, Arab versus Israel versus Arab versus America, and the EU and now China—all a certain brand of imperialism. All are competing for African and PAD shares of private property and vast wealth using who has the biggest trick to fuck us all comes to mind. If I had to bet on one for an ally, it would be China as it is certainly working at being an ally to Russia. They realize they both are for self first, but with a twist of humanity, something the Europeans, Americans, and Arabs fail at to the point of zero in African and in other areas with people of color. These are corrupt deals and illegal doctored 99-year-to-life millennium age deals to foreigners, children of the past, and in some cases, present slavers, oppressors, and terrorists to African freedom fighters. They are illegally awarded concessions and contracts voided of black youth in and outside Africa at all levels. These undeserving foreign carpetbaggers are growing in number, and this is in full view of the French, Americans, Chinese, British, Arabs, Russians, Germans, Lebanese, and others who have been illegally granted land concessions by self-appointed or foreign-installed African "pop art" leaders who don't even know what minerals are on the land. These African representatives seemingly could care less for the use of satellite technology to research the content of the soil areas the foreigners have pegged before signing contracts for a fistful of dollars, but the soil is worth trillions of US dollars in cash, jobs, and development funds. African leaders are not the people. The youth are mostly blind to foreigners, and multinational companies get away with murder and slavery, so the wealth of the forest and minerals are placed under or remain in foreign control. I have witnessed this firsthand: the selfish, blind acts on the part of over fifty-two and growing African divided states leaving nothing for the PAD or African youth if we Africans accept this crime against humanity. I say over fifty-two because it seems breakaway areas of the continent caused by the partnership between foreigners and African leaders happen so often it's hard to keep track. In Uganda and across Africa, Chinese, Arabs, and Jews trailing safely behind Europeans are fencing off large areas of the continent to keep Africans out. Yes, we Africans are in an African inheritance war. To win, we must defeat all attempted renewed colonial wars for Africa and the people's right to self-determination.

Chapter 48

The African Inheritance War

In the end, the Republic of the Congo minister of justice said at our historic meeting that he would inform the proper officials, meaning the minister of foreign relations and the president, if need be. In any case, the fight was not yet over, and I sure as hell was not about to give up the fight we had won. Had our visit caused the minister of justice to turn up the heat to release the crude oil the state had commissioned? That remained to be seen. At the end of the day, it was the multinationals and American greed that backed the World Bank and IMF-funded mafia hands. John Perkins wrote about this in his 2004 book *Confessions of an Economic Hit Man* published a year before the meeting with the minister of justice. They held the patents that American taxpayers and Africans paid for in cash to create the African diamonds on the head of drilling equipment and pay as much as US $50.000 a week to non-African workers on the oil rigs while black youth scrambled to exit their homeland and paradise. And here I was trying with all my energy and funding to get back into my paradise.

Africans and the leaders do not know how much of our oil leaves the sea bed through the tiny oil rigs and wellheads that lead to the waiting massive sea on ships bound for ports in Europe, Asia, and America with the proceeds going into white-owned and white bank accounts as black youth are being gunned down and sent to prison for smoking weed, a joint due to the fact the black youth were bared from working in their own development. This human right violation is at the core of going without a proper bed, food, clean water, housing, education, and employment when Africans are so very rich.

By birthright, we Africans collectively own the land and the resources, and we are moving to unite the cultural revolution, march it as we are doing right across the continent as China did to rebuild our once-wretched lives. There are some five hundred million PAD in the diaspora and some eight hundred million in Africa, making a billion-plus Africans of which 60 to 70 percent are under the age of thirty-six. Young black men and women will not take no in exchange for a grand future with land to fare better. A lot better. Thanks to the World Wide Web, no longer are the black youth cut off from knowledge about their vast African wealth that till now they were denied due to jacked-up loans, school fees, or no schools at all due to apartheid, the US government, British and Jewish banning, and Arab cultures that deny young women from education at the age of eleven.

The struggle across the planet being waged by Africans is the final cultural revolution aimed at rebuilding lives and taking management control of our land and freeing our people from ignorance. Continue to enlighten the people, and I do not mean with the Cross and the Koran. Start with saving, redirecting, and relocating our brave and fit youth from the hands of unfit rules. Teach people and institutions, including streets gangs and prison inmates, from being misguided, and welcome them back into society with no belief system if all they are offered is the Cross or the Koran. This is a misdirection for many, forcing them away from their natural African cultures and vast land and wealth that states they can be whatever they wish to be or not be. A certain way to ensure that this happens is to show by example the African youth and adults a path to the African new world with the prize they have already won.

The taking of political control and economic control is a must by African youth. To hell with America and the world crying dependency on Africa's wealth while holding on to African private property. These foreign to Africa aim to hang on as long as they are tolerated to steal skills, land, and resources belonging to African youth, not African leaders and multinationals protected by biased, corrupt bilateral trade agreements, investment agreements, and trilateral agreements used to make false claims on who is in charge in Africa. It is five hundred million African diaspora people and eight hundred million Africans who own the land, wealth, and opportunities. The African youth's mind is not wasted; rather the mind and body are now free to escape and relearn to swim in the sea of plenty.

Visiting their African homeland, as I did when younger, is like having sex in the backseat of a brand new car a proud parent has gifted you made of African minerals and fueled by African energy. Claiming African ownership is the same as owning dual citizenship, which I owned but did not realize until late in life. Now that I do realize it, knowing this true fact enables and enlightens me so I could and did develop into a proud and powerful African man. I am now a man of wisdom and will continue to visit the land I own and witness firsthand as I and many others have done to retake the vast land, wealth, and freedom we Africans own to a whole new level. And we have our ancestors to thank for this new beginning. The ancestors that first stood upright and looked out over the African plains that bordered the great African forest, much of which still stands that created the young King Tut and others before and since went on to raise the first civilization and with these gains for the human race and the planet went on to create the first computer codes (hieroglyphic writing) that taught the world to read and write. Africans educated and raised humanity to the highest level we know today. Africa's youth and new qualified leaders that must be the learned must not fall for the so-called Western European, Asian, Arab, Jewish, and East Indian free aid plot that kills more than it could ever possibly give or heal. An insult is what the foreign aid must now be called because it is a trick. The people who operate these scams are clans out to grab Africa's vast land and wealth in exchange for dead aid or death to the people they claim to be assisting but cannot help themselves or save their own homes.

The likes of foreign institutions owned and driven by white Wall Street CEOs and America's former presidents' biased, anti-black, and now poor white youth economic clubs and their failed states partnership; the youth of all cultures must see their world being ripped apart by these 1 percent goons from greed hell. A just new world must open their eyes as should African people if we wish to survive. We all must witness these economic KKK apartheid clans for what they truly are: killers of planet Earth.

What Is Money Made From?

Now going broke, America is losing its Moody's Aaa first-class rating. The last time it was checked, it was at an Aa rating and diving lower, some say with only the military to back up the American dollar. America's system is going bust, causing once-major American cities and allies to go bust. This suggests America is holding a bad hand in the poker game in the superpower's game of chance with its enemies and allies. What money and power are made of and where they come from is the quest. What is driving China and giving China its rise and much of Asia and its trading partners? Knowledge and Africa are feeding China.

It's now 2015. The news about Africa's rise to world power is flooding the global economic system popping up all over, and this has started a rush on minerals held in abundance in Africa, the stuff money and power is made from. African youth must educate themselves as fast as they can because their future is going to need all the advanced education they can get. Africa is the private property of African people, and at the head of the list are the African youth who will and must make the call as it is not the call for any foreigner to make.

What I am saying is US treasury debts will rise as a result of the downgrade, and rates on short-term debt could fall as investors throw money at safe-haven assets. My bet will be on gold, the mineral that grew ancient Egypt to be a back-to-back global millennium superpower. Even Egypt's state of decline survives on gold from Nubia, the land of the blacks (Sudan), and from its golden age of life-giving treasures yet to be seen. Egypt awaits the return of the Nubians.

These times have us all witnessing unpredictable actions in us all. As a result, even white Americans, Europeans, Asians, and Arabs are jumping once dependable homeland ships and running for the borders, any border. In Zimbabwe and South Africa, the foreigners like the Dutch, Arabs, English, and Portuguese among others (even Africans) took silver from invaders for African lives before the invaders enslaved the traitors. The history of these invaders and nations proves they defiled in human blood and lives the name of all that is holy in Christianity and Islamic beliefs these invading slavers used to terrorize Africans as they carried the evil forward into Africa; slaughtering countless millions of Africans who remained in Africa on the land. This is not counting the millions of African families stolen and those tossed overboard at sea. The worst human right violators, such as the Dutch, Arabs, French, Spanish, Germans, English, Americans, and Portuguese, are now suing the government of Zimbabwe in an attempt to force the people to give up the victory won at liberation to keep the remaining white settlers on farmland; homelands taken centuries earlier at the point of guns. at the cost of countless lives, millions of African men, women, and children; and land rich in farming with soil and mineral wealth so vast the land glows with green life and riches.

I was invited back to black-controlled Zimbabwe in 1989 nine years after independence and was asked to appear on Z-TV .to help the blacks force the whites from the land. They were trying again to invade and take control of Zimbabwe and the people's lives. The land had its hero President Robert Mugabe who reminded the queen and prime minister of England and the world that the people of Zimbabwe had their Zimbabwe and they had their England, EU, and America. Zimbabwe and African land is not white owned and will never be for sale to the former murdering occupiers who refused before and after independency. African white brothers and sisters who never gave a good damn about black human rights must get themselves a return ticket and move back to where they have roots, so say the people of Zimbabwe and Africans in the diaspora who must also get a return ticket and must to paraphrase the Holy Bible "return to the land of your birth and develop." The English, Dutch, Germans, and Europeans have land to return to, and as we can witness, Africans are not welcomed in Europe or any white-controlled land beyond certain extreme limits. African youth everywhere, listen up! Escaping the Western and African nightmare in Africa by running for cover to Europe is not a solution if it can be avoided. Escaping the Western nightmare system into African paradise to rebuild a new Africa is a sound welcome solution. However, traveling from Africa for education, business, and tourism are reasons that should be carefully reviewed.

In conclusion, I will share just a bit more of those obstructions tossed at African people to sabotage and impede their development and give suggestions on what to do about them in order to live long and have some golden years left to kick back in the sun. In my travels, I have learned and witnessed from people, cultures, and personal experiences as in the 1989 telexes and letters I received from the African Union. It's best to remember we have not had the proper opportunity to communicate, so the one institution PAD need the most is proper qualified representation in political and economic areas on a community level. The right to self-determination qualifies PAD in the diaspora to establish self-governing systems if only to help manage their vast shares of African land and wealth and to communicate directly with African nations' leaders and foreigners having any relations and links with PAD shares of Africa's vast private property to ensure PAD a quality of life and a protected lifestyle wherever we live as a human right. I suggest these changes be supported immediately and IMSCO as one institution PAD should call for to make all possible efforts to help bring about positive change and help manage and control Africa's vast land, wealth, and opportunities for the people at all chosen speeds.

The Republic of the Congo minister of justice I met that hot summer afternoon in 2005 in Brazzaville was as clear as pure Congo mountain spring water with his last statement to Mr. Balla and me: "African men and women must maintain management control of African land and wealth!"

Since the 1500s, the Europeans have pegged every inch of Africa and African lives with guns, the Bible, and lies. It's time for the invaders and all who partner with them to go home, stay home, and make room for the new Africa and the PAD who are returning. There is no need to panic. Africans will continue trading and interacting with foreigners. The African inheritance and black man's renewal are now powerful with allies enough to push superpowers and invaders aside as we must produce global change that made China possible, except for the Western nightmare. No matter how it cuts, this is a new beginning for African people globally. In the end, even the invaders must obtain return tickets home and take their oppressive biased cultures and models of imperialism with them, with no insults intended. Respect for the rising African culture is strongly advised as interference will not be tolerated. Nature calls and needs the original African woman and man to renew the seed of life only the African can bring forth as free as the migrating great herds on the great Serengeti Plain of Africa's East Eden, birthplace of mankind.

Land of the Blacks

In 2006, I traveled by car with two other people: an African Muslim woman named Fatima and a very capable local Arab driver from Khartoum. We crossed the 120-degree desert deep into South Sudan. We drove along the banks of the epic Great Nile River from historic Khartoum seated just below Egypt. I was in Khartoum to sign another African-to-African codevelopment agreement established to purchase and sell gum arabic to be purchased from African Sudanese farmers. The agreement stood to be worth billions of US dollars over time on the world market, and it carried near unlimited political power just waiting to be tapped. The local Sudanese farmers who discovered the gum millennia past knew its properties and used the priceless natural gum. Today it is the foundation of much of the world economies, more valuable and stable on the international market than 24-karat gold. I did not realize it at the time of signing and announcing the agreement on Sudanese national TV that it was by all accounts because of the vast resources found here that it caused a major concern among the many hidden hands that were here in the business and keeping the value of this vital resources to themselves.

It was all true. I was there and there to stay armed with my United Nations ECOSOC accreditation with the aim of assisting as many blacks and impeded people as possible to reenter major business and to be able to trade and codevelop worldwide. This was my own personal aim as well, and to hell with those who did not like the moves being made as we the people had lives to live and live our lives we should and will. PAD from all over are returning and claiming our birthright, rite of passage, and stakeholder right. We, IMSCO and our affiliate companies, were running the rails, underfunded, and hungry for lost lives over the millennia. What we needed were resources, and the trail of the needed resources led to and ended in Africa. I had no chance of ever doing business with Europeans on any level in America, Europe, or the Western world, and nor did the Africans in Sudan, all Africa that would amount to a wooden nickel. We all are oppressed and locked out of real business connecting ownership in the Western world, and I will be damned as long as I was standing and alive if these sons of slavers were going to ride my ass and the backs of the people a day longer without the fight of their wretched lives.

I am attempting to show proof to young marginalized black people everywhere that the value of their land and inheritance truly is worth saving, owning, and managing, worth learning about and designing careers around in universities, worth living for, and worth dying for. Indeed to the black youth and the elderly, the strong, the sick, the meek, the unlearned, and the professionals, know that you are the largest and richest land and resources owners and holders on earth. You must now step forward and take full control of the management of the land that establishes who you are. The youth, and all African people who wish and are aware, must realize this is it! African people need to realize reality, and like reality or not, Africans, you are in a resource business war over the control and management of the largest wealth source on the planet. That African land and wealth, the vast inheritance left to you by the ancestors who paid the ultimate price to leave it after great suffering, should not be insulted. Some of us accept one too many insults daily from outside problems being imposed when in fact the solution to the problems rests waiting for you: the solution is in your own internal self and community.

To prove African people are at war, keep in mind that it was African people's free labor that the United States and Europe have yet to pay on the hour for the work that was performed under the whip and chain. The guilty foreigners have yet to return stolen property from banks now in he hands of only one percent of the Western mostly vanishing white population all over the Western world. As a black man once said on one of the TV shows I was invited to appear on in Zimbabwe, "You have to take it out of them!" Some of this European stolen African wealth is now being used to pay the growing Western debt due to China and China use the funds to lend trillions back to America and a sinking Europe all on the backs of an enslaved white population replacing black enslavement. But China needs to be reminded that her African welcome can be limited is limited if all the African players PAD are not at the table in all the deals it cut in Africa and in the Western world when African wealth, resources and global interest are at stake. Receiving stolen property even if only half the African owners are at the table is still a crime against humanity. PAD are original full partner owners. China must realize that it cannot just walk into Africa with its youth and half-educated professionals who shun Africans hoping to develop a Chinese Africa. It insults black youth and PAD's right to self-determination as equal African leaders. PAD are not any ones property to insult as black spooks who sit in the wing of a bias African Union (AU) blind to reality of PAD trying to sell us a "Sixth African Region." The "Sixth African Region" is an attempt by African leaders and representatives in Africa and their foreign lenders who call the shots at the AU until PAD representatives are seated. The AU and a hand full of mindless PAD Africans blindly attempt to rob, trick PAD people to settle for less, in a separate but equal deal that gives foreigners time to return reclaim and settle in Africa! Some leaders in Africa just cannot let go of the old colonial bloodsuckers ways. Where have we heard that before? The African presidents and representatives involved wont get away with it at any level. Qualified PAD teams and supported by IMSCO have demanded PAD right to share our voice on our own behalf and cut our own deals for all that we own in Africa and that Africa trades, sells and develops.

Speaking of seats at the table. In the fifties and sixties in America, thanks to sister Rosa Parks the African Queen that took a seat in a racist Alabama on a bus that refuse to tolerate a black person sitting in the front seat of the public taxpayers funded city bus, exhausted from a long day's work as a servant, sister Rosa Parks sat down in the first seat she came to on the bus and refused to move. The white bus driver demanded she move to the back of the bus and sister Parks stayed put. From that hour and day on all PAD in America faced off with a white American system over the right to vote, to be free human beings and live free where we damn well wished. We won that battle. But most PAD (cannot afford even a bus ride today let alone quality medical, food and housing), and most of all to get an education. The men and women behind the African Union leaders insult of granting what is called the "Sixth African Region" while blocking for now the PAD right to vote and seat at the AU table. To protect our hard earn rights to land, and our wealth, soaked in our blood there is only one-way: take the African Union seat by force if need be and hold the meager power seat. Real power is never given; it's always taken! Today that same passive weapon can be used, and it should in some cases be used to take down nations, but it will take too long as we all will be dead by then. Sanctions are the weapons to use today as we have the resources to deny and guns where needed to protect; but the tool of choice I suggest is sanctions that truly bite! There are other even greater weapons, but it is better to keep them off the table for now as the reader may have even better suggestions.

The tool or weapon is the state-to-state bilateral trade agreement. Before you vote for any US or foreign president, insist that PAD own a fifty-fifty stakeholder share in Africa and even more in foreign business interest and trade between the PAD and your homeland. Demand that all be written into the foreign bilateral trade agreements or any agreement both ways with all state and private organizations doing business with Africa and allied partners. Make certain that PAD lawyers, stakeholder representatives, and IMSCO are at the table on both sides of the deal in Africa and the US, and that other nations signing such bilateral trade agreement that have anything to do with PAD land, wealth, and future business share dealings. Believe it or not a PAD government is slowly emerging to offer guidance to the huge PAD population. This is certain to ensure your community has their shares of the resources, businesses, and opportunities to progress now and in the future. If the community cannot or does not know how to properly carry out the management, contact representatives and private organization to watch each other and serve PAD's best interests in and outside the PAD community, such as IMSCO and AMRE Trade Oil Inc. that have a track record. Business is war, and to win a people, in this case, African people must first claim what territory is theirs and then defend it and the property to the death using any means in reach.

Chapter 49

African Human Rights, Shoot to kill!

In 2008, I was back in New York City, standing at my window looking east toward the East River and holding a sizzling "RED HOT" e-mail I had just printed out. It was a copy of a secret e-mail exchange that had been sent to the American embassy in Khartoum, Sudan with my name all over it. There were five e-mails (bullets with my name on them); in all containing a detailed discussion between five people (traitor's) in Washington, DC, and Khartoum and carried a message that confirmed my team and I as suspicious. Mind you the NGO IMSCO I headed was supported upon entering the United Nations ECOSOC UN affiliate by the US Department of State. Certain this plot was cooked up years early 1989 during my visit to Zimbabwe. It took a while but this all came to a head Soon after I had returned to America from signing the cooperation agreement with the black farmers and their agents in Sudan, it was suggested that I obtain a license from the US Treasury Department even though an NGO like IMSCO already had approval from all UN member States to carry out the work mandated by the UN. I would have had no objection to applying for a license had the information been provided by the United Nations and had the US government given proper guidance stating that

NGOs with aims such as IMSCO had needed to do so. When I was in Sudan, I witnessed firsthand and was presented proof that larger Asian and EU companies and the US did not have such conditions placed on them. Even Ex-US present Jimmy Carter, white Hollywood stars and from impeded Africans from Israel to corrupt anti-black control Brazil was in Sudan, North and South racing ahead of wretched PAD and the local wretched wealthy Africans to save us from success. These foreign countries did what they wished to Africa. I could use some foul language here but my book editor would not have it. Well, I was a coowner of Africa; it was my land, my resources, and my people, and I was heading a United Nations ECOSOC-affiliated NGO that like all other NGOs had already received permission to assist the people of Sudan and beyond. I did not see the reason to ask foreign permission from the US or anyone for the right to trade with my own family and wealth. Hell, I had not asked to come to America as the enslaved. I never gave up my human right to America, Europe, China, or the US Treasury Department. I may not have been planning to bring gum Arabic back to the US in the first place especially if the price had not been right. American companies were sending the gum to Mexico or just paying for the supply and letting England, France, Poland, or Germany purchase it under the table, refine it, and then ship it in into the United States as a finished product to sell at prices with no questions asked. The commodities game of locking out African people is the most corrupt game in the world ranking high with the crude oil business. Anything goes or went as nothing is shared with PAD except political and police bullets in the black man back! The shooters objective, the PAD and African land and wealth.

Neither the US or EU officials knew my plan to enter South Sudan under their ever-watchful radar to cut a deal for natural resources reaching the success and amounts I had. The multinationals and American-biased food companies and their agents and brokers serving the pharmaceutical industry, vitamins, cosmetics, high-fiber formulations, beverages, fancy French wines and global spirits of all kinds, confectionary, medical, advanced military explosives, encapsulated flavors, even the nail polish industry, and Hollywood artist representatives must have seen our deal as a threat. Gum Arabic, crude oil deposits, and the gold supply were all pegged by these same guys that had pegged the rest of Africa using the US Department of State and our hard-earned tax dollars to carry out their dirty tricks, called foreign policy, to keep the field clear of so-called troublemakers, smart asses, and freeloaders like me and my team.

I had walked into a mix of bad two legged animals and their multinational agents dividing the kill, devouring the spoils of Sudan people alive after having placed the Arabic president Omar al-Bashir's head on the chopping block for human rights violations later bribing the World Court to back off Omar al-Bashir's. It seems they needed him. In spite of the charges, the Africa funded superpowers were refusing to go in and take al-Bashir down because they needed the Arab dictator to hold his bloody pack of killers in place to keep slaughtering black Sudanese; they wanted black Sudanese dead, and they wanted their super greed jaws to take over Sudan's north and south the way they did with Libya and its late president Muammar Gaddafi. The move by the Western world to grab Libya African land and property is now a mess to be witnessed. What they did not want was African Americans or others to get in on the feed. The Western world blew their one chance in a million during the enslavement of Africans in the fifteenth to sixteenth and nineteenth century because they were just too greedy to see beyond hand to mouth. There had been enslavement before throughout human history even largely across Europe in the millions, and all one has to do is look at the Romans using slaves to build the empire. But this Western greed was different; this was blindness on a scale found in outer space.

As it turns out, like billions of others, my team and I was within our human right to take on outer space. I was following United Nations' protocol and mandate to do what I could for marginalized people of which I was a member and stakeholder in the club, so I already had a license. I had an African stakeholder license and did not need a dog-eat-dog human-rights-violating imperialist group of Western states interfering with my linking and developing with my African family. The United Nations had very clear rules on this. The people in the US Department of State and EU I would soon learn were out to take IMSCO and me down a peg; they were following orders from outside influences who should take a moment to read the UN Charter. The United Nations, meaning 193 UN member nations had approved NGOs, such as IMSCO, to operate in all member states without passing through governmental biased red tape. I did not need a license. Had the US Department of State employees and the people on the *"African Desk"* done their jobs and properly served the people of America, the taxpayers, and not some monopoly gang pulling strings and bribing lower-level US government employees behind closed doors, they would have respected African Americans' human rights. I later discovered attacks on me and IMSCO were coming directly from the US Department of State in a most biased clandestine manner. Judging from the biased tone of the five e-mails passed to me from the US embassy in Khartoum, Sudan, they were meant to block, starve and even bury an ECOSOC United Nations–mandated organization IMSCO and my reputation. The tool of slander in the business and diplomatic global community is used in order to sabotage the human rights of African people. But they failed because some very alert US citizens at the US embassy in Khartoum, Sudan, got their hands on the secret e-mails and sent them to me in New York City.

The ringleaders who sent the e-mails were following guidance trying to block blacks in America and Africans right across the African diaspora from doing business with their family members and homeland. Just as blacks in America are having major problems trying to enter directly into postcolonial Arab Sudan, I was trying to make business in Africa to avoid the denials of lily-white Silicon Valley, California, to achieve business shares, higher learning, and advancement. I had studied in university but was overlooked when the computer technology organizations came calling, so there I was in Africa and learned yet another door stopper was being shoved in my path. Black youth must not ever be found kissing white male mob business ring fingers instead of bargaining on a level playing field as long as they have to enter our Africa, black Africa, black Silicon Valley in search of vital gold, coltan, and gum Nubia.

Resources are the power for driving the

engines of every plane, electronic device, and advanced equipment on and off the planet, and 80 percent of the coltan that drives the electronic industry comes from the DRC. Vital coltan and gum arabic are just two of the ten vital resources from countless other vital resources that money is made from, driving development and human survival. Coltan makes the hard body inner and outer shells of items that are sold to make Africans educated or not when they show the will to (take control regardless of the price and cost) in the right areas between Africa and where they reside or live. CNN promoted shows like *Blacks in America*, which reported on how African Americans who are legal stakeholders in Africa are denied access to advanced electronic technology and creative designing in Silicon Valley and universities. Black youth must ask themselves how many roads they must walk down before they become men respected in this Western society.

As soon as copies of the five infamous e-mails you are about to read for yourself reached me in New York City, shot out of the American embassy in Khartoum by a hidden hand, I contacted the US Treasury Department and confronted the officials. They denied having anything to do with the e-mail attack. I did not think that office had been involved, but on the other hand it's the same US system. It was my way of sending a message back to the employees at the US Department of State's "African Desk" that I had a copy of the telling e-mails. I wanted to send shock waves hoping someone or all players should lose their job. I had been waiting for a reply from the US Treasury Department on the request for a license to import gum arabic after my return from Sudan, and I had been back a year or more and had not received even a phone call.

I should have received approval, a green light, long ago. My case was different, since I was representing an NGO. I was representing the United Nations to help solve humanitarian problems, and these guys on the African Desk were trying to sabotage that work. The reason was clear. Stop Africans in the diaspora from getting a foothold in life and the economic gains to be made in Africa as they had in the Western world. Hell, I was just as black as the blacks in Sudan, and the blacks in Sudan had invited me in. I was only doing my job, a job that was and is supported by the United Nations members, or so I thought. While the US Department of State had not, the US Treasury Department did finally respond to me.

The letter read in part as follows:

> We have consulted with the US Department of State for foreign policy guidance on this matter. Based on the information provided, the State Department determined IMSCO's proposed activities with a Khartoum-based company on such a large commercial project could provide economic benefits to the non Specified Areas of Sudan. Therefore, the State Department recommended that it would be inconsistent with US foreign policy to issue a License authorizing the proposed transactions rout by IMSCO. For the foregoing reasons, your request for a specific license is denied at this time.

There was only one route to move any goods in and out of Sudan: Khartoum. The whole world was moving crude oil and commodities through Arab-held

Khartoum, and they were not being denied. Meanwhile, big business from all nations was importing the gum like it was pot.

What I learned from the e-mails was that these foreign nations, multinationals, and agents (some Arabs) were working for them just as I suspected people at the US Department of State were doing. We all know that many who work for governments often end up selling out the people, including the CIA, and when they leave the government, many hire out to private companies with chests full of taxpayer advantages to boost their inflated salary. Frankly, I have no idea what they plan to do beyond trying to block Africans and other people of color from linking with family and codeveloping in trade. The weapon is dual citizenship!

When you read the following e-mails, you can decide for yourself what they are planning.

The letter from Treasury also stated, "Furthermore, while Sanction 1464 of the Tariff Suspension and Trade Act of 2000 (P.L. 106-476) (the "act") notes that the Secretary of Treasury and Secretary of State will consider license applications by U.S. Gum Arabic processors to import Gum Arabic in raw form from Sudan, the Act does not apply to IMSCO because it is not a processor of Gum Arabic..."

I am a student, not a specialist of crude oil, gold, diamond, or any other raw materials; I am a new breed of trader and for good reason. I, like millions of other Africans in the West and in Africa, have been banned from owning any type of foreign business for centuries and so have all Africans, Chinese in many ways, and Indians in the Americas and the East. Gum arabic is coowned by all African people, thanks now to the meddling in African affairs centuries ago that has come back to bite the meddlers' descendants in the pocket and butt. African people are not American or European subjects or slaves, and based on human rights, they never have been.

If anything, we are an awesome people, badass, determined, supportive, and cool. At the same time, we can take the heat and have for centuries. I don't blame the enemy. I would be a pissed and concerned enemy to blacks as well. Blacks are faithful to each other to a flaw. Africans to PAD, business and trade is moving forward. We did not ask to come to Europe, South America, or North America. What most of us are trying to do is trade and obtain the price of a ticket out of the white world so we can go home in style as peacefully as we can, any way we can; pay for the return ticket with our own resources, as we will. As European and Western economies reach their end of days, one wonders why the former slave empires now fallen are interfering with Africans as they return home knowing full well one should never interfere with an army going home. Trying to understand the plight of the fears of those sporting nuclear weapons, one thing comes to mind: "It's a terrible thing to have to live in fear; having been there once myself."

Remember now, someone had to be bringing in tons and tons of gum arabic from or through the restricted areas in Sudan because the only infrastructure, passable roads, and rail lines were in the north and ran through Khartoum, the area I was forbidden to export the gum from. Instead I was told that I could truck it hundreds of miles over land through a war zone with bandits so pissed at the world, darkness feared to enter the region. If the drivers and trucks survived the unpaved paths because there are still no roads (even in 2015), it would take months and an extreme amount of cash only the Western world print that would drive our market price for the gum arabic sky high and out of the market's reach. Talk about a need for fairness and a level playing field. "Checkmate" is what the guys and girls at the US Department of State (African Desk) behind the e-mails wanted to say. Enjoy and deny life to blacks in Africa and in the diaspora from Brazil to Mississippi to African black bloody streets of America, England, and France and across the still wishful, colonial-minded Germany. Stop us cold in our hot tracks. Not a chance. We are still here going strong.

The following e-mail was released to me from an unknown person inside the United States embassy of Khartoum, Sudan.

I was actually thinking more in terms of cover. If post could turn up something shady on the Sudan end, it would make our case for denial stronger if Mr. Weston chooses to sue OFAC over the denial. When balked he becomes quite irate. It would also help differentiate this guidance from others if we get other applications that seem more credible that we want to approve.

But yes we do have enough grounds for denial now on the basis that we think benefits will accrue to parties in the non-exempt areas and that the quantities involved seem excessive.

US Department of State 2008 email. Our Mission—"Stop Frank Weston!"

*Subject: RE: License Request—
Importation of gum arabic—IMSCO
From: Clark, Owen A Sent Wednesday,
November 05, 2008 11:45 a.m. To: Klein
John Marshall; Young, LaToya M*

The reader will find the entire five e-mails and the outcome at the conclusion of the book.

The above secret e-mail was sent from the US Department of State's "African Desk" in Washington, DC, to the American embassy in Khartoum, Sudan, designed to slander and by any means stop an honorable discharged African American war veteran and his team mandated by the United Nations from carrying out humanitarian work and development projects in Africa that assist African people and American allies and from entering business and trade agreements with Africa and beyond. This list of five e-mails proved to be just the beginning of almost seemingly insurmountable obstacles and near-death experiences (nothing will stop the people) we had to face in my efforts to escape America, the Cross and the Koran, and economic apartheid. To review in full copy of the original US Department of State, five, no doubt countless other emails sent secretly into Africa designed to kill any attempt between PAD and Africans (family) to link in business and trade see page 452.

US Dept. of State Employees, Shoot to Kill!

"Combating racism, racial discrimination, xenophobia, and related intolerance represent the new stage set by IMSCO and PAD NGO's to enforce United Nations and the international community and public funding to ensure the rights and dignity of people of African descent." IMSCO

***

The bias US and European linked systems e-mails (see page 452,) sent by employees of the US Department of State is proof Western the system promotes treason and state sponsored Xenophobia; and that the employee's were being ordered, paid by governments and private outside companies, lobbyist through these employees willingness to take part and to inflict slander, bias, horrors, and terror on five hundred, some say the number is three hundred million PAD and Africans in the diaspora wanting to trade, go home and be rid of the western nightmare. The United Nations answered the call of those five hundred million plus PAD to place the matter of "Combating racism, racial discrimination, xenophobia, and related intolerance, and represent a new stage in the efforts of the United Nations and the international community to restore the rights and dignity of people of African descent" before the world. The PAD people included IMSCO and me that had helped lobby for the historic day and event on December 10, 2014, called the "International Decade of People of African Descent" requested that every nation on earth that had taken any part in the enslavement and violation of PAD and African people in exile to come to the United Nations and own up. Many UN member states (the United States, Brazil, Russia, China, and the EU) were present and played a limited role for representatives of the criminal states or just there to lend Africans' support, I hope. The guilty nations, the United States, EU, and Portugal, whose representatives claimed Brazilian citizenship to try and escape, did show respect but left their bankbooks at home. The nations representatives instead delivered their sad lip service about poverty and forgiving and forgetting your pain. They suggested they exchange it for peace, taking the time of the attending PAD, living and dead souls seated in the packed UN Trusteeship Council conference room, as the floor turned red dripping with the blood of the ancestors from the words of PAD spokespersons.

The attending nation representatives showed signs they did not have approval to give up a dime of the trillions of money to the victims and sat down under shame and extreme pressure. PAD called time and time again for full immediate payment of the trillions of US dollars due, taken, and stolen from their labor, property, and the dead. So who are they when nearly five hundred million PAD live and vote in the Western world and wider African diaspora nations? They are still expecting attacks to increase, raining like missiles from above as we Africans trapped in the diaspora turn and look homeward to Africa and our vast wealth I have personally witnessed. They see Africa as the only place we could hope to start to rebuild and earn a sustainable living, have a sound family and future, and survive with cultures that created humans and civilizations as original and old as nature is. When our right to self-determination and management of most of the wealth shares are under our control, then we can collect our just due from a cold-hearted Western system, if it is still around. Being trapped between the Cross and Koran, you converted or died! I chose to escape back into myself and then returned to Africa where I learned most living baobab trees were older than the deities of Christ, Mohammed, and all others. After decades and centuries all together fighting against all attempts by the enemies of humanity to be pulled back into their Dark Ages, Western imperialists were pulling back from Africa and other lands, and people were struggling to escape the greed and the abyss. But do not be fooled. The new imperialists and colonial Nazis still have a few tricks tucked up their sleeves. But then so do the people.

The US Shoot to Kill Black business

***

United States Embassy of Khartoum, Sudan 11/6/2008
Struble, John W: Economic Officer
From: Clark, Owen A
Sent Wednesday, November 05, 2008 9:20.
To: Struble, John W
Cc: Klein John Marshall; Fierst, Pamela D
Subject: RE: License Request—Importation of Gum Arabic—IMSCO John,

I can engage Mr. Frank Weston one last time and get him to give me contact information for his group in Khartoum. We would then request that you contact them, meet with them and determine:
a. The bona fides of the group—are they a genuine group of cultivators, exporters, financial managers,

businessmen, etc;

b. The Group's plans for cultivation, harvesting, transportation to Port and export of Gum Arabic on behalf of IMSCO (the NGO seeking the License);

c. The Group's responses to questions about their remuneration (how will they be paid for the services provided). Once you have met the group and we have the responses to the above we can determine next steps.

JC Owen "Jimmy" Clark Desk Officer—Sudan—Programs—Group (AF/ SPG) Bureau of African Affairs U.S. Department of State, 2201

C Street, NW Room 5819 Washington, D.C. 20520.

From: Klein John Marshall;

Sent Wednesday, November 05, 2008 11:58 AM. To: Clark, Owen

Cc: Struble, John W

Subject: RE: License Request—Importation of Gum Arabic - IMSCO

I was actually thinking more in terms of cover. If post could turn up something shady on the Sudan end, it would make our case for denial stronger if Mr. Weston chooses to sue OFAC over the denial. When balked he becomes quite irate. It would also help differentiate this guidance from others if we get other applications that seem more credible that we want to approve.

But yes we do have enough grounds for denial now on the basis that we think benefits will accrue to parties in the non-exempt areas and that the quantities involved seem excessive.

From: Clark, Owen A

Sent Wednesday, November 05, 2008 11:45 AM. To: Klein John Marshall; Young, LaToya M

Cc: Struble, John W Subject: RE: License Request—

Importation of Gum Arabic—IMSCO I am truly tempted to say let's draft the denial memo and be done with this, just to stop this man from calling me 5 times a day, he has called twice this morning and is becoming abusive and even more erratic than normal!

The original State Department's slanderous e-mails sent from the Department African Desk, 2008 that support a policy that attempts to deny PAD people the human right to be a part of the African family. The core reason behind the human right and criminal act is keeping the vast knowledge, wealth, land and power out of African people reach. Divide and conquer! The Western world should remember what goes around comes around. There is not a single European Empire Rome of Greece or France or England still standing with any real value still attached. America an exception only due to its large and able PAD pollution wealth being stolen aided by employees such as we witnessed and how far will that take a Chinese govern fading United States of America? I mean really guys these bias email being sent over the web is lame.

End, of biased, slanderous e-mails from the US Department of State "Africa Desk" in Washington, DC. To review the emails (see page 452).

Mr. Owen A Clark labeled me "erratic" for seeking my people's wealth and trade with total freedom from a nightmare slave system he represents yet his actions make he and his teams more enslaved in then Africans yet he cant see it.

Since gum arabic is a major part of America's and much of the world's working economy today, it says that black Africa was feeding America and much of Europe and China, and black people, Africans, worldwide, wanted their land and wealth back, under their control, every grain of gold, diamond, and coltan minerals in Africa. Will this change the world? The world will always be changing, and our few seconds passing through the planet will not stop it.

What did I do about the infamous e-mails? I contacted US Attorney General Eric H. Holder Jr. and requested guidance on the illegal slanderous matter. The US Attorney General's office referred the matter back to the US Department of State and cc'd me a copy of the letter suggesting the State Department should clean up its own mess. I sent a copy of attorney Holder's reply letter to my Congresswoman Carolyn B. Maloney (14th New York Congressional District). She wrote a letter to the assistant secretary at the US Department of State Legislative Affairs requesting an investigation. The congresswoman's letter read:

> *"Dear Mr. Verma, Assistant Secretary US Department of State Legislative Affairs, I am writing on behalf of Frank Weston who work in the 14th Congressional District, which I represent. Mr. Weston contacted me regarding the denial of his request to import crude oil and gum Arabic into the United States for his company AMRE Trade Oil Inc. Stated in the enclosed correspondence, Mr. Weston contacted the Department of Justice on the matter, which subsequently referred it to the Department of State on April*

28, 2011. Please review Mr. Weston's concern and advise me as to your conclusions, consistent with all applicable rules and regulations. Thank you for your attention to this matter. If you have any questions, please do not hesitate to contact my office. Sincerely, Sign Carolyn B. Maloney Member of Congress."

The reason for sharing these e-mails, documents, and letters with the reader is for much the same reason the WikiLeaks group released its documents: to help the world learn some of the hidden hands impeding all humanity. In this case, it is African peoples' development by the one nation's representatives that travel the world declaring freedom for all when most of its veterans fought and were discharged from service with injuries. Many died fighting for that freedom. Those who survived now find themselves impeded and denied a quality of life, gainful employment, or right to own a business by the United States of America and its allies. If this is not a nightmare, then what is? It is important for the world to know what Africans, young and old, are up against as we turn away from the Western abyss of horrors and terror outlawed to defend ourselves as we turn homeward to Africa. We are changing our world for the better as we move forward and strive to be all that we can be as human beings.

I report this information to inform and motivate Africans Americans, Africans, all PAD, and anyone who may be concerned about their own lives so they too can better stand and fight to win the African inheritance war and their own personal war for a better society, and governments. At the end of this book report, this most extraordinary journey, my team and I did succeed in obtaining many goals set. It's not over yet. We have helped set in motion vast opportunities for a great many people and our own. I now can have a home most any place I wish in Africa, but I am not at all pleased with that unless all the people can feel the same. Thanks to the IMSCO Establishment Agreements being passed on to the younger generation and being signed by nations with vast land and wealth and dual citizenship attached for many; African governments and the people that welcome all PAD with keys to Africa our continent, our home. Over the decades, I have made so many friends, partners, and coworkers among all cultures, and I cannot name or thank them enough.

Dual citizenship is the best present any exiled Africa can own as a weapon, as other cultures enjoy and use it to better survive with. Dual citizenship is an all-empowering birthright and a human rights tool that African students, young people, and businesspeople can own as a link to a vastly wealthy Africa. Dual citizenship provides the owner the key to seasons hot and cold and near and far and gives reasons to be motivated as I was to enter higher learning and win at the game of a higher life form. African people, most especially the youth, must now start and develop business as a certain way of escaping the present nightmare in their lives. The Western world and cultural and economic apartheid systems will not end until Africans end them by just walking away to a better life and to the land you own in body, mind, or spirit. Dual citizenship birthright with Africa is the only ticket needed to reach the unlimited amount of wealth to build the cash-generating institutions so that we can afford to just walk away. I shared information with the reader regarding the e-mails written by the US Department of State employees and information regarding the World Bank and the IMF to help people be more at ease as they advance. The major oil companies also see us as their economic competitors believe it or not and we are. An Exxon Mobil employee phoned me once to report on the bias of the company that it would not do business with me or people and companies like ours, regardless if the business is a private business, or veteran or American owned.

The World Bank and IMF wrote nearly those very words to say they would not support or do business with IMSCO or its affiliates, the people, even though I never asked for their cooperation. It seems the World Bank sees PAD, any African in the diaspora, and Africa as competitors based on the kind of deals being cut that are ripping off African peoples' wealth and lives. Keep in mind the World Bank and IMF are NGOs the same as IMSCO, but the bank has big clients like the United States, the EU, and China. Wall Street and its global corrupt system, pulling down America as it has Europe and others for greed, are said to be controlled by 1 percent of the Western world's population that presently exists. Are they saying Africans around the globe are competitors? You're damn right we are! Africans are rich enough to reestablish a global economic system and a pharaoh, like a King Tut, to help unite Africa and protect and manage the continent. "Confessions of an Economic Hit Man," John Perkins, author, book was written to expose the likes of the World Bank and IMF that fail to inform us or address corrupt dealings.

Conclusion

Through it all as it turns out, I would hope I have helped my people see a way back to the land with a lot of help from my teams. Africans have the tools, economic clout, and political savvy to really level the playing field. The African people's vast land, market, and wealth are strong enough to override any racism, racial discrimination, xenophobia, and related intolerance and represent a new meaning to the words "disrespect," "impediment," and "sabotage" tossed at them. In the new world we Africans have inherited and created for ourselves, we can now select our own trading partners. We have taken power as only real power can be had, and African have lots of real power.

It's true that the long African liberation war left a bit of a mess in the African community, but considering the horrors Africans just came through and are going through, the challenges of acquiring the vast wealth we coown as a people, reconnecting the family, driving out the carpetbaggers interfering in African human rights and codevelopment, and getting rid of the related intolerance should be a walk in the park.

This book was researched and written over decades as a guide to help motivate the youth, all who have youthful minds; most of all to the battered, but by no means the alone and down-and-out African families everywhere, youth, good, bad, and the not so good to him or herself, and African businesspeople seeking a better deal, a better world, and a better way of life. African business entrepreneurs and adventurers must now go

all out for the gold! African youth, this is

your time in our time. I cannot say enough with proof that we Africans have the wealth and know-how. Solutions, creativity even designing the genes. A way forward for all humanity has been in us Africans since our ancestors first lit the first fire on the African plains to make dinner to feed the hunters and shelter the hungry and the children, to get the jobs of building earth's first civilization done, and to write it all down to be remembered and repeated if need be. We did it all once; we can and will do it all again. Step into the lead role as we are needed. Take what was stolen from us back, and use it to manage our share of the planet and future with all qualified inhabitants willing to cooperate and build in a whole new direction to a new world where all who wish to can prosper. Own your unlimited life, Africans; that is what this mission in life is all about. Do not let the US government, European Union, Asia, or African Union get away with any more stealing or grabbing African wealth and minerals that young men and women need to build and grow their future. Africans' vast resources are what global wealth and employment progress are made from, so to hell with getting a job. You have the wealth and space to grow business that creates sustainable employment. Being impeded, sabotaged denying in this case PAD, cultural identity links to family back in Africa and rights to education denied our resent African ancestors has turned out a success story; after all over so many years, the denial has come back to haunt the Western world that cannot live without African vital resources and wealth. So who is in control of African lives? Africans! From here on, all who wish to play must and will pay.

Africans must now be very aware of offers of friendship laced with lies and brotherhood. In a letter from the US Department of State

Am I suggesting seeking revenge? Africans have already won their sweet revenge: victory. In any case, Africans do not promote race games as solutions as there is only one race: the human race. Now it's time to "build anew" as James Baldwin reported at the First Harlem Jazz Festival in 1978. Most black folks just want to get on with their lives and be done with Western and foreign cultural and economic interferences. Africans in America and around the globe are tired of the insults of living someone else's culture, dreams, and nightmarish lifestyles.

Linking with Africa and having proof of your ownership rights to the African continent and all that is there is a right for the youth and all Africans in exile as you have so very much to take home and share, even if some of us never make it back and many may not. For those who do or can get back, dual citizenship is the one "return ticket" stub all PAD Africans must now obtain and can obtain with IMSCO's help as one of a few immediate key avenues. Take it!

IMSCO-signed establishment agreements are the protection African people will need when returning and remaining without fear of being harassed or impeded unless one billion and two hundred million Africans and allies will have your back and come to that person's aid. This is how PAD in the diaspora from Brazil to New York City to Alabama to France to Haiti must take their political, business, and cultural seats in Africa and the Western world in any and all areas of power concerning African people's land, vast wealth, and now golden future. Control foreign policy through owning the right to vote in the diaspora, Africa, and the outside world where you now or may reside in the future.

It has been many miles, hours, and years since Paris, France, that first trip to West Africa, and Rock from the Congo stumbling through my door in 1998. I first crossed the ocean to Paris in 1967 and then on to Africa in search of myself; I found self and much, much more. From the start of the book when Rock and I first met, our ancestors had survived African slavery and the bloody centuries-long Congolese and European-created wars. I had survived Western-exiled enslavement in the Americas and all the lies about freedom, liberty, and justice for all that never came and I think never will for the dreamers since America the great superpower is broken with few friends left to be trusted, so the Western empires are falling. Rock and I were not just messengers in time, but warriors in battle whose endless efforts with countless others will continue on into the future.

Rock would attend an American university where a few years earlier all African Americans had been forbidden to attend; that is until African Americans kicked in the doors to every locked institution in the biased country only to find we didn't have the money to attend to reload our minds bodies and souls. Rock received a master's in finance at the University of Missouri. Blessed with dual citizenship, Rock had the opportunity to remain in America, marry, open a business, and have a lovely daughter who is now a teenager. Moreover, Rock, Jeffry, Anita and I to name a few have teamed up to carry on the work Balla, Jules, Rock and countless others not name here helped introduce me to in Congo, Cameroon, Zimbabwe Mississippi, Alabama,

Brazil, across South America and onward. Rock, Mr. Vital Balla, and I were now all a team with PAD in all areas of the world numbering tens of millions on the continent and in the PAD diaspora. We all pooled efforts to develop an Africa rising. We wanted nothing to do with dead aid from the World Bank and aid agencies or donors that think they are slick, smarter than Africans when in fact all the not wanted foreign aid pushers seek African people's wealth to aid themselves. All parties might now try trading with Africans to gain access to Africa's vast wealth and warm-hearted people.

It's been one hell of a struggle even to reach this point in the African inheritance war to advance taking of full control. We Africans have retaken Africa; we have proven we are organized enough to have influenced political control of America with the help and open minds of mostly American youth from most cultures in America who helped place the first black man into the White House, which is huge by any means. So far, Africans have freed themselves more from physical bondage than psychological that have far too many of us working for Big Mac. Mental bondage must now be broken like the iron chains placed there in some cases by our own African chiefs, some of whom still sell out the people in Africa and in exile. They must be removed immediately if progress is to move forward. African youth and adults must now free themselves from a lack of education and economic bondage.

Not to worry, the funds to assist and help get African youth through the education needed and living process will be there is there as IMSCO and its team and many, many others are demanding implementing with IMSCO Establishment Agreements being signed with African states ensuring that PAD shares of African vast wealth be fully shared within the planned international decade for PAD; and these regained wealth shares are to be presented to the people on a monthly basis from all parts of the world for those who wish to take part in the African business rise and trade for profit. From here on in, it's all about owning and living a quality life. The matters of finance, property management, and trade are key for Africans, the largest and wealthiest land owners from North America to South America, the Caribbean, and Brazil. So envied are we that much of the world wishes they were in Africa's seat.

In April 2014, *60 Minutes* reported on the corruption of Wall Street, which most informed people knew. Wall Street was ripping off its own clients in part because Africans have retaken Africa and have more than one group to cut deals with other than the biased, European, greed-stricken 1 percent that butt bash all who are dependent on Wall Street and the death to investors game. Partnering with Wall Street, just like the Work Bank and IMF all are, and stealing, exploiting, and wasting the planet's resources, and for what? The Western billion-dollar clubs produce little or nothing worthwhile for the masses.

African youth can and must step up and save Africa and comanage their vast wealth, which is the only way they can save themselves and their families. America is not the future for black people; Africa is. The Wall Street clan is hopelessly corrupt, so much so that the rules must be changed, as suggested by Brad Katsuyama in a 2014 *New York Times* article that blew the eye-opening smoke to the world. Brad Katsuyama worked for the Royal Bank of Canada until he left to pull the plug on Wall

Street corruption. Naturally, African youth seeking opportunities as business professionals must make every effort to pull the plug on Wall Street and foreigners running amok in and across Africa. African youth with IMSCO guidance and business professionals must jump on in and make the foreigners pay to play on their land and with their opportunities regardless of the project. White American companies, Europeans, and most non-African foreigners have no other place to invest but in the corrupt system of Wall Street. Factories are going, going, gone to China in this case, and the good China depends mostly on African wealth and resources. America owes China a trillion plus US dollars, and China is dependent on Africa and its global African owners: the black PAD youth. Get the picture, youth. Jump in now African youth and do it by demanding with IMSCO back-up a full 51% ownership as done in the Republic of Zimbabwe of every company and business in Africa and those conducting business and trade in between. Do it now! America's economic ranking is reduced to Aa down from a Aaa rating, and Europe is headed to hell in a basket of greed, flat broke, and they did it to themselves. Refusing to cooperate with Africans and PAD in the diaspora has proven to be America and European Union undoing, while China is grabbing every opportunity it can carry in a bowl of rice. But do not try to play their game. Introduce your own linked African new business culture and games. That is how I plotted researched and wrote this book; from an African mind set prospective.

Africans in the diaspora and PAD must and can ensure that all important vital goods are manufactured in Africa and are controlled by African people by new rising institutions. At least Africans will be in every deal, with no exceptions, if the lights are to remain on, the rent is paid, and food is on the table in foreign communities and our own. Most foreigners, while trying to deny Africans their cultural rights, have learned they have lost their own and have no "return ticket" to get back across the "bridge too far" they crossed when being deported and escaping out of their Europe as prisoners or victims of oppression and genocide, then and now. The matters in Europe then and now were and are so bad that many Europeans have cut ties, had ties cut, or blown up the bridge due to bad family relations when leaving or fleeing their homeland. There it is again: that six degrees of separation I spoke about at the start of the book. So in many ways we all are in the same boat, only Africans never gave up any part of their rights to a return ticket. The world must learn, and Africans must demand that the world respect, cooperate, and invest in PAD when doing business, buying stocks, trading between Africa, or get out! Or witness the world Wall Street corruption crash as suggested by Mr. Brad Katsuyama. I would love to partner up with him and select others who think like him; we might make a grand team. The foreigners now are playing a death game by trying in most cases to cut Africans out of the wheels of progress. Well, I am here to inform all that the shoe is now on the other foot. Yes, Europeans have what they call the best jobs, but Africans own what the best all be they limited jobs are made of and are working on obtaining the best sustainable business that grow jobs for our youth in Africa and PAD nations. When I first arrived in China in 1998, I saw grand newly developed roadways with no cars, and then in the blink of a Chinese bird eye, the smog was thick from the millions of cars made from African metals, resources, and rare earth. The local coal industries are causing the Chinese major health problems in the advancing Asian nation of one billion plus people who are running out of land and resources fast. They too were once colonized and impeded by the greed of the now falling Western world: England, America, and Germany to name three that teamed to stick it to China. These three super packs all of whom are standing in line and seeking handouts from the former enslaved Chinese who depend on PAD and black Africa's trillions of US dollars we blacks in the West toss into China via the Western economy annually; we are keeping both parties alive. What happens when PAD dual citizenship and voting rights in African young growing political systems opens direct trade links with the vastly wealth Africa the PAD own? Answer, check out the results of China and India state sponsored billion people global dual citizenship policy pumping trillions of soon to be Bit Coins; I mean US dollars into the hands of the out cast. Now factor in direct political and foreign trade between PAD Africans in Africa. Starting to get the point?

Biased foreign policies won't get the Western world the best bang for their inflated bucks. Only trade cooperation with Africans, PAD partners, coowners of Africa, and the Chinese, East Indians, and Russians can save the world, not bombs and drones.

Last but not least of this super African power is the rare version of refined rare uranium, known as U-235, that must be distilled or enriched. Vast amounts of raw uranium like the mineral that drives the electric industries, medical needs, and military can be found across Africa, so we Africans have the brains and the bomb. This is why the DRC, Rwanda, the Central Africa Republic, Niger, Ivory Coast, Angola, and Zimbabwe to name a few, have sky spies, US and NATO drones buzzing about and killing unarmed Africans because they are themselves as superpowers trapped between the Cross and the Koran. Africa holds much of the world's raw supply of uranium that America and Europe would like to keep out of Africa development hands, but good luck with that as five hundred million PAD and their billions of allies (or soon to be) will say good luck with that. Here is a key reason why dual citizenship for PAD is urgent! As seen below, PAD can and will establish peace in Africa as it is our family members being droned and shot to death as unarmed people, students all trapped between the Cross and the Koran, and our youth from the streets of New York to Mississippi to Alabama to Brazil to the dreaded streets of Spain, France, and England where Africans are dying, being attacked and terrorized, and murdered by cops and politicians. The lucky ones are forced into prisons for life. On behalf of the people, IMSCO as demanded by the UN and concern humanity demands the black youth and man be freed from the whites self made psychological fears of self made bondage and left alone.

The problem is global for black people. In Australia, reports are reaching IMSCO that the white-led European government is oppressing and murdering our Aborigines, Africans by blood and cultures, our first earth brothers and sisters. They were inhabitants of the region for forty thousand years before England dumped its unwanted there with no return tickets back. The eyewitness professional reporters to IMSCO state the Aborigines' water resources are being poisoned along with other drinking spirits as a way of ridding Australia of the last of earth's first humans, linking us all to our origins just so the Aborigines cannot come back later and claim their stolen blood-drenched land and cultural wealth. This genocide can now end and will as all other concerned humans take a stand to protect nature and the right of all cultures. America and Europe pretending to be the planet police like the local corrupt ones are doing more to abuse people of color than assist, and I am one who knows firsthand. America, the EU, and China along with PAD assisted IMSCO and Africans in the diaspora must now hammer out immediate agreements to include PAD and ensure peace and solutions among us for Africa because sure as hell is burning, PAD are coming home. China and the world cannot say that African people PAD trapped for now in the West are property of Europeans as it is more likely, based on the large debt Europeans owe African people, that Europe is the property of African people. African people own and are holding the economic markers of the United States and the EU with trillions of American and European debt held for now by China.

China and the Western world depend on African resources, wealth, and the cooperation of the very people they disrespect for their survival. The world and the Western system must now pay their debt due Africa and its global people with no protestations; stepping back as was attempted in the goose dance at the UN on 10 December 2014 in the Trusteeship Council during the International Decade for PAD is not acceptable. Refusals will not wash because Africans can now write their own past due payback checks with interest attached. Africans can also provide credit at an interest rate that could bankrupt most of the planet's present biased economic system. What is that old saying? "My enemy's enemy is my friend." Africa's black global youth owns a future now with opportunities that most other opportunities are linked to, and these African opportunities are as big as the known universe. The future wealth and land will be developed as the people require that development and will be managed by African youth; so proper cooperation and education for African youth is urgent for the world as we know to continue witnessing peaceful human development and survival. It would be wise for the rest of the youth of the world to wake up to this reality as African youth are in the spirit of Vin Diesel the actor and cast as family and team leaders, if you will: in the driver's seat in the fast lanes where African youth should be. So please stop and think, black youth and Africans. Stop thinking you are poor African youth, get control of your wealth, get even and stop letting others call black people poor because they are not! Do the research please, and educate yourself on the facts. And it may be the Western world and China's last chance to get it right team with African professionals, up-starts and youth because African people, starting with the youth and ending with the youth at the head are owners and are headed home to their Africa. The Western and Asian world need to own up to these facts and start partnering or leaving, knowing the owners have the lion's share.

EPILOGUE, A New Beginning

It's April 23, 2013, at 5:00 p.m. just hours before my flight departs back to New York City. I had arrived back in Cameroon a week before by invitation from the government via the minister of external relations to sign yet another IMSCO Establishment Agreement. Along with an extended list of other African nations, they were signing to link for life with PAD in business, trade, and all other linking African family matters. A call had just arrived on my cell phone, and the voice on the other end was an excited member of our IMSCO team that had invited me here. The voice was shaky and unsteady as it informed me I must be ready to meet the prime minister of Cameroon under orders from President Paul Biya to receive me in his office before leaving for New York City in a matter of hours.

I depart the Hilton Hotel in Yaoundé with members I hope will be on my future team, headed by advanced-thinking Cameroonians, the people who were the driving force behind inviting IMSCO into Cameroon officially after IMSCO's field team established contact a year or so earlier. I had returned to the Republic of Cameroon to sign the IMSCO Establishment Agreement with the government of Cameroon and set the record straight that Africans in the diaspora whose ancestors were forced to leave their homeland were returning as powerful intuitions in the name of IMSCO to codevelop with the people.

IMSCO's aim is to march across Africa and open doors for African people to enter and get their land and wealth back and, in the end, their golden lives to have and own a future. IMSCO is signing agreements with a growing number of African states that outrank any US, EU, or other foreign bilateral trade and investment agreements signed by superpowers mainly because the foreign agreements signed with the African governments have not honored the birthrights and property rights of PAD or their human rights. IMSCO Establishment Agreements are opening doors and welcoming PAD and families back for the first time after millennia of being in exile and from being enslaved in recent centuries to link as families. As I am exiting the hotel my cell phone rings. Its Jeffry an IMSCO representative next President calling. Before I departed NYC I had been dropped at JFK airport by Jeffry a youth of 22 years from Haiti, Vice President of IMSCO left in charge of IMSCO global operations while I travel. Jeffry is checking on me. I assure him all is going well and that I am headed to meet Cameroon Prime Minister. In Cameroon the people like Jeffry and others hope their work will enable IMSCO to starting driving the enemy of African people lives, ending American, EU biased political and economic policies meddling in African private lives and business. Most African Americans, like the people of Cameroon, are not even aware of the huge amount of damage being done to them by nation states that PAD and Africans on the continent are living in, nor of the trillions of US dollars African family members are losing monthly and annually including international reputations by foreign hands.

As we departed the hotel, keeping in mind that every undercover spy agent in Central Africa stayed at the Hilton Hotel, the presence of a well-dressed African American captured the attention of most of the eyes as we crossed the lobby to enter a waiting car, one in a long line of cars led by two police motorcycles and security vans parked just outside the hotel door. A group of well-dressed Cameroonian business people had received me at the airport and had been escorting me everywhere I went for the past week, stopping at nothing until I was delivered safely to my targeted locations in Yaoundé; this time, to the office of the nation's Prime Minister His Excellency Philemon Yang in charge of the business operation of the Cameroon government. We arrived five minutes before 6:00 p.m., the time set for me to meet face to face with the man who could seal my trip with a victory never possible in America or Europe. Black man gives black man (woman) power would be the theme of my meeting with His Excellency. The news of this meeting and reunion ended up on the global web and front pages of national news with the same billing as the US and EU representatives with African prime ministers, only my meeting was historic and carried its weight in gold and opportunities for PAD, Cameroon, and the continent. The aim of IMSCO Establishment Agreements are to ensure access to business and opportunities in Central Africa for all African people through business culture, the right to vote in elections that affect African human rights and wealth shares.

"African-Americans, all PAD people are pooling efforts to assist the development of Africa."

The world president of the International Multiracial Shared Cultural Organization (IMSCO) was received in audience by the prime minister on Tuesday April 23, 2013, at the Star Building.

Frank Weston left Prime Minister Right
Back to power and being Royal in an African kingdom

IMSCO CEO Frank Weston is welcomed by Cameroon S.E. Prime. Minister Philemon Yang; black man gives black man power.

The historic news story began with...

On behalf of the Head of State, the Prime Minister, Head of Government, His Excellency Philemon Yang granted audience to the World President of IMSCO on Tuesday the 23rd of April

2013 at the star building, in the person of Mr. Frank Weston, following the signing of a Convention between the Non-Governmental Organization and Cameroon. Weston is signing the IMSCO Establishment Agreements across Africa.

Accompanied by four other members of the local IMSCO group, Mr. Weston told the Cameroon press after the audience that the plan was to open a branch of the organization in Cameroon entailing the facilitating of the return of the economic gains of African Americans to the continent, and particularly to Cameroon to link up after centuries torn apart and assist in giving a boot to racism, racial discrimination, xenophobia, and related intolerance. End of News report.

Frank Weston left CEO of IMSCO / Cameroon Minister of External Relations S.E. Prime Minister MBONJO at signing of IMSCO/Cameroon Establishment Agreement 18 April 2015.

The mission, though aimed at establishing business and cultural ties between PAD and Africans across Africa with trade with foreign partners; via the IMSCO Establishment Agreement is also a united agreement that ensures Bilateral Trade and Investment policy with diplomatic status and insurance to be included and trade with any company in the regardless the nation size and commodities and nationally, among brothers and sisters and foreign business cultures; Belief systems not withstanding all to ensure representation in a new era supported by the United Nations agenda 2063 introduced on December 10, 2014 with the international community. The UN-linked aim is to expose the world to the reality of demands being made by PAD and Africans for unconditional respect for human rights, the right to self-determination ensuring stakeholders dignity as they move forward with their lives free of intolerance.

Something even more extraordinary happened; something that stopped many closet racists in their tracks. It took place two months before the United Nations December 10 event for the International Decade for PAD. In August 2014, President Barack Obama welcomed fifty mostly African heads of state into the White House and served them dinner. I called it "The Big Sit-In." Missing, however, was one of my most favorite African living heroes: President Robert Mugabe of Zimbabwe. He wasn't invited for his representative status of a fearsome Zimbabwean people who were facing piercing, inhuman American and EU system sanctions meant to kill. The sanctions were because the people stood their ground, IMSCO and me among them, against recolonization attempts by English, American, and EU greed. It was a greed aimed at retaking the vastly rich Zimbabwean land removed from white racist control since the 1600s that would not walk a black dog to assist a black person's comeback to hunt the impeders after enslavement, and colonization was forced to an end by the people. I am proud to say my IMSCO team assisted in Zimbabwe's liberation in 1980. Many nonblack Americans were completely stunned. Many had voted for Obama's landslide victory two years earlier and had voted in the November 2014 midterm national elections. Mostly whites had teamed to turn back the clock on American cultural progress and moved to take Klan control of the US legislature from the president's power base. It was a move that sent shock waves to black and white youth, evident by the growing white support for "black lives matter."

In Obama's speech to the visiting African presidents, he reportedly said, "I do not see the countries and peoples of Africa as a world apart; I see Africa as a fundamental part of our interconnected world—partners with America on behalf of the future we want for all of our children. That partnership must be grounded in mutual responsibility and mutual respect..."

What was the reason for the turncoat white Tea Party vote to toss the N-word out of our White House? Only those who voted to end the first black president's control over the House of Representatives know the reason why.

President Obama had welcomed leaders from across the African continent to the nation's capital for a three-day US–Africa Leaders' Summit, the first such event of its kind in history. The summit, the largest event any US president has held with African heads of state and government, was built on the president's trip to Africa in the summer of 2013 and aimed to strengthen ties between the

United States and one of the world's most dynamic and fastest-growing regions: PAD homeland. Specifically, the summit advanced the administration's focus on trade and investment in Africa and highlighted America's commitment to Africa's security, its democratic development, and its people. At the same time, it highlighted the depth of the United States' commitment to the African continent, advanced shared priorities, and enabled discussions of concrete ideas to deepen the partnership. At its core, the summit was about fostering stronger ties between the United States and Africa.

The theme of the summit was "Investing in the Next Generation." Focusing on the next generation is at the core of a government's responsibility and work, and this summit provided an opportunity to discuss ways of stimulating growth, unlocking opportunities, creating level playing fields, and enabling growth environments for the next generation. What was wrong with President Barack Obama's historic speech in my researched opinion was that it was only a speech; the president failed to include or lobby the contributions and African rights of PAD who have been locked out of past generations for centuries depending on who the foreigners were. It will take an African solution to place black professionals and youth in the discourse at the table and in any and all business and political decision making as a right to lead the way in any and all African development projects. How else can the owners of the great Africa learn and do it for themselves if they are not at the table, included, and deeply involved from bottom to top of the future the president spoke of? Without ownership control of their African wealth, can there be other qualified black men for president and for the likes of Obama's daughters to select for marriage to build a strong community? Under a foreigner's controlled plan to develop Africa or when the African Union members are pushing the foreigners' flawed plan of impeding PAD, African youth, and the global African community, black people lose. Young people of color owning their African birthright and inherited African future is the only solution, just as other non-African cultures should control their culture, property, and land if they own what they claim after going a "bridge too far," in most cases, like America and Africa. Black (male) youth motivation will be included from this point on in all African and societal discourse concerning African people's development at all levels. Power, real power, is taken and never given! Africans have retaken their land and the power that comes with it, and we coown the American and European weapons to ensure protection of what we own while now working at developing our own advanced weapons. But enough talk of war. Let's talk of peace and development for all.

Thankfully, the black youth do have a return ticket home and can now start over with new identities to replace their stolen ones. In the end, all the African presidents left Washington without taking a single youth of African descent prisoners of the Western world even though President Obama called for black youth to be released from US and Western cultural and biased criminal justice imprisonment. The African and Arab presidents came seeking, using the opportunities that the enslaved labor of PAD created from centuries of forced labor with no mention of including the black youth. President Obama made no mention of African

American and other black youth across the globe to be included in the international agenda being addressed: an African diaspora birthright to all that Africa is or will be. The president spoke of the Young Men's Initiative in New York City though nothing was said to my knowledge about the faith of young black men at the White House. Blacks need to feel their initiative is being empowered by elected leaders.

American presidents past and present just did not have African concerns, were avoiding urgent concerns others have or the right team around them to make such calls for black and Spanish youth. IMSCO suggests and calls for real motivating initiatives for young black people to be supported all over the world where they live and dream of being. Opportunities and institutions are already in place that can jump-start many of these young people's careers. African youth must be informed they are coowners of these foreign institutions based on the minerals and resources these institutions need and require to exist since they were created on the backs of black people and their property. As I have mentioned, Western companies would not have a market or product to sell without gum arabic. It's this gum and other resources that wars are fought over and why nations fall. This was the main reason the US Department of State employees attacked IMSCO's aim to link with this commodity in Sudan in 2008. I suspect the employees of the US Department of State's "African Desk" are working behind closed doors and moonlighting for the likes of Coca-Cola and other lobbyist who attack the human rights of African organizations and their representatives using economic, slander in e-mails and even more deadly weapons to deny mentioned earlier in the book.

The Coca-Cola Company is dependent on natural gum, which can only be obtained from Africa. Many other important foreign industries that are springing up in Africa and South America and grabbing illegal land belonging to the people are in the same resource-dependent boat; this is all while attempting to avoid or lock out African people and African Americans. The ancestors of PAD never gave up any parts of their birthright and property rights when they were forced to depart Africa as enslaved human beings. Westerners and Asians are now attempting to slither back into Africa, taking advantage of the access for the impeded black youth and their families. As others have done in the past, China demanded the return of any and all land and property America, England, Germany, and others grabbed. Africans in the diaspora are teaming with their African family and allies to demand the return of the same and will use any and all means on earth to make it happen. It is important for the world to realize Africa is "not for sale" at any price. How can the private property, birthright, and homeland of criminally exiled, enslaved people be stripped from a whole people still holding legal title? African land and resources being illegally sold and grabbed will not be accepted ever. These grabbers are claiming what they know is a human rights violations and a crime. They are claiming that the attempted sales of PAD's and African property, our youth's inheritance, are legal under foreign and African corrupt partnership that in fact amounts to development terrorism. This African and PAD stolen property is hijacking. It is nonsense that these foreign leaders, backers, and presidents of Africa of foreign nations using the African Union to drive Africa deeper into debt and wars. It is important to remember what President Obama said when he lost both houses of the Senate and Congress in the nationwide election. "I do not have to run for office again," said Obama, smiling broadly. It was in his second to last speech to his critics and the American people, leaving many a stranded African American community facing an uncertain dreams of American system present or future cooperation when Obama's term is over in less than two years. That somewhat sneering remark at his critics sent shivers down my spine and the spines of most aware and concerned African Americans, PAD, and much of Africa who invested so much to place Obama in the seat of power at the White House in 2008. Is this the beginning of the new era of deadly games of kill or be killed? Will the new the global African societies find a safe path and cooperation from an old world dying foreign system around them to move forward in peace?

What are the old fifty-four African heads of state saying, and what worth while messages if any are being sent to the PAD and their families in Africa? We men and women in and outside Africa don't need to sleep with our enemy to develop our lives and homes again after surviving the destruction of slavery and the denial of our human rights, rights to rise and earn a living, and to learn to read and write about the very history our ancestors created millennia ago. What is truly taking place, or should I say attempting to take place, is that these African presidents in seats of limited power are questioning African youth and the people's ability to know they are taking down their own youth and their own divided communities and nations by such dealings. Such leaders need to step aside or be forced out now as maybe they have no idea of the new kinds of power and wealth Africans own, are dealing with: 1.5 billion black lives around the world have in their hands and pockets.

Black lives have fought for millennia to retake Africa. A few areas still remain to be brought back into the fold. They do have wealth and land enough and power with built-in markets for empires to rise again and build as fast if not faster than China, but most of all, they will serve the African people and people of the world with the very best that life has to offer. But if we keeping ordering power from foreigners when we have enough water and sun power to produce any amount of power needed, we do ourselves and Africa great harm. When I started out on this journey, I had to be half crazy because I had nothing. Not even a return ticket to the Western world I was escaping from to save my life, so it did not matter because my life was already at risk in the Western world. I made it out and back and out again where I can now remain outside the impeding Western grid. I was younger then, but age doesn't matter in this game. Winning is what matters by using your own education, power grid, and energy source, and Africa has it all. African people are free men, women, and children because of Africa.

Why is it that after all these years, the foreign investors never shared a dime worth of energy until the Chinese entered the African picture? Africa is feeding much of Europe and now China. In spite of the bad deals, we Africans are educating the Chinese and European youth, while many of the receivers of African resources are denying training to black youth that in the end send them to prisons or to die at sea. Meanwhile, they are trying to escape the foreigner-promoted terrors that the "Power

African" teams sent to "help." Africa cannot survive another century of that madness. Foreigners come and depart, leaving behind broken and burned infrastructures that cost the people trillions of US dollars not to mention the lives of youth; the PAD cannot afford to lose them. Research suggests the present presidents and leaders (as the buck stops with them) are all to blame for black youth having to select petty crimes over hitting the books. Owning and protecting resources is real power on this planet, so ally with those who can help protect resources.

Like China, India, and an economically and morally bankrupt, busted European Union dictated to by greedy companies, President Obama is aiding these centuries-old African presidents including the USA out dated models. The actions of many African men and now women, when you factor in the African Union, are helping replant colonialism and worse yet the enslavement of African people who are now ready to go to global war; are in a save the homeland and an inheritance war to prevent their fall again. Real modern African leaders and leadership is beyond petty greed and tribalism! PAD and people of Africa, you are stakeholders and owners of a land, wealth, and power so vast you can call your own shots and must! IMSCO and many other rising African institutions is here to assist; in fact, IMSCO was established for the people, the youth.

Establish your international business institutions and trade deals, rules, and laws using at first your IMSCO Establishment Agreements and IMSCO's newly formed business office of prime minister. The prime minister and foreign minister office for PAD represents the people, communities, and industry affairs when it comes to African people's vast private property and wealth shares.

Foreign governments have no right to claim they have the right or power to legally represent PAD or African people's private property. Africa is private property having been paid for in slavery and blood demanded by the people's oppressors and enemies.

International political business affairs linking these rights and power to dual citizenship to all African nations with the right to vote for who you wish to represent you on both sides of the ocean should be highly prized, and IMSCO recommends the African parties be willing to die protecting these human rights. Sing the American, foreign, and African national anthems, and be citizens of all political worlds you have won back, but stop the bleeding of your life and that of the people by being ready to defend your human right even at the price of death. A better personal life helps develop the person, society, and government. Finally, if any black youth wish to know how to change things and make better opportunities in life, build and support IMSCO and read all bilateral trade and investment agreements between Africa and the Western or Asian nations you are trading with. While "IMSCO Establishment Agreements" are PAD all African people (bilateral trade agreements) that over ride any foreign bilateral trade and investment agreements that does not include the birthrights and ownership rights of PAD and Africans in Africa. "IMSCO Establishment Agreements" are being welcomed across Africa and we urge all nations and people to respect these human and property rights being reestablished for Africans by Africans.

Managing PAD Wealth and Land Shares

A hard fought for and won "International Decade of the People of African Descent" event took place at the United Nations in New York City on December 10, 2014, to address the unique needs for protecting PAD from further government political attacks: end racism, racial discrimination, xenophobia, and related intolerance, and draw the world's attention to the objectives of these aims. It took UN member states, including the African Union, since 1960, and the other founding nations of the UN since 1945. The UN member nations raised, collected, and stole trillions of US dollars annually in PAD people and African names needed for African development. It is urgent for African youth to research and recognize their own human rights and refuse to be controlled and held against their will by UN member states, who deny cultural, political, and economic rights and justice as a right to self-determination. A PAD prime minister economic office is now required.

Solutions for the Future

Everything, and I mean everything possible, is being done by the western system, allies, and organizations to prevent African people and PAD from returning to Africa as stakeholders. The United States and its allies are using biased, doctored bilateral trade and investment agreements to lock PAD and Africans out from stakeholder trading in an ongoing attempt to grab the land that is not for sale and drive African youth out of Africa into the sea or prisons. This include PAD people who hold substantial educational and economic resources to assist Africa in the only sustainable manner. The World Bank, IMF, and an endless trail of donors with their own interests claim to be friends but in truth seek only what Africa has to offer. They don't give a damn about the people and the natural land our planet needs to breathe.

This is followed by nation states' actions called "Sister Cities International" projects. These cultural exchange projects are funded by taxpayer dollars and slum-captured African and Spanish people to establish ties with Africa and its vastness of life without the knowledge of the oppressed Africans. All real knowledge of stolen and nearly destroyed African cultures is kept conjointly hidden from the impeded people: PAD and homeland Africans. African youth are passed over. Quality education is blocked as it was for my own parents and nearly all Africans; even knowledge of their hard-working parents and community contributions to serve the interest of non-African Europeans in the Western world who really wish they were Africans and could remain on the African land is hidden. PAD youth own half the African continent and have the right to tax each and every foreign business for every action taken on their private land and for use of their private resources up to and after the products are manufactured. So no door is now locked to the African youth after all.

IMSCO can and has set new paths across the danger and impediments by establishing the IMSCO Prime Minister Office in order to provide access; from a seat at the African Union, their land

and resource shares pay for the official documents that will help the African people survive the coming Western, Arab, and Asian storms. IMSCO and its global teams strongly urge all African professionals and entrepreneurs to link with IMSCO and each other (or any proven allies as well). From America to Brazil, across South America, Asia, Europe, the Middle East, and Africa, as one resource power unites regardless of beliefs, whether it's the Cross or the Koran or any other African belief systems, focus on the power within oneself and in one's family, team, and African land and resources we all coown. "He who controls the resources controls the power." That power, that African power, is also the 1.3 billion African people in a strong market.

In the United States alone, African Americans dish out over $1 trillion a year to non-African businesses and the states that prey on African Americans as the foreigners do on Africans. Imagine if that money was spent within the family from Queens to Los Angeles and across Africa, what a wonderful life it would be; it will be!

The latest crimes against humanity being forced on African Americans are now led at street level by the police force from Ferguson, Missouri, into New York City, Mississippi, and across the Western world as police are taking instructions from the one percent colonial bosses extending right across America and Europe. The orders are coming from the same Western postcolonial funding bosses who still hold trillions stolen from the backs of enslaved Africans over the past centuries and are now struggling to hold on to the lost cause to contain blacks. They are given permission via the mostly Irish, German, Italian, and Jewish accountants to take down black opportunities to progress. They even insulted President Obama by letting the Israeli prime minister stand before Congress to try and make their point that no black man was better than them. This all came to a head in the United States in March 2015, but that is not the direction I want to take this book—focusing on a dead cause. This book is about the western world's dream of holding black men and women in global prison or slavery if only in their own demented states of mind.

Western bilateral trade and investment agreements being signed are illegal and worthless on paper in the face of the just ownership power of Africans returning home to their families, land, and future and escaping a nightmarish western failure. Mostly European citizens are being taken down by the Western lost dream by refusing to open their eyes to the last reality they may have to survive in the new world order with friends. These "Sister Cities International" projects in New York and other programs in other cities are often based inside governor and mayoral offices and paid for by taxpayers' last cents used by America, Europe, Africa, and Asian nation states and local city governments. They divert trillions of US dollars annually away from taxpayers and Africans. The states are seeking the governments' ways to claim vast African resources to shore up the worthless US dollar in the face of gold and mineral resources. The African merger bank's power is now in the hands of African people and backed up by the all-mighty PAD on the rise second by second as they take over Brazil, America, and South America as trading partners and better yet family. These Western, Asian, and now Middle Eastern resources and land-grabbing scams are designed to deny black youth, indigenous people, and their families' knowledge of their development abilities and resources. For example, the Western and Asian global travel industry into Africa and PAD states are designed first to build private hotels using the cover of foreign embassies to plant invaders for their clients to stay with protection when they arrive, eating foreign-made, processed, imported foods after traveling in on foreign airlines with western refined fuel led by foreign tour guides who collected all payments in advance before landing in Africa.

International business in and out of Africa is priceless, and travel profit must also benefit African people in the diaspora. This trade can now be taxed alone with any and all resources for trillions of USD each month, all directed at the pockets of African people. What is achievable now is black youth across the globe have proper guidance and power from institutions like IMSCO and other qualified Africans to issue operating documents and licenses to obtain resources to trade from America to Brazil, across South America, Asia, Europe, the Middle East, and Africa.

African youth should and must reach out to each other as they own the solution. They must work their magic through African institutions such as IMSCO and AMRE Trade Inc. or build their own and not depend on the World Bank, IMF, or any others as Africans are too rich to have true friends. Get started in controlling these rightful ownership shares of Africa's vast resources. Gold, diamonds, platinum, and land are all cash, and the world cannot operate without these and many other African-held resources. Yes, African youth and African people worldwide are very, very wealthy.

We have the numbers, and we have the resources to rebuild our empires and great cultures including Egypt. For those who wish links with the Cross and the Koran, if you wish to drift, do not think that the rest of us are going to stand by and just watch while more non-African believers die. Belief systems are ok if you are so weak not to believe in the natural state of life as nature presents what can help advance humanity. Just do not try and take humanity back to the foreign Dark Ages as there is only one race: the human race. Banning education is a crime against humanity and nature. Banning education to women and the youth is the worse crime one can commit, and the people or state committing such a crime must be banned forever from our African part of the blue planet. The African youth owe it to themselves to wise up to the fact that they have the power and wealth to manage their own future and present their worth to humanity.

Any African nation attempts to deny PAD dual citizenship is economic and political attacks, racism, racial discrimination, xenophobia, and related intolerance. African youth and the wider concern community is within their human right as coowners of all that is Africa world wide including shares of all business and trade. The PAD and African youth coown the African continent and rights to place levy, TAX and control lion shares of all foreign business and trade. Owning ones business culture is life and the key to direct self determination for PAD Africans is dual citizenship. Its economic and political power all rolled up into one mighty global people! Our African dual citizenship is one of the Western world worse nightmare, demand it!

Rights for Self-Determination

PAD have little choice but to obtain and exercise their human right to self-determination and assist IMSCO in demanding dual citizenship and political and economic access to every African nation immediately as the PAD power is there to ensure that this is done. Dual citizenship gives the holder the access to unlimited international business and political leverage. To that end, on behalf of PAD, IMSCO has established an office of prime minister. This office will serve to develop and carry out a guidance system to assist PAD people in managing their guaranteed dual citizenship and self-determination path to vast African wealth and global opportunity shares in Africa and its global future.

The vast Africa wealth and private property of PAD is being produced in the trillions of US dollars annually and can best be managed by an elected PAD prime minister and staff to ensure transparency and full human rights to self-determination. Management of this vast inheritance wealth in the hands of both the PAD prime minister linked with the African Union Sixth African Region and all PAD institutions as needed and required to serve by and for the people through official branch offices, directors, and representatives throughout Africa and the world. This is the much sort after human right by all Africans and it is the only way to ensure the entire PAD's global interest to track and defeat foes and implement the PAD many needs.

The first prime minister representative is selected from inside IMSCO qualified team members. Elections will be held in the future throughout the PAD global community, and the elected person(s) will serve for an appointed number of years. The prime minister's duties with its own official seal and stamp will be many and far reaching, including managing international affairs, being a voice and vote, and establishing an official agency. This agency will be empowered to appoint accounting, management, and security services and forces to protect agents for PAD, assets, and interests regarding how their assets are developed, managed, traded, and kept. Protecting the vast PAD and African wealth, resources, and economic shares will be contracted to PAD. Through qualified African people, institutions, and black own banks and trading institutions owning what money is made from African people will now enjoy their time in the SUN. The duties of the PAD prime minister's office will seek to assist and serve some five hundred million PADS and Africans in Africa.

The PAD Prime Minister Office was established to ensure PAD vast inheritance order, fair and just inclusion, and land and wealth distribution having gained land and mineral wealth concessions in the hundreds of billions of US dollars in assets so far. The prime minister's economic office call on the whole of the PAD and Africans on the continent to assist the office in guidance and not to accept an anything less than full complete ownership partnering in Africa and where ever African trade and business is carried out. PAD young and old must step up and help select leadership for PAD's right to an African Union seat, voice, and vote linked to owning dual citizenship for PAD in the diaspora and in all exiled residence nations as a human right to self-determination. In the US Constitution Africans are still addressed as none human void of US nationality but then the question remain who gave whites fleeing or being forced out of Europe to the Americas the right to give or deny civilization building Africans who were in the Americas long before Europeans. Only African people can give black man and woman power. This human right matter has been demonstrated by IMSCO and other partner PAD NGOs at the United Nations event "International Decade for PAD," held in New York City on December 10, 2014. "International Decade for PAD," demanded respect for African and PAD-managed justice, unique cultural rights, and past-due shares of Africa and reparation payments required for protecting PAD from further foreign government, self appointed human right law brakes, rogue settlers be they in Africa or Asia or the Western world, multinational companies (private and government), economic and political attacks, racism, racial discrimination, xenophobia, and related intolerance. It will also draw the just world's attention to the objectives of these aims. The IMSCO prime minister office will ensure with the power of PAD human right a seat the AU table and all tables that concern PAD rights including the annual Asia African Conference.

Regardless of the present-day and historical impediments, Africans are back and moving forward, led by an increasingly able youth-wisdom power. Africans are raising empires again to last millennia beyond the millennia of the first African civilization built. African PAD have the land, wealth, and knowledge to fend off any foe—even the enemies within—for the good of all mankind. Human rights and African inclusive ideologies and the youth will lead the way. Africans in Africa and in exile have won! The matter is now between African family members.

PAD FLAG OF UNITY

F. Weston award PAD Flag to Mother Hale, Harlem, NY
President CEO FRANK WESTON of IMSCO,
designer of the Copyright ©, PAD flag, honour award
to Mother Hale of Hale House. PAD flag, unifying
symbol for all PAD people and nations.

Key to Africa Honour PAD by Republic Cameroon

The Africa key was granted to IMSCO for PAD via the Republic of Cameroon. Now that is what youth have been waiting to hear. Finally, we Africans in the diaspora are seen as real players and competitors owning vast land, wealth, and a continent that will level any playing field. "Fasten your seat belts," says a tall, lovely, African sky angel with joy. Africans and PAD families from across the world are on board. Finally, the once-lost family members are coming home to Africa! They are coming by the millions from South America, Brazil, the Caribbean, Europe, Asia, and America to pool efforts to relink with family and at long last to help rebuild their personal African empires.

Africans have won the long liberation struggles only to face an inheritance war with the same enemies. It's time to return, manage, and control the new Africa. And kick back in a new African kingdom! As Winnie Mandela said,

"When we win, we will win forever."

Where to from here? My team in the diaspora and Africa need me to travel back to Africa as soon as possible on some urgent business. So I step into the shower and let the water run. I look down and notice I do not this time have my socks on in the tub. That is a certain sign I am more relax now and start planning my trip back to my African paradise in need of all the cooperation PAD can offer and we have a hell of a lot to offer each other for our bright black future.

A golden inheritance and an abundant future await African people from around the world. James Baldwin got it right in Harlem so long ago when he said, "That inheritance produced by the unprecedented travail and triumphs of our ancestors on these shores as a universal inheritance and place us in the vanguard of a new morality and a new world."

Author F. Weston at the Great Pyramids of Giza

***

Thanks to all:

It's been a hell of a journey but many PAD are returning to Africa. There are far too many to name to list here, so I will just say thanks and a job well done to the brave, bold, warm-hearted people that make Africa and its global family freedom possible to be realized. Now, we Africans and allies must manage and share Africa and its people's vast land, resources, wealth, and opportunities to lead to a golden future. It's like I said from the start: if you believe in the six degrees of separation, this is your story as well.

Frank Weston and Ms. Rosa Parks, Harlem, New York, 1986.
        "Frank, please help link our people with Africa and our wealth." Rosa Parks.

"One last seat is needed before the people of African descent can relax. IMSCO suggest the AU seat be named in honor of our hero Ms.- Sister Rosa Parks. The people of African Descent rightly own the seat and right to manage self-determination demanded a seat and decision making at the African Union.

447

Africa's Seychelles, "East side of Heaven"

"I am back in Paradise!"

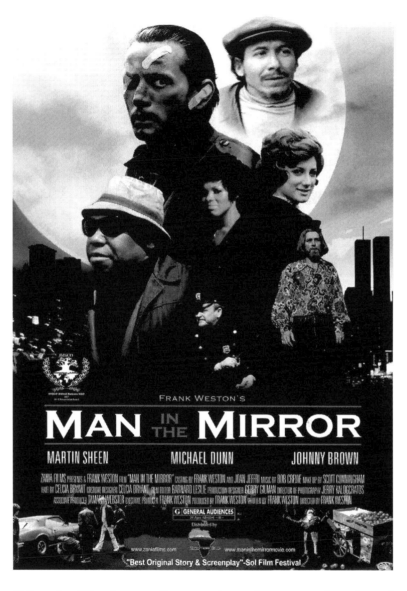

"Man In The Mirror," a movie written, produced and directed by Frank Weston. <u>The American Dream?</u>

IMSCO

The baobab tree, African people success story
***
Africa like China is "Not for Sale!"

African and PAD youth, return home, build empires by managing your vast land and wealth. <u>Take</u> what is yours, partner needed to create African business and jobs. Education is the KEY to control and protect.

IMSCO

Struble, John W : ECONOMICS OFFICER - USA EMBASSY - KHARTOUM

From: Clarke, Owen A

Sent: Wednesday, November 05, 2008 9:20 PM

To: Struble, John W

Cc: Klein, John Marshall; Fierst, Pamela D

Subject: RE: License Request - Importation of Gum Arabic - IMSCO

John,

I can engage Mr. Frank Weston one last time and get him to give me contact information for this group in Khartoum. We would then request that you contact them, meet with them and determine:
a. The bona fides of the group – are they a genuine group of cultivators, exporters, financial managers, businessmen, etc;
b. The Group's plans for cultivation, harvesting, transportation to Port and export of Gum Arabic on behalf of IMSCO (the NGO seeking the license);
c. The Group's responses to questions about their remuneration (how will they be paid for the services provided).

Once you have met with the group and we have the responses to the above we can determine next steps.

jc

Owen "Jimmy" Clarke
Desk Officer-Sudan Programs Group (AF/SPG)
Bureau of African Affairs
U.S. Department of State
2201 C Street, NW Room 5819
Washington, DC 20520
202-647-4248

From: Klein, John Marshall
Sent: Wednesday, November 05, 2008 11:58 AM
To: Clarke, Owen A
Cc: Struble, John W
Subject: RE: License Request - Importation of Gum Arabic - IMSCO

I was actually thinking more in terms of cover. If post could turn up something shady on the Sudan end, it would make our case for denial stronger if Mr. Weston chooses to sue OFAC over a denial. When balked he becomes quite irate. It would also help differentiate this guidance from others if we get other applications that seem more credible that we want to approve.

But yes we do have enough grounds for denial now on the basis that we think benefits will acrue to parties in the non-exempt areas and that the quantities involved seem excessive.

From: Clarke, Owen A
Sent: Wednesday, November 05, 2008 11:45 AM
To: Klein, John Marshall; Young, LaToya M
Cc: Struble, John W
Subject: RE: License Request - Importation of Gum Arabic - IMSCO

I'm truly tempted to say let's draft the denial memo and be done with this, just to stop this man from calling me 5 times a day; he has called twice this morning and is becoming abusive and even more erratic than normal!

11/6/2008

ZIMBABWE BROADCASTING CORPORATION

Ref: GTM/B.3/vm

THE BROADCASTING CENTRE
HIGHLANDS
HARARE
ZIMBABWE

19 May 1989

Frank Weston
Chairman
Committee For The United Nations
Diplomatic and Consular Corps
Four Park Avenue
NEW YORK
N.Y. 10016

Dear Sir

BUSINESS IN ZIMBABWE - 9 YEARS AFTER

The above named programme which we recorded with you has finally been edited and ready for broadcast.

There will be a delay of some 4 weeks before the programme is transmitted. This is due to administrative proceedure and not pressure from the white business community and their backers in America and Europe.

ZBC is in total agreement with the views you expressed in this programme and infact our view is that the programme in question is a follow up to the one we did with you in January, 1989.

You will agree with me that the first programme raised a stir in Zimbabwe. We were questioned why we screened this programme but we believe these are schemes by some circles to prevent the establishment of close links between blacks throughout the world.

Let me assure you that we will resist all pressures intended to stop the screening of the second programme. Looking forward to further co-operation between your organisation and ZBC,

Regards

G. TICHATONGA
ASSISTANT DIRECTOR GENERAL : PROGRAMMES
NEWS AND CURRENT AFFAIRS

PS. I wish you could be around when the programme is screened. We may need to record a follow up episode.

/VM

Box HG 444 Highlands Telephone: 707222, 729661 Harare Telegrams: "Broadcasts" Telex: 4175 ZBC HOV ZW, 4223 ZBC HOR ZW

Notes to Pages

Books reference:

"No Longer at Ease," "Things Fall Apart." Chinua Achebe, author publisher Fawcett Crest . New York 1959, pp. 133
"Dead Aid," author, Dambisa Moyo, publisher Farrar, Straus and Giroux, New York, 2004 pp.71.
Salman Rushdie's book: "The Satanic Verses" pp. 238
"Heart of Darkness," Joseph Conrad, author publisher Barnes & Noble, 1994, pp. 16, 20, 44, 290
"Confessions of an Economic Hit Man," John Perkins, author, publisher A Plume Book,
"The Wretched Of The Earth," Frantz Fanon, author, Grove Press.1963.
"King Leopold's Ghost," Adam Hochschild, Houghton Mifflin Company, 1998, pp. 59.

Introduction and Map

"The Middle Passage", the map in public domain, depict the main route where countless millions of young African men and women traveled while being kidnapped into slavery and transported to evil-by-evil men chained to the bottoms on ships from their African paradise to a European managed hell. It is suggested by "The Middle Passage" map untold millions died were forced over board into the sea while the stronger survived only to end up as force labor for centuries into what the mentally unstable Queen of Spain and Kings of Portuguese, France, Germans and Americans all Europeans slavers call their property: whose bloodied hands and criminal intents hunts humanity still to this day insulting humanity and planet earth, pp. 20.

Chapters and pages:

*"The Road Home": Enters "Rock" from the
Republic of Congo with a message. Contact made, come
home to Africa you are need urgently. Pp. 12.*

"Into the Unknown": I had no cultural rights as long
as I remained chained to the burning cross by Bible-
carrying Ku Klux Klan members in America. pp. 25.

"Crossing the Mediterranean Sea": "Benin, Land
of the Blacks." First, the postcolonialists withdraw the
funds if any and then break or ship out any equipment
that might assist the Africans before ordering their
personnel to bust every latrine and burn all important
records, even the birthday certificates of some
frican presidents. pp. 38.

"Landing at Maya Maya Airport Congo": Meeting Vital
Balla, inside Brazzaville, the Europeans last frantic
view of Africa Heart of Darkness," pp.43.

"A Coded Message to Black Men": Ballot or the
bullet, signing the first "IMSCO Establishment
Agreement, a first step the signing by Frank Weston
author and the Congo, Brazzaville ambassador approved
by the Congo Republic (Cabinet) designed to help unite
the African family bullet free. "Think dual citizenship."
*First signing of the "IMSCO Establishment
Agreement" to begin peacefully resettling in Africa and
reclaiming PAD shares of Congo wealth the same year a
book written by Adam Hochschild, "King Leopold's
Ghost," published by Houghton Mifflin Company 1998
about the deranged Belgium King Leopold who with the
economic part taking of his associated, all Europeans and*

Americans who butchered Africans and African development far beyond present day researchers ability to contemplate the horrors reported by first hand by Joseph Conrad in his book Heart of Darkness a narrative about evils done to Africans and rape of Africa in the Congo. Pp. 57 published by Houghton Mifflin Company 1998. pp. 68.

"Land of the Dragons": Invitation too the Peoples Republic of China, 1998 pp. 72.

"The Ugly European": "So you think you can make a difference?" European efforts to block African and PAD linkage. pp. 80.

"Inside Man": "Touch of Evil," Western Companies refuses to cooperate with PAD Africans home coming. Europeans went a "Bridge too far," more facts drawn out in author John Perkins book "Confessions of an Economic Hit Man," 2004, a Plume Book. pp.84.

"Washington, We Have A Problem": US Department role. pp. 88.

"Purchasing Power": World Bank and IMF divide and push African countries into debt to grab Africa. Pp. 90.

"Survival Instincts Early Years": No Health Care, Blues singer Bessie Smith, 1898 sing blues for a stolen child hood. pp. 95

"Sex in a Hen House": I know your Mama boy." pp. 100.

"Getting Out of Dixie": "Back of the Bus!" pp.108.

"New York City": "No thanks President John F. Kennedy." pp. 113.

"Go Kill the Yellow Man": "Kidnapped by US Army," 1960, pp. 116.

"Escape on the Underground Railroad to Europe:

starve, pp. 222.

"Black Hope versus White Hope, Author, Frank Weston, debate Zimbabwe white settlers 1989, "Hit Man," taking a political bullet. p.233.

"Cut to the Chase: "Do Africans Boycott Blacks" PBS TV debate between author Frank Weston and OAU / African Union ambassador over who own Africa, pp. 240.

"Running Cash to Struggle": Author F. Weston transport diamonds, cash and information to assist ANC / PAD, in apartheid South Africa 1990's pp.252.

"Nelson Mandela's Vision": Are all Africans not included? Pp. 259.

"Warrior Winnie Mandela": Rosa Parks on steroids, and author Frank Weston team to take on apartheid in South Africa! pp. 273.

"Rise of Civilization": Author Frank Weston visits roots of African civilization, Egypt, to document and find path back to his people culture, pp.275.

"Harlem, Black Soul of America": pp.281.

"Apartheid South Africa": 1992 look into apartheid South Africa, pp. 285.

"African Wealth and Power": African people vast wealth, pp. 290.

Return Ticket?: "Do You Have A Return Ticket?" pp. 302.

7.) "A Dry Black Season": pp. 318.

Diamonds, Chocolate, and Sex: Unexpected allies, pp.321.

Downtime: An evening with Sam, pp.329.

Reloading: New York University, education never too old or late, pp. 334.

"Queen Winnie Mandela"": America's imperialism under President R. Reagan force Winnie then South

Africa "Deputy Minister of Art, Culture Science and Technology to loose post, pp.338.
9/11 Wake-Up Call: **"Wake up call,"** pp. 290.

WikiLeaks Takes Note: on US Department of State employees caught with red handed sabotaging PAD and African trade links, pp. 356.
"African Inheritance War:" American, European and Asia greed quest for Africa, pp. 371.
"War on African Human Rights, impeded trade between the African people sabotage economic development and Shoot to kill black men, all to protect a Western world system that has failed itself while totally dependent on foreign resources largely owned by Africans, PAD and Russia, pp. 385.

Conclusion:
Human rights, development and Dual Citizenship is the ultimate PAD Weapon for African people and struggling African / PAD youth, Africa's most valued assets and future managers of Africa's vast land and wealth are all summed up here. This may well as the sum total of any African, PAD oppressor fear.
"Man In The Mirror": A Movie depicting the American dream, a Zania Films LLC. Picture pp. 449.
"Imperialist Portrayal Drawing," pp. 454 © By IMSCO

****

African People Inheritance Business Treaty (APIBT)
The IMSCO – AFRICAN / PAD PEOPLE TREATY
"People of African descent (PAD: <u>exiled</u>)"
(African people to people independent trade agreement)

Under the legal mandate and Guidance of: IMSCO

66896828R00253

Made in the USA
Charleston, SC
30 January 2017